NEW
DOORS *in*
MINISTRY
to WOMEN

NEW DOORS *in* DOORS *in* MINISTRY *to* WOMEN

A Fresh Model for Transforming Your
Church, Campus, or Mission Field

Sue Edwards & Kelley Mathews

Kregel
Publications

*New Doors in Ministry to Women: A Fresh Model for
Transforming Your Church, Campus, or Mission Field*

© 2002 by Sue Edwards and Kelley Mathews

Published by Kregel Publications, a division of Kregel, Inc., P.O.
Box 2607, Grand Rapids, MI 49501. Kregel Publications provides trusted, biblical publications for Christian growth and service. Your comments and suggestions are valued.

Unless otherwise indicated, Scripture quotations are from the *Holy
Bible, New International Version®*. © 1973, 1978, 1984 by International Bible Society. Used by permission of Zondervan Pub-
lishing House. All rights reserved.

Scripture quotations marked NASB are from the *New American
Standard Bible,* © the Lockman Foundation 1960, 1962, 1963,
1968, 1971, 1972, 1973, 1975, 1977.

For more information about Kregel Publications, visit our Web
site: www.kregel.com.

Cover design: John M. Lucas

ISBN 0-8254-2508-5

Printed in the United States of America

03 04 05 06 07 / 5 4 3 2 1

To our sisters,
mentors, and spiritual mothers:
the women of Dallas Theological Seminary,
Creekside Bible Fellowship, and
Irving Bible Church

CONTENTS

FOREWORD

Women's ministry is coming of age in our local churches. Sue Edwards and Kelley Mathews have written a book that will assist the church to be even more relevant and fruitful in ministry to women today. While various forms of women's ministry have existed for decades, especially in denominational churches, many of the present forms have lost their effectiveness and appeal. They are not as effective in reaching the next generation because they don't seem relevant to the issues and needs of women today. To reach a new generation we, with a heart for women, must be open to change, flexible in our methods while firmly holding to the center, the Word of God.

This book contains a concise and clear explanation of the differences between the modern and the postmodern women of our culture. Then the Transformation Model, which addresses and adapts to the needs of the postmodern woman, is offered as a solution. However, Sue and Kelley maintain a fine balance between the necessity to minister to the needs of young women while not neglecting the valuable resource found in older women. These experienced, mature women must be encouraged to obey the Titus

2:3–5 command to be the mentors and role models for the generations following them.

The importance of their emphasis that the teaching of Scripture must be the core focus of any program cannot be overestimated. Without consistent Bible teaching with application to women's lives, spiritual growth will not be constant. Every other activity finds its source in this focus. Consequently the relationships that develop among women are not shallow and superficial, but are genuinely caring and nurturing.

Since Sue ministers in a large church and Kelley in a small one, they offer valuable insights on how these new methods can be adapted to churches of any size. They are practical and honest in describing their own experiences and the methods and activities they've tried. Some were successful, some were not. This gives the book credibility you can trust. It has been forged from years of experience.

The scope of the book is not limited to the local church. Ideas on starting ministries on college campuses, both Christian and secular, are given. An excellent chapter on using the model cross-culturally will be very useful in creatively planning a missions outreach.

This book is a valuable resource for anyone involved in women's ministries, whether it's a church, campus, or missions program, and even for those ministering one-on-one. I'm happy to recommend it as an essential ministry tool for communicating the Word of God and building life-sustaining relationships.

—VICKIE KRAFT

ACKNOWLEDGMENTS

*T*here is a sense in which no gift is ours until we have thanked the giver. Thank you, Lord Jesus, for You are the greatest Giver of all. You surround us with teams of friends who share the joy and lighten the load.

Sue Edwards:

The HOME Team: To David, my husband of thirty years, *"the wind beneath my wings."* Without your encouragement, flexibility, unselfishness, and expertise with the computer, this book would not exist. To our daughters Heather and Rachel, for lighting our world as we watched you grow into beautiful women inside and out. To Tom and Matt, for loving them the way we do and for being God's men. And thanks for a new generation of joy, grandchildren Becca and Luke. And to my parents for passing on their passion for life.

The CHURCH Team: To Pastors Steve Roese and Andy McQuitty, for open doors and wholehearted support! To the women's ministry staff, Mary Dean, Mary Bodien, and Cindy Mann, for your friendship, prayers, and for teaching me how much fun ministry can be. Kathy Appleton, your contribution on the missions section was invaluable. To women leaders, thanks for joining us in the journey and transforming women's lives.

The DTS Team: What a joy to serve with David Cotten, Beverly Lucas, Bob Garippa, Chaplain Bill Bryan, and the Student Services staff. Thanks for your help in developing a women's ministry on campus and for all you teach me about ministering effectively to students. And to Gail Seidel, Joye Baker, and Carolyn Hannah who share my heart for DTS women.

The MENTORING Team: Heartfelt gratitude to Kathy Hyde and Bible Discussion Groups, Inc., for the early years when I was floundering. You lifted me up and equipped me for today. And to women's ministers Vickie Kraft, JoAnn Hummel, and Julie Parton who were wise counselors and encouragers through dark days. I treasure your friendship and value your expertise. To my friend Dianne Miller, who continues to trailblaze for women today. And to dear Tommie White for all you are teaching me in your victory over breast cancer. And finally to my grandmother who gave me my first glimpse of God.

The WRITING Team: Thanks, Kelley, for sharing your writing skills, your fine mind, and your heart for women on this project. God brought us together and I could not have orchestrated a better team. Your flexibility and maturity beyond your years made working with you a joy every step of the way. And thanks for the computer shortcuts you taught me. You can teach an old dog new tricks!

Kelley Mathews:
My journey to this moment would not have happened without the support and encouragement of many people. First, my thanks

to Sue, for being willing to share with me her dream of writing a book about women's ministry. And to Sandi, for pointing her my way. Trying to articulate my feelings regarding your dear friendship, Sandi, has been much too difficult for someone who is supposed to be a writer! Thank you for the invaluable advice, constant encouragement, and many laughs. This one is for you.

To Maellen, my deepest gratitude for your willingness to babysit Nate regularly so that this work could take place. He loves his Granny! To Bill and Sara Blaydes—yes, you too had a part in this work. Thank you for providing me with a home away from home during my seminary years, and for loving me as your own. I cherish you both. To my mentors, formal and informal—Jeanne Carter, Mary Margaret Bains, Edie Mitchell, Sonya Ragusa, Sandi Glahn, Carolyn Hannah, and to all the other influential women in my life—Mom (I love you!), dear friends Erin Anderson, Amy Roberts, Jeni Ward—thank you *all* for letting God work through you to make me more like Him. To the leadership of Creekside, past and present, thank you for honoring women as you do, acknowledging them as coheirs in Christ. I appreciate the opportunities to serve and lead (aren't they the same thing?) through the women's ministry.

Finally, to my husband, John, thank you for believing in me so wholeheartedly. Your love and encouragement give me the push I need to stretch, risk, and seek God's purpose for this gift He's given me. Who would have thought this would happen so quickly! Thank you also for Nate—my delight—so much like you in many ways. I love you.

A dual thank-you to all the women's ministry directors, missionaries, and campus directors who made time for us in their busy schedules to share their experiences and expertise. To Amy Joy Warner, for your helpful research and insight into postmodernism. To Dennis Hillman and Kregel Publications, we salute you for your integrity and kindness. Most of all, to our first love, Jesus, for guiding us on this adventure. If this book is helpful, may the glory go to Him!

Information about the authors:

Sue and Kelley are a perfect team to collaborate on this book. Both Dallas Theological Seminary grads, Sue is a modern woman with twenty-five years experience while Kelley is postmodern, just beginning to oversee her church's women's ministry. Sue, in addition to being adjunct faculty at Dallas Theological Seminary, ministers in a large church; Kelley in a small church. Sue is a new grandmother, and Kelley is a new mom. Although they enjoy different life stages, they share the same passion: to see women won, grown, and unleashed for God's glory. And they bring different perspectives that benefit the variety of readers. Both live in Dallas, Texas—Sue with her husband, David, and Kelley with husband, John, and toddler son, Nate.

Sue is a founding member of the Association of Women's Ministry Professionals, an organization that promotes personal and professional growth in their members, all salaried as women's ministry directors, pastors, consultants, educators, and trainers. For information on AWMP, see our Web site, www.newdoors.info.

INTRODUCTION

Amy was twenty-eight, attractive, and earned $80,000 a year writing software. But she was estranged from her mother, never knew her father, and recently ended a four-year relationship with a live-in boyfriend. A coworker deposited her in my office with a plea: "Help her. She's missed two weeks of work and she can't stop crying."

As I looked into Amy's swollen eyes, I saw myself thirty years earlier, I remembered the hopelessness. But God provided a spiritual mother named Kathy Hyde who nursed me back to health by introducing me to Jesus and reparenting me as I learned to lean on Him. I was transformed by their love. When I reflect on the difference Jesus has made in my life over the past quarter century, I am overwhelmed with gratitude.

Now I am the spiritual mother. But will the same methods and models used to help me work for Amy? Yes and no. Amy and I were both in our mid-twenties when we turned to Christ for help. Our fundamental needs were the same—we both needed an intimate relationship with Jesus. We needed to know the Bible, to be part of His family. We needed women to model what a godly woman looked like. We needed a push to risk ministering to others in a way that complemented our design and gifts. Our needs were the same, but what worked for me thirty years ago will *not* work for Amy. Why? Amy is a postmodern woman.

What does that mean? This book was written to answer that question and to show you how to include Amy in your ministry. Here's a breakdown of the book.

How to Use This Book

Part 1: The Transformation Model and Why It's Working

Part 1 characterizes the postmodern woman to help you understand her mind-set. You must know who she is before you can reach her. But there are dangers as you make changes to include postmoderns. We'll alert you to these dangers and show you how to minimize them.

We also introduce you to the Transformation Model. This model meets the needs of today's women, both modern and postmodern. We will examine seven pillars of the model that work whether you minister in the church, on campuses, or around the world. In part 1, we examine this model in general terms. Later, in parts 2, 3, and 4, we'll adapt these pillars and principles to specific areas of ministry.

Part 2: Taking the Transformation Model to the Church

In part 2, we'll examine what's happening in the church and how to apply the Transformation Model there. More and more women are joining church staffs as pastors to women, ministers to women, and directors of women's ministries. Megachurches are awakening to the Titus 2 mandate that women are responsible for the women in their churches. Women attend staff meetings and enjoy their place on the team. Some churches pay their women what men in comparable positions make. Many do not.

Women in smaller churches observe the exciting ministries in the megachurches and struggle to attain the same effectiveness despite their lack of resources. Most small churches cannot afford to bring on staff a minister/pastor to women (or any other assistant pastor position), so women labor as lay ministers with hopes that their pastors value their work, trusting that they are doing what they can with what they have.

Whether you are already on staff or serve as a lay minister, these principles will help you build a ministry that works today. Whether you are part of a small church or a larger church with more resources, we'll show you how to implement these ideas in your setting. One size does not fit all, but the same principles apply everywhere.

Part 3: Taking the Transformation Model to the Campus

Part 3 takes the Transformation Model to the campus, where women of all ages desire training. Colleges, universities, and seminaries are packed with women preparing for meaningful work or ministry. Wherever women congregate they want to connect. But the exclusive sorority model grates against Christ's ways. Women are instigating new organizations on campuses that will address the specific needs of women there. Explore with us what women are actually doing and how to begin a women's ministry on your campus.

Part 4: Converting the Transformation Model Cross-Culturally

Finally, in part 4, we will take the Transformation Model to the mission field. Women all over the world hear what's happening in America and want a women's ministry too. Is the Transformation Model applicable to other cultures? Absolutely! But missionaries must "tweak" these principles to fit the culture and contexts where they serve.

For centuries women missionaries blazed trails in other lands. They evangelized, planted churches, taught, and worked in medicine. Today they continue their noble labor. But now women also teach nationals how to minister to their women. Whether on short-term trips or long-term commitments, women equip their sisters around the world. We'll look at cross-cultural strategies that work today.

In Addition . . .

We'll share stories of women pioneers engaged in the glorious adventure of serving God in places women have never served before. Dozens of women ministers and missionaries will reveal their experiences and what they learned as a result. Whether you have years invested in women's lives or you hear a faint call and want to explore the possibilities, this book can help.

As a resource, we will maintain a Web site with e-mail addresses of many of the women we interviewed. You can ask your questions and learn from their experiences. Just access the Web site www.newdoors.info to find updated addresses and resources.

But before we examine the multifaceted world of women's ministry in the new millennium, let's take a look at where we've been.

Where We've Been

Models of Women's Ministry in America

Women have ministered to one another through the centuries, but most of that ministry occurred informally. From the frontier days until the mid-1900s, women formed the heart of communities around the country. They visited over the fence while hanging out their laundry, birthed each other's babies, kept watch over the neighborhood or town children—no matter whose they were. Before our culture dismantled the nuclear family, women cooked, canned, and cried together. They trained the younger women by example.

Many women grew up in church. The ten commandments hung on the walls of every classroom and the Lord's prayer began the school day. Please don't misunderstand. This was not the golden age for women. They often felt the brunt of prejudice and opportunities were limited. But sisterhood flourished and women were seldom alone.

In the mid- to late-1800s various models of women's ministry emerged that took on the flavor of the times. Here is what they looked like.

The Tea Party Model

Women gathered for social events and activities. They drank tea and enjoyed each other's company. At these gatherings, women were expected to behave with proper etiquette and propriety. Such opportunities provided excellent training for younger women, who learned social graces, and gave everyone a chance to show off that new hat.

Today holiday parties, mother-daughter banquets, and fashion shows meet a social need, and women still love to gather and celebrate. But they want much more, and they want it packaged differently.

The Social Activism Model

Christian women of the nineteenth century were service-minded. The mid-1800s saw the rise of voluntary associations designed by and for women, dedicated to the betterment of American society. We will use two still-existing movements to illustrate this model.

As rural America gave way to the Industrial Revolution and the urban experience, women found themselves thrust into unfamiliar and sometimes dangerous territory on college campuses, in the factories, on the streets. They needed support, training, and a place of refuge. In 1858, the Young Women's Christian Association (YWCA) began providing boarding houses for young working women, political lobbying for better working conditions and equal protection under law (remember: women could not vote until the 1920s), and a variety of recreational activities for these young women living away from home. The YWCA gave women an opportunity to serve other women on a broader social stage.

In 1874 women concerned about the destructive power of alcohol founded the Women's Christian Temperance Union (WCTU). They met in churches to pray and then marched to the saloons to ask the owners to close their establishments. They were a driving force in the push to make Prohibition law. But behind the WCTU's temperance reform was "protection of the home." Through education and example, the women of WCTU hoped to encourage total abstinence from alcohol, and later, tobacco and recreational drugs. Today the WCTU remains active in the fight against drug and alcohol abuse.

These organizations, and others like them, arose out of a biblically based concern for the welfare of women and families. The founding women had a knowledge of Christ and the Bible. Postmodern women rarely have that foundation of faith. And these women aren't coming to you, whether in the church or on campuses, for an opportunity to right the wrongs of the world—they are needy themselves. More than mere service, they need knowledge of Christ, the One who gives purpose to whatever service they may enter later.

The Missions Model

Until perhaps the past thirty years, women called by God served on the mission field because there were few meaningful opportunities for them to serve God at home. As a result, churches designed programs to learn about women missionaries and support them. In many churches, women's ministry had a missions focus. While that focus was appropriate for that day, daughters of the new millennium fail to see the need for world missions. They are desperate to heal before they can concern themselves with women around the world.

While fostering a global perspective is a worthy goal of all women's ministries today, it cannot be first priority. It should be an arm of every women's ministry, but not the core. We cannot help others until we are healed ourselves. But watch out—when today's woman experiences healing, she doesn't just want to learn about missions. She wants to *do* missions.

The Parachurch Bible Study Model

Women love to study the Bible. But because churches did not provide the opportunity, Bible studies outside the church began to flourish in the 1950s. Bible Study Fellowship and other Bible classes exploded, attracting women from all denominations and backgrounds. I (Sue) came to Christ in a parachurch Bible study. The teacher became my spiritual mother, and she taught me to teach the Bible. I served as a teaching leader and teacher trainer in Dallas-based Bible Discussion Groups, Inc. for more than fifteen years and considered this ministry my spiritual home. More than my church, it nourished, fed, and challenged me.

I was so loyal that I refused to consider ministry in a church. The people I served with were lifelong friends. I attended seminary to be a better teacher there. But after seminary God began to open doors in the church. For several years I ministered in both places, unable to break away from the place where I grew up and from the women I loved. Gradually God made it clear He was moving me into church ministry, but it was heart wrenching. Some of my friends there still cannot understand why I left. I consider that Bible study my training ground, and I am grateful.

These parachurch studies can be valuable for equipping women in churches without women's ministries. But we believe that women can be better served within the church. For, within the church, as we teach and help women mature we walk with them in a variety of other arenas. We give women varied opportunities to use their gifts in the service of the Body. We partner with other ministries in the church, working under the authority of God's appointed leaders. We participate in God's key instrument on earth—the church. As churches awaken to women's ministry within their own walls, parachurch women's Bible studies will, and should, be less and less needed.

The Formal Model

Have you noticed that formal is out and casual is in? How many restaurants require a tie? My husband's ties hang on the tie rack in the closet. He actually likes to wear ties, but he seldom has the chance. Both at work and at church they are out of place now. He saves them for weddings and funerals.

And when did you last see the majority of women wearing dresses and high heels every Sunday to church? Or to the office? Khakis or jeans seem to be the preferred dress of the postmodern woman. The new trend in clothing is just one indication that a casual approach is appealing to the daughters of contemporary culture. And God commands us to woo them!

There are foundations of our faith that we must protect, but formality is not one of them. How does this formality look in women's ministry? It is expressed in rules that no longer serve any purpose—rigid structures and formats seldom evaluated—and teaching methods that aren't effective with postmodern women. It is fear of experience and an unhealthy worship of women leaders. It is refusing to dig deep into the ugly complexities of life and instead being content with simplistic answers. A formal approach fit with women of the 1900s, but is ineffective if we want to reach all the generations for Christ.

A note of caution, however: we must guard against extremes. How tragic it would be to alienate the women of earlier generations because of so shallow an issue as clothing styles or structure preferences. Modern women often model a gracious and godly spirit for all to emulate. Their love of structure and discipline is desperately needed to rescue many postmodern women from chaotic lives. Women's ministries that blend the best of the formal model with an informal style will attract and retain the variety of women God brings to our doorstep.

The One-Size-Fits-All Model

Churches used to schedule women's activities and Bible studies during the day. The vast majority of women stayed home, even after their children grew up and moved away. Most women were married. Not so today.

American has been described as a "melting pot," where different races, nationalities, and genders are expected to conform and think alike. Women in church today don't resemble a melting pot. They look more like a green salad. They look and think differently. They like to be distinct. They enjoy variety and request to be with women of different ages and stages.

The 2000 census found 12.9 million households headed by single women. Three out of five children in the United States are in childcare.[1] What are the demographics in your church? At Irving Bible Church (where Sue ministers), out of 2,500 weekly attendees, 36 percent of women are single. Kelley's church, Creekside Bible Fellowship in Rowlett, Texas, counts 170 members total. The vast majority of the women, 74 percent, are married with children. Another 12 percent are single mothers. Both churches minister to widows, mothers, divorcees, and professional women. Women of different races and nationalities enrich us by participating in everything we do for women.

Many of the mothers in our churches are working outside the home, some out of necessity and some because they want to. We encourage those mothers whose husbands earn a sufficient income to stay home with their young children. But some refuse. Should we simply write them off? No! God asks us to teach and train them with the hope that they will make their family a priority— even if they choose to continue working.

Women ministering in the new millennium serve every woman or they neglect their call. That complicates everything we do. As a result, we change our meeting times and formats to honor working women's schedules. Teachers learn to use illustrations that aren't always about the stay-at-home mom with 2.2 children. Our workshops address issues besides training toddlers and surviving teens. No longer does one size fit all in the church, but variety adds zest and spice to our work. The challenge can be a blessing if we choose to see it that way.

How Do You Feel About What You Have Just Read?

As you contemplate the different models, do you observe any that dominate your women's ministry? Most women's ministries today can identify with aspects of each model. IBC's women's ministry enjoys an occasional tea party. We have a missions chairperson on our women's board. We employ structure when it suits our purposes, and we have a mom's ministry for our mothers of young children.

But the overall flavor of our ministry no longer reflects any of these models. We changed gradually, as the church was also making these kinds of changes over time. Change is a painful process. Approach it with wisdom and a gentle spirit. Our missions director has a sign on her door that reads, "Blessed are the flexible for they will not get bent out of shape." If you tend toward inflexibility, we suggest *Who Moved My Cheese* by Spencer Johnson, M.D.— a delightful parable that reveals profound truth about change.

Keep in step with your pastoral leaders, but remember that God may call *you* to point the way. Although change is hard, we have found God faithful when we knew He was leading us. Get on your knees, and if you are sure, enact change with God's blessing and strength. Remember: your changing may win women to Christ for eternity. And that's the bottom line.

PART 1

THE TRANSFORMATION MODEL AND WHY IT'S WORKING

Chapter 1

WHO IS THE POSTMODERN WOMAN?

The phenomenon of the generation gap reaches beyond familial relationships—mothers and daughters, grandfathers and grandsons—into the church body as well. Older women, content with their traditional, didactic method of Bible study, are puzzled and sometimes threatened by the younger generation's desire for creativity, diversity, and spontaneity. "We know our way works—why change it?" they wonder. Likewise, teens and college-aged girls observe their mothers and grandmothers in church and say, "Boring! That is *not* for me." And they walk away from relevant truth because they can't relate to an antiquated method. Many postmoderns (for our purposes those under thirty years of age), believe they have little in common with the "moderns" (their parents' and grandparents' generations). It is an unfortunate and potentially destructive misconception.

The labels affixed here to the generations in question are, by nature, general; they don't fit each individual. Many women in their sixties think like postmodern women. And young women who grew up in Christian homes often take on the attributes of modern women. But for the sake of our discussion, these labels are handy. They help us as we search for methods to minister to the different generations.

Are Your Methods Reaching the Postmodern Woman?

Many postmoderns view life from a different perspective than moderns—yet many women attempting ministry use obsolete methods that won't work with young women. Highly structured formats, academic Bible teaching without application, and simplistic thinking don't interest the Oprah generation. They are relationally starved and looking for spirituality, but not if it is packaged in yesterday's styles.

The postmodern, non-Christian woman wants transformation. She wants authentic relationships and deep spiritual experiences. She demands we address the complexities of life and refuses to settle for pat answers and superficial explanations, insisting that we take off our masks and get real. She wants substantial change— a new life that works.

Many are wounded and fear trusting anyone. These are the daughters of feminism. In many cases, their mothers left them behind to follow their own dreams, and these latchkey kids want a home. They come to the church searching for authentic community and family.

Many call several women "mom" and several men "dad." Adults played musical chairs in their lives, so they learned independence for survival. They experienced the emptiness of isolation and are desperate to connect. And so they come to Jesus. We must seriously consider their needs as we plan our ministries. But there are dangers we can't overlook as we seek to woo and win them!

Be Alert to the Dangers!

Danger 1: Don't Marginalize or Offend Moderns

Imagine the results if we changed our methods to attract young women and lost the older women in the process. Our challenge is

to embrace the postmodern woman while retaining the generations of women who came before her. Why? Because these earlier
generations are our army of spiritual mothers. They will teach and
train the younger women God is sending us. They will enfold
postmoderns when the leaders run out of arms. Only a fool would
tailor-make ministry to the needs of one generation and forget the
other.

Danger 2: Don't Capitulate to the Culture

Aspects of both modern and postmodern cultures fly in the face
of biblical truth. For example, typical postmoderns believe truth is
relative. Secular education is founded on that premise, affecting
every academic discipline. But the Bible teaches absolute truth. In
our attempts to attract postmoderns, should we abandon teaching
absolute truth because they resist? Absolutely not! That would be
capitulating to postmodern culture.

But we can teach biblical truth using methods that appeal to
postmoderns. How? By using more stories, images, and art—and
by making the main points of our messages applicational rather
than academic. Postmoderns aren't impressed that we can conju-
gate Greek verbs. First, they want to know if our faith works.

Remember: modernism also contradicts Scripture. For example,
in the past, relationships and families have been sacrificed on the
altar of modernity's materialism. Dr. Alice Mathews, Lois W.
Bennett Associate Professor of Educational and Women's Ministries at Gordon-Conwell Theological Seminary, comments,

> Having done some useful course work and a lot of reading
> in my Ph.D. studies on postmodernism, I see many great
> dangers in modernism as well as in postmodernism. So I
> see myself as a "premodern" woman living in the midst of
> the ongoing assumptions of modernity and almost wel-
> coming postmodernism as a way of forcing Christians to

see how much we've bought into the culture of modernity in community-destroying ways. No, I am *not* postmodern. But nothing less than postmodern thought could force us to question the tenets of modernity which are in the air we breathe. I know that I bought into modernity for the first six decades of my life, and only in the last decade I have come to see how that ethos, modernity, has been at odds with the gospel of our Lord Jesus Christ.[1]

Are you considering the needs of postmodern women in your ministry? If not, is it time for a change? But be careful not to capitulate to either culture or unnecessarily offend either group as you do.

Awaken to the Need for Change

I (Sue) am not a fan of change. I'm in my fifties and comfortable with the way things are. But as adviser to women students at Dallas Theological Seminary and pastor to women at Irving Bible Church, I lead ministries to hundreds of postmodern women. To answer my calling I have been forced to change. Why? Because it's not about me—it's about them!

Actually I resisted the idea of changing the way I had always done ministry until three years ago. I attended a women's ministry conference at Multnomah Bible College and Seminary in Portland, Oregon. Before me sat a panel of Christian women, all under thirty. Most were students in the women's ministry track.

Several had grown up in Christian homes and the others came to Christ through youth ministry or in their early twenties. I listened intently as they answered questions that revealed a different worldview than mine. One raised in a Christian home expressed that she felt disenfranchised from her generation. But she also looked at the world differently from her mother. She felt caught between two worlds. Others identified with their generation and talked about their struggle to see life "biblically." Each one challenged us to understand them and their lost generation.

A modern woman once asked me, "Why should I change? Why can't the postmoderns change instead?" DTS student Amy Joy Warner has an answer.

"For the Christian, Jesus Christ offers the ultimate example for approaching the postmodern culture. John, in his Gospel, clearly illuminates Jesus' method when he writes, 'The Word became flesh and made his dwelling among us' (1:14). In Jesus Christ, God approached humanity in terms it could understand. In doing so, God established a pattern for those who would follow after Christ. God's Incarnation creates the necessity and appropriateness of a postmodern approach to Christian ministry. If we are to follow His example, we have no excuse for not accommodating ourselves to the postmodern culture in such a way that Christ is evident once again."

The postmodern women at the conference came to faith because someone reached out to them in terms they could understand. I left the conference knowing God was calling me to change the way I approached women's ministry.

Is Jesus Asking You to Change?

We need a new model because our old models, as we have shown, don't reach the postmodern world in which we now live. God loves this world and asks us to woo them to Him. Jesus' last words on earth are still our chief concern.

> Therefore go and make disciples of all nations, baptizing them in the name of the Father and of the Son and of the Holy Spirit, and teaching them to obey everything I have commanded you. (Matthew 28:19–20)

Postmoderns sometimes seem like they come from other nations, but Jesus commanded us to reach and teach them too. As God brings these postmodern women into our churches, Titus 2:3–5 clearly calls the *older* women of the church to ministry.

> Likewise, teach the older women to be reverent in the way they live, not to be slanderers or addicted to much wine, but to teach what is good. Then they can train the younger women to love their husbands and children, to be self-controlled and pure, to be busy at home, to be kind, and to be subject to their husbands, so that no one will malign the word of God.

Understanding this passage has energized armies of women and men to take women's ministry seriously. Titus 2 mandates mature women in the Lord to mother and mentor new women. Mature women come from every generation, but many are older in years and need to know how to embrace women of other mind-sets.

How Do Moderns View the World?

Both modernism and postmodernism strive to make meaning of the cultural, economic, political, and social changes taking place in art, architecture, literature, the social sciences, popular culture, industry, business, technology, and education. Modernism is committed to logic, reason, and the scientific method and assumes that these are the tools that lead to truth and reality. Modernists have long believed that the scientific method is capable of producing solutions to the problems of the world and that there are no limits to where the search for truth may lead. They equate change with progress and believe that democracy leads to freedom, equality, justice, and prosperity. For modernists, education and professionalism are seen as keys to upward mobility and the attainment of the American

Dream. . . . But there is a darker side to modernism, which is the object of much of the criticism aimed its way by the postmodernists. Modernism has produced rampant materialism, a consumer society, a ravaged environment, and unrestrained technology. It can be associated with oppression, exploitation, repression, violence, and even terror.[2]

For many postmoderns, previous generations have not solved the world's problems. Science and technology have not provided the answers. They are right! But neither will secular postmodern philosophy give them the answers they seek. What is true for moderns is also true for postmoderns, and all people who ever lived or will live—only Jesus can fill the need in their souls.

Nevertheless, postmodern thinking is going to turn our world upside down! Len Sweet writes, "A flood tide of a revolution is cutting its swath across our world and is gathering prodigious momentum."[3] We must view our world as a postmodern world.

So ready or not . . . if we desire to have a successful ministry to today's woman, we must change our tactics to win her. We are called to approach her in a way she can understand. What characterizes the postmodern woman?

Four Attributes of the Postmodern Woman

Although I often dislike what is happening, I must admit that I observe postmodernism in the women who come into my office off the streets. I see these trends in the media and in my neighbors. I now consider these factors as I prepare to teach the Bible and design ministry programs. For a thorough treatment on the dramatic changes ravaging our world, read Len Sweet's *SoulTsunami*— a book that changed my (Sue's) perception of today's world. We are indebted to Len Sweet for these attributes and many of the terms and concepts used here.

1. *"Double Loop Thinking"*

Life is so complex that the postmodern woman has learned to feel comfortable believing two contradictory ideas at the same time and not be bothered by the contradiction. She believes our ability to understand truth is limited, so when faced with different facets of opposing truth, she isn't concerned about the inconsistencies. Life is so fast and full of mystery that many postmoderns believe it is beyond comprehension. Here are some examples:

- This is an "in your face" society but "get out of my face" society.[4]
- The sexiest lingerie is marketed by a company that promotes Victorian ambiance.[5]
- Communication technology is pulling us together and pulling us apart.
- They think community and global at the same time.
- They are connected through electronics but fascinated with the past.
- They love extremes but are drawn to simplicity.
- They are closed off from the world by the Net, yet surfing the Net only makes them want to go to Australia—and they go.

Soon after I became aware of double loop thinking, a talented young singing group performed a concert at our church. They called themselves *Altogether Separately.*

2. *Three Times HOT (HOT has three distinct meanings for the postmodern)*

The First Is "High-Online Technology"

More has changed in the past fifty years than in the past five hundred years. Our changing times parallel the transition from the Middle Ages to the Renaissance.[6] It is estimated that more information has been generated in the past three decades than in the previous five thousand years. One weekday edition of the *New York Times* contains more information than the average person encountered in an entire lifetime in seventeenth-century England.[7] The Internet is changing our world.

I have a love-hate relationship with technology. I love the services it performs as I write to you, but I hate when my computer acts up. I use e-mail only because I am forced to. Picking up the phone is my first inclination. But Kelley, for instance, is at home behind the screen. To connect with younger women I must be HOT. I do admit that the more I use e-mail, the more I like it!

Do you realize that if your car is less than ten years old, it has at least thirty computers in it? Already some textbooks are online and updated daily. If you have a digital watch, it contains more computing power than existed in the world before 1962. Speech recognition systems can identify 230,000 words with 95 percent accuracy. Think of the changes in technology when voice activation becomes standard. Before long your computer will speak, your TV will listen, and your telephone will show you pictures. There's a cartoon in which a man says to his wife, "Answer the TV, honey, I'm watching the phone."[8]

The way technology is changing our world leaves us breathless. We need to get connected quickly, or we will be out of touch. In fact, the Barna Research Group reports that "by 2010 we will probably have 10% to 20% of the population relying primarily or exclusively upon the Internet for its religious input. Those people will never set foot on a church campus because their religious and spiritual needs will be met through other means, including the Internet."[9] It's time to be HOT instead of ostriches.

The Second Is "Hands-On Truth"

Postmoderns grew up learning that there was no absolute truth. Secular education assumed this fact and most postmoderns don't question it. They will go to the wall for a few principles—animal rights, the environment, and freedom of speech—but generally the concept of truth is hard for them. As a result they aren't easily reached by intellectual, linear arguments. The evangelist will need more than principles and propositions to win the postmodern. This is bad news for those of us who love truth and were trained to communicate it through propositions, three points, and a poem. Those skills will help us, but we need more.

Does this mean we no longer teach truth? Not at all. The postmodern needs truth desperately. But it does mean we adapt our teaching methods to reach the postmodern mind, remembering that moderns also sit listening. We will dig into these methods in part 2.

"Hands-On Truth" requires that we live out the principles we teach *before* we expect our listeners to believe us. Above all other criteria, a postmodern ministry must be relational. First and foremost, Christians must show themselves to be fully integrated personally. Mayers asserts that

> John 17 is the most distinctive of many texts that call for Christians to be authentic in word and deed i.e. lifestyle. . . . Jesus is praying that the oneness He shares with the Father might be the same kind of oneness that we share within our own persons. There is to be no artificialness or hypocrisy! Christians must be truly caring, genuine, transparent. It is for such irrefutable authentic lives, not cold rationalistic assertions, that Jesus prays. . . . Jesus wants us set apart in truth. That is our outward claim is identical with our inward reality.[10]

When the postmodern observes consistency in our lives, then we begin to earn the opportunity to engage in dialogue with her about the hope that we have.

Sweet writes that postmoderns are "dealers in love more than dealers in dogma. But in classic double-ring fashion, postmodern culture needs more truth, not less. The difference is that Truth is not a principle or a proposition but a Person. Truth is not rules and regulations but a relationship. God did not send a statement but a Savior."[11] Although biblical truths are stated and learned as propositions and principles, at the heart of Christianity is a relationship with Jesus. This is actually good news for us!

The Third Is "High On Touch"

Postmoderns want experience, relationships, community, and interaction. They aren't content to sit and listen to someone speak to them. They want to participate. Many postmoderns are desperate for relationships.

During the panel discussion at the Oregon conference, the young women continually used the word *home*. Those who grew up without faith kept reiterating, "We never really had a home." "We want to know what a home feels like." "Could you make us part of your home?" There is value in inviting these women into our homes, but that is not all they are asking. Their pleas center on being drawn into healthy, intimate relationships. They want to be touched—physically, emotionally, and spiritually. They want to belong.

Postmoderns think that hunger will be satisfied by belonging to a community of people. They don't understand that only a relationship with Christ quenches our spiritual thirst. While they are learning, we envelop them in our authentic community to show them the difference Christ makes in our relationships. And there we teach them the truth—not only about Jesus, but also all the other truths from God's Word. To embrace them we need an army of arms that are HOT—High On Touch. We need women from multiple generations. We need every single one to surround the mass of postmodern women seeking Christ, to reach out and embrace them where they are.

To reach the postmodern woman, we need to be HOT—High-Online Technology, Hands On Truth, and High On Touch!

3. Chaord

What is chaord? Len Sweet coined this term. It's a mixture of chaos and order. As a modern woman I learned that chaos was bad and order was next to godliness. I love structure. When my daughter Rachel studied on her bed with the radio playing in the background, I would insist she turn off the music and sit at her desk. The next day I would find her on her bed again, background music playing away. The battle raged until I heard an expert teach on different learning styles. I recognized that my daughter's learning style is different from mine. She excelled in school and I learned to let her study in ways that worked for her.

I have also observed that her generation is more comfortable in chaos. The world is so complex that they are used to several things going on at once. They seem to like it. They exist within the tension of order and chaos with far greater ease than my generation. Flexibility is more natural to the postmodern woman.

I force myself to look at our ministry not as a rigid organization but rather as an organism that moves and bends in response to its environment. It is fluid and flexible. We are no longer wedded to methods out of habit or tradition. Now we try to adapt when we see it is appropriate. Of course, we never change the foundations of our ministry—our commitment to teach God's Word and to live out Titus 2—but now we value creative ways to better serve all the generations.

We call it *chaord*—a willingness to function without such rigid walls of structure. We will address the practical details of this concept in part 2.

4. Spiritual Hunger

"For the first time in US history, we are in the midst of a massive spiritual awakening that the Christian church is not leading.

Americans are exhibiting the highest interest in spiritual matters in fifty years and Christianity is registering the least amount of interest and energy in fifty years."[12] For believers that is frightening! I grew up learning that science would solve all our problems and give us all the answers. People who believed in a real God or a real devil were considered ignorant in my childhood home. Fifty years later, we now enjoy the comforts science and medicine bring, but we know science is limited. Where do Americans go for answers?

Postmoderns are looking to the spiritual. The Barna Research Group reports that 75 percent of Americans "believe that angels exist and have an effect on people's lives."[13] But the spiritual takes many forms today, and many are naïve enough to be drawn into anything that offers a high experience or a sense of community. Postmoderns want to know God, but they are suspicious of organized "religion." They don't trust bureaucracy, government, organizations, and institutions. Traditional forms are suspect.

Some fear that in our zeal to woo the postmodern crowd, we will sacrifice the heart of our ministry, making it unrecognizable. Not so! We adjust our methods in order to further our reach. In the first century, the mission of the early church was to win souls and grow converts. As a result, they were loosely structured and met in homes (see Acts). Likewise, in a postmodern world, what outdated programs might we alter to woo young people? Would those changes affect the heart and focus of our faith? No. But isn't it time to consider how to bring postmoderns into our ministries? They are spiritually starved. We have spiritual food. Let's present this food in a way that is palatable because we know it will nourish them now and forever. If we don't, the charlatans and frauds are serving up poison around the corner. To minister to postmoderns, we need a new model.

Chapter 2

WHAT IS THE TRANSFORMATION MODEL?

*W*e need a ministry model that meets the needs of today's women, both modern and postmodern. We call this model the Transformation Model because it has one goal—life change in women for their fulfillment and God's glory!

Postmodern women demand that our ministries offer authentic, substantial opportunities to grow and serve. We find that modern women want that too. The Transformation Model incorporates both their needs. What might this model offer women of all generations that they have not experienced before?

The Seven Pillars of the Transformation Model

1. The Transformation Model Centers on Scripture

If we envision women's ministry as a wheel, the hub of the wheel is the study of God's Word. Bible study is the primary activity of the ministry. It is the one component that is designed with all the women of the church in mind. All other ministries are the spokes of the wheel. These spokes give women opportunities to use what they have learned in God's Word. And they are the place we narrow the focus and minister to women with specific needs.

The truths of Scripture nourish all women, for all their lives. We have found that when postmoderns finally discover absolute truth on which to build their lives, they love truth as much as moderns do. So, when a woman asks me how to get involved in women's ministries, I almost always direct her to our Bible studies. That's where she will find the spiritual food she needs.

In Matthew 22 when the Pharisee asks Jesus to place a priority on the commandments, Jesus models this wheel. He answers the lawyer with, "'Love the Lord your God with all your heart and with all your soul and with all your mind.' This is the first and greatest commandment. And the second is like it: 'Love your neighbor as yourself'" (vv. 37–39). Jesus reveals that God's desire is to transform us through our relationship with Him so that He can transform our relationship with others, that they may be transformed also. The greatest transformation tool is the Bible!

2. The Transformation Model Builds Relationships

Although the Scriptures are the focus of a life-changing women's ministry, mere knowledge of the Bible is not the desired goal. Rather it is first a deeper relationship with God and then healthy, intimate relationships with other women.

Women love to connect—some more than others. On leadership style and personality tests, both of us come out task-oriented. At the Bible classes, I (Sue) enjoy people but I am there for Bible study! During my first years at IBC, I made sure the Bible study format was heavy on task and light on fellowship. I paid the price. Some of our more relational women left looking for genuine friendships. I have learned that God values relationship too.

He created the church so that we could belong to one another. When our ministries give women time to connect as well as meaningful tools to deepen their friendships, everyone is blessed. Most postmodern women demand it—even if they are more task-oriented. Many, because of their backgrounds, need spiritual mothering as well as exposure to genuine relationships. It gives them a sense of home and proves that Christianity works.

Women on campuses are also hungry for connection. They also need a relationship with Jesus first. But often they are not aware of that need. They will join in just to make meaningful friendships. Many campuses lack a ministry that offers both a relationship with Christ and also with other women. We will talk about how to implement such a ministry in part 3.

Around the world, women have the same needs. Missionaries find that bonding between American teams and nationals is a number-one priority. Different languages and cultures complicate the relationships, but the basics don't change. Growing to love one another and building relationships is second only to centering on Scripture.

3. The Transformation Model Accommodates Differences

Segregating women by ages and categories violates the Titus 2 mandate in Scripture. Most women enjoy being with women from different backgrounds and life stages.

Consider these real-life examples:

- In a small group, a single woman sees the tears and hears the woes of a woman who married carelessly. The single woman thinks seriously about whether or not to accept an invitation from a nonbeliever at work who has invited her to dinner.
- A young mother shares her struggles with her strong-willed two-year-old. An older mother explains what worked in her child's life. She cautions her not to overreact and comforts her with the knowledge that all two-year-olds throw tantrums.

- An African-American woman prays for a white woman's ailing mother. The white woman has never experienced the delight of sisterhood with a woman of a different color. Both are blessed. The white woman views a racially motivated crime on the news with a new perspective.
- A working woman vents frustration at her boss's inappropriate advances—but she loves her job. A professional woman with thirty years experience takes her aside and helps her discover her options. She provides resources that will help if necessary. And she prays with her.
- The mother of a prodigal connects with a young woman who resembles her daughter. Together they talk through some of the issues that have estranged them and the mother begins to understand her daughter in ways she never had before. The mother takes steps toward her daughter and in time the relationship is healed.

These are the benefits of bringing different women together. Some resist the idea. We lost a few young mothers from our Bible study because they wanted to be with other young moms. The next year we offered a small group just for them. But we recruited two older mothers to lead it. As we prayed for ways to retain our young mothers, God brought us a woman with a heart to begin a "moms" ministry.

This ministry helped our moms connect with other moms and learn more about parenting. They seemed more content in heterogeneous groups the next year. When we have surveyed women, most want to be in a mixed group. They have discovered the blessing these groups offer.

4. The Transformation Model Makes Every Minute Meaningful

We live in a 24/7, all-the-time world. People expect to be able to buy anything twenty-four hours a day, seven days a week. Work follows us home on the Internet. We wake up in a different world than the one in which we went to sleep. Change happens so fast, we can't learn about it before it is obsolete. The pace of modern life isn't healthy. When people come into the church, we want to offer them a haven where the rhythm slows down. We want to turn our thoughts to God, relationships, and meaningful endeavors. We want to rest and focus on what's really important in life. And we should.

But time is tricky in ministry today. Women won't tolerate your wasting their time. They are busy, and most have multiple choices concerning how they will spend their free time. Some women have almost no free time, and joining your ministry comes with great sacrifice. They schedule in only what they believe is valuable. You will only waste their time once—maybe twice. As a result, the standards are high. We must plan what we do carefully.

I am not suggesting that we entertain the women or try to outdo the competition. But I am saying that if our ministry is not covered in prayer, well planned, and expertly executed, women will not participate. It had better be worth their time.

But there is a twist! The postmodern woman doesn't want to be rushed. Too much structure makes her uncomfortable. For several years I used a bell in our Bible study to signal when it was almost time to finish our table discussion. I also used it in our prayer time to let the women know when we were going to move on to a new subject. Many of the younger women did not like that bell! Women today want to know the time is well planned, but they also want the flexibility to "let the Spirit lead" at times. We'll talk about ways to incorporate *chaord* in your format later while still making every minute meaningful.

5. The Transformation Model Builds Teams

Team expert Don Simmons defines a team as "an enthusiastic group of people with complementary skills and gifts who work together toward common purposes and have a high level of trust and accountability."[1]

You need a team! Our world is in desperate need of Jesus. The numbers are huge. Are you praying that God will enlarge your influence and bring you women of all generations? When He does, you will need an army of women at your side. You will never be able to meet those needs by yourself.

Building a team and delegating the ministry means you give up control. And you will invest countless hours recruiting, training, and encouraging your team. They will need you to oversee—not micromanage—their work. As a result, many leaders refuse to put in the time up front to build teams. Don't be one of them!

Teams are not an option—especially in a postmodern world. Teams and community are an effective witnessing tool to post-moderns. They won't be impressed if you are a one-woman show. No matter how gifted or passionate you are, ultimately you can't do it alone.

Lone Ranger Alert!

Wherever you work, there will always be lone rangers—women who insist on doing their own thing. They refuse to work with others. Instead of agonizing over their loss, learn to let them go. God probably can't use them to their full potential, but that is their choice.

6. The Transformation Model Adds Variety

Have you noticed during your weekly grocery run how many options you have to choose from? One missionary who returned home on furlough was so overwhelmed by the vast array of choices, she wanted to flee the store. Do you wish life were simpler? Although many of us do, it isn't. Americans expect variety.

What does that mean for ministry? In the church and on the campus, women expect a medley of ministries—especially the postmoderns. However, your ministry will look different depending on your size. Small churches and campuses are foolish to overextend resources. But variety comes packaged in different ways. We'll examine when and how to add variety in later sections.

7. The Transformation Model Prepares for Conflict

"I can't believe the lies he is telling about our pastor," moaned Ellen, a seminary student who served on the missions committee of her church. She grieved over a conflict between the senior pastor and the missions pastor, Sam. What happened? The senior pastor asked Sam to resign. They were mismatched from the beginning. Sam was a retired missionary and insisted on ministering "the way it had always been done." The senior pastor believed Sam's methods were outdated and ineffective.

For three years, they tried to work out their differences. The senior pastor sent Sam to training seminars. He suggested Sam plan a short-term missions trip to expose church members to missions. Sam refused. Nothing worked and now Sam was packing up his office.

Even before his last day at the church, Sam began to slander the senior pastor. He invited each member of the missions committee to dinner and used the time to defend his position and attack the integrity and character of the senior pastor. Sam used words like "evil" and "dangerous."

Ellen and her husband had accepted Sam's invitation to dinner—and Ellen was devastated. She had invested years in missions only to see it near destruction due to the controversy. "What does God want me to do?" she asked.

Unfortunately, this scenario is common. Whether you minister in a church, on a campus, or on the mission field, you will encounter conflict. Even if you make wise decisions, not everyone will agree with you. Those who aren't prepared reap consequences that break hearts, drive women from ministry, and damage God's good name.

Conflict is like a country road. You never know where it will lead. In my experience, unless you prepare ahead, conflict will take you where you don't want to go.

Many women assume that they can avoid conflict by making everyone happy. They think that because we are Christians, we won't disagree. Both assumptions are wrong. No matter what you do, you can't make everyone happy. And believers do disagree, sometimes so fiercely they dishonor God and damage the church or ministry they love.

At IBC, women who serve with Sue sign a pledge that they will handle conflict biblically. We study principles from Matthew 18 and we equip ourselves beforehand so we know how to respond when conflict erupts.

Part 2, *Taking the Transformation Model to the Church,* contains instruction and resources to help you learn the skill of conflict resolution. Although this section is directed at those in church ministry, it is equally valuable for women on the campus, on the mission field, or in other kinds of ministry. Learn to survive conflict without casualties.

These seven pillars of the Transformation Model—center on Scripture, build relationships, accommodate differences, make every minute meaningful, build teams, add variety, and prepare for conflict—are basic to ministering to both postmodern and modern women. Details follow to help you apply these principles. Are you called to the church, the campus, the mission field, or another facet of women's ministry? Maybe you have the opportunity to minister in several of these arenas. It is our heartfelt prayer that God will use the principles, stories, and pioneer profiles ahead to transform lives and bring unspeakable joy.

TAKING THE TRANSFORMATION MODEL TO THE CHURCH

*O*ver the past fifteen years, the Transformation Model has emerged in cutting-edge women's ministries in American churches. You could fly around the country and visit a variety of exceptional women's ministries. Unfortunately, few of us have the time or resources for such a trip. But this book can help you design your own innovative ministry for both postmodern and modern women in your church.

Part 2 contains strategies and examples from experienced church leaders as well as our own ideas. Are you sold out to women's ministry as a full-time woman on staff? Or are you a lay leader with a passion to implement a dynamic women's ministry in your church even though you won't be financially compensated? Maybe you aren't sure God is calling you, but you sense a gentle stirring in your soul when you envision yourself impacting women for Christ. No matter your circumstances, this section will show you how to get off to a great start.

Chapter 3

BEGIN RIGHT!

omen today find themselves facing different scenarios. How you begin and how you minister is shaped by the size of your church, the leadership's attitude toward women, and whether there is an existing women's ministry. In this chapter, we will explore several real-life examples, learn from their experiences, and then glean some principles that apply to everyone.

A Large Church Without a "Transforming" Women's Ministry

I (Sue) planted my first women's ministry in this scenario, at a megachurch of ten thousand members in a large denomination. Having no woman on staff due to the pastor's views on that matter, different lay women tried each year to organize the women of the church. Several circles met in homes. Volunteers hosted spectacular dinners and fashion shows. But the deep needs of women were not addressed. And each year after she concluded her term, a different lay leader left in disappointment. My immediate predecessor was so discouraged that we couldn't get her to join us when we implemented the Transformation Model. Her experience had been painful and she wanted nothing to do with women's ministry. Sadly, I have observed this pattern repeatedly. When women receive little training or support, they often leave, vowing "Never again!"

A New Beginning

Liz was an elder's wife. From experience in a former church, she knew the impact a thriving women's ministry could have on women—and she wanted it for her church. A gifted leader, Liz hadn't used her gifts in the church because there were few opportunities for women with gifts of leadership and vision. Instead she started her own business and worked in community organizations.

But God sparked a passion in her heart to begin a ministry that would transform women in her church. After brainstorming with local women experienced in ministry, she formed her plan, made an appointment with the pastor, and received his blessing. He even gave her a budget and a staff member as the women's ministry liaison. God was laying the foundation and Liz's enthusiasm grew.

A New Team

The Sunday my family joined Liz's church, she ran down the aisle and embraced me. Immediately her women's ministry plans spilled out. She heard I just graduated from seminary. She knew I was an experienced Bible teacher. Would I join her? My passion was her passion and it was God's timing. Liz and I were a team for the next seven years.

We recruited women to pray. Liz knew those who had a heart for women. She met with each one and shared her vision. Then she asked them to consider joining us for periodic prayer.

Ten of us prayed together every other week over the next six months. We asked God for guidance on the structure of the ministry. We asked for leaders. We asked for God to send us the women to participate. We asked for credibility so that the leadership would ultimately hire a woman director. We understood that without a trained leader to bring consistency to the ministry, it would not flourish long-term—and our church had the resources to bring a woman on staff. We committed the entire ministry to Him. In addition to prayer, we dreamed about a women's ministry uniquely designed for our church and what it would take for that dream to come true.

During those six months, God revealed the hearts and gifts of the women who faithfully prayed with us, and they became the new women's ministry board. The foundation for a team was laid.

This step is crucial. However long yours is, a time of prayer and planning will provide a solid foundation for your future ministry. Don't skip this important element!

Who Are Your Women?

In most large churches, you will minister to women of all ages, stages, and backgrounds. You must consider these differences even as you plan for the first year. It is important not to grow too quickly, however. Focus on the core of your ministry first.

How can you learn the demographics of women in your church? If you have been a part of the church for many years, you may be familiar enough with its makeup. If not, ask a staff member. Those charged with integrating new members or with publicity may know statistics that would help you.

Surveys can be useful. When a woman fills out a survey she knows you care about what she thinks. However, unless you give them out and take them up at the same time, the results are usually limited. We experienced a 10 percent return on our surveys. You might try a survey in your church bulletin to be returned in the offering plate or to an usher. However you do it, find out who your women are. Otherwise, you can't plan a ministry for them.

Invite Leaders' Wives

As we began, it was important to enlist as many staff and deacon wives as possible. We hosted a lovely lunch for them and introduced them to the ministry. Some joined in. Many did not. One hindrance that plagued us through the years was that the senior pastor's wife never got on board. She was a godly woman with many fine qualities, but she chose not to participate. This and years without a women's ministry director on staff were our two greatest hurdles.

Woo your leadership's wives; share your vision with them and invite their participation. They are vital!

Build a Solid Relationship with the Staff Liaison

Many churches that have not yet added a woman on staff will provide the women's ministry with a liaison to the pastoral staff. Your relationship with him must thrive if your ministry is to succeed. Communication is key.

At our church, Liz communicated with our staff liaison at least once a month in a memo. We didn't include him in the day to day details or even the major decisions. We believed God gave women greater insight into the needs of other women. But we always explained our ideas clearly and asked his blessing before we proceeded. If he objected, we stopped. He always had good reasons and we valued his counsel and direction.

Communicate the Exciting News!

Because our church was huge, we needed a way to communicate with the women in the church. In large churches, the challenge is letting everyone know that you are about to launch. Will your pastor announce your new ministry from the pulpit? That's a great help! Pulpit announcements were rare in our church because there was so much going on. So we researched another possibility. The church produced a monthly magazine that was mailed to the entire church. Our staff liaison asked for space. Not only did they give us space, but also the church's graphic artist created an attractive page introducing the new ministry. We were off!

A Small Church Without an Organized Women's Ministry

I (Kelley) discovered Creekside Bible Fellowship as it celebrated its first year anniversary. The congregation of ninety-plus people (including the growing nursery) had just begun renting space in a local business park. The façade of the young church resembled a plain white office building. Perhaps you are familiar with such a "store-front" church in your area. There are thousands across the nation.

Don't let small numbers discourage you from initiating a women's ministry. From the beginning, Creekside women held semester Bible studies and, within two years, had established an annual fall retreat. Wives of the pastor and elders were involved in this process, but they by no means ran the show exclusively. Over the years, we have applied some of the principles found here—to great effect. The methods will look different for each small church, but the same end product is still the goal—a ministry that changes lives.

Bigger Isn't Better!

Half of all American congregations have fewer than one hundred regularly participating adults.[1] Your resources may be limited, but God will furnish all you need. Don't sell yourself short just because you aren't a megachurch. You'll enjoy unique advantages because of your intimate size.

The Same Principles Apply

You begin by selling your leadership on your vision. Write a proposal. Is a woman on staff a possibility? Would your budget allow it? Maybe it is impossible now, but what about in the future?

At Creekside, the long-range plan included a paid women's minister, when the right person came along and the church was able to pay her salary. In our eight years, we have had one women's director—on staff, but paid virtually nothing due to financial constraints. It worked for us for a while. Be flexible with your leadership and remember your goals. But plant the seed for such a director early, because sustaining quality and consistency without a woman on staff is difficult and frustrating. Be gracious. Assure your pastor you will work diligently whatever the resources.

Then enlist the women who show an interest in ministry to women in your church. Are there women who have taken the initiative to invite women into their homes? Is there an older woman that the younger women go to for advice or encouragement? Does anyone distinguish herself as a woman who knows the Word? Are there professional women with skills in administration and leadership? Gather these women together to pray and brainstorm.

Do you know the demographics of your church? How many women are single? working? widowed? mothers of young children? In a small church, many of your women know one another. Is your church composed mainly of one group of women? That is more likely in a small church. Should you focus on ministry to them first?

Publicizing your new ministry is easier in a small church. Will your pastor announce it from the pulpit? You don't have as much competition as in a larger church. Post flyers on the doors, stick them in the stalls of the restroom. Divide up your roster and make personal phone calls. What about a bulletin insert? A skit before a worship service? All of these methods continue to work for Creekside. Find out what works with your church.

Will your pastor's wife be involved? In a small church her absence is even more noticeable. Invite her graciously, but give her the freedom to participate or not according to her interests and other responsibilities. Don't expect her to teach the Bible or head up the ministry just because she is the pastor's wife. Neither should she run the ministry from the sideline or use her influence without discretion. Give her opportunities to serve with her unique gifts. Respect and protect her privacy. If she is part of the team, that will help your ministry. If not, don't resent her.

A Church with an Existing Women's Ministry

When I (Sue) was hired as pastor to women at Irving Bible Church, a healthy women's ministry was taking shape. Mary had been the women's ministry director for two years, although women's ministry existed long before she joined the staff. She brought a heart for women and expertise in events, but as much as she enjoyed ministry, her husband and two young sons needed her at home, so she made the decision to work part-time.

With our children grown, my husband and I believed God was calling me into full-time ministry. I came on staff to partner with Mary and to focus on building the Bible study. God paved the way for the transition.

Navigating Change

It wasn't easy for Mary to report to a newcomer. She was gracious, but I know that at times she found it difficult to watch me take the ministry in new directions. We differ in our gifts, personality, and leadership styles, but in many ways we complement one another. I did not undo what was in place. I simply added to it. Nor did I try to change the way she worked. Fortunately, we have melded as a team. Mary and I share a common vision and model for ministry—the Transformation Model. And we are united in our commitment to both the postmodern and the modern women God sends us.

Mary had recruited influential women to serve and the pastor's wife supported us completely. Many of the initial steps were bypassed because of Mary's groundwork. I came on board in March and we were up and running with a new board and Bible study in September.

If You Encounter Resistance

Our experience is unusual. Often when a ministry already exists and newcomers appear with fresh ideas, there is conflict. That is especially true when women don't agree on the ministry model. In several denominations, older women are wedded to "modern" models that fit their generation but don't work with younger women now. Changing these denominational models means letting go of the past. They don't want to!

Some older women struggle to understand why these models don't work anymore. They are easily wounded when younger women want to try a new model. How do you plant a new model against this kind of resistance? How do you honor women with different perspectives while not allowing them to dictate an outdated model?

First you confirm that you have your leadership's blessing. The pastor won't want women in the church feuding. Bring him a clear, written proposal of your vision, explain your reasoning, and assure him you want to work under his authority. If he agrees, move ahead. If he resists, this is not the time. God has other plans for you.

Next, connect with women you think may resist your efforts. Try not to see them as the enemy. One at a time, take them to lunch and share your ideas. When you pray over the meal, ask God to help you understand each other. Kindly inform them that the pastor knows and supports your vision. Ask for their ideas. If possible, include them in your plans. You may be surprised at the encouragement you receive. You may have to adjust some of your plans to win their support, but it will probably pay off long-term. If you can win these women over, the ministry will benefit.

If your views are irreconcilable, hopefully you can agree to disagree. Can your ministries coexist side by side, giving women the choice of attending either or both? That may be your best option. If these women attempt to discredit you or your ministry, then you should follow the steps to healthy conflict resolution shared later in this section. Just be sure that you never say or do anything that might be perceived as criticism of their ministry. God will work it out over time.

If you have won them over or agreed to disagree, you are ready to begin. Gather women to pray. Visit other churches to observe their women's ministry. Read books on the subject. Follow the pattern already laid out in this section. Even though there is already a women's ministry in your church, in essence you are starting over.

In a Nutshell . . .

Whether God calls you to a large or small church, or a church with or without an existing women's ministry, the principles are the same. You simply adjust them to your situation. Here in a nutshell is the way to begin a women's ministry:

- Propose your dream to church leadership and receive their blessing and support.
- Meet with influential women in the church and share your vision.
- Enlist women with a heart for women to pray regularly with you for God's direction.
- Know your demographics so you can tailor-make your plans to their needs.
- Communicate the exciting news that you will soon launch!

How Northwest Bible Church
First Hired a Women's Minister

"A key step in organizing a Women's Ministry program is to inform and educate the male leadership of the church, if they do not share the vision. It is a rare exception to find leadership that has a Women's Ministries program high on its agenda," writes Vickie Kraft who served Northwest Bible Church in Dallas as women's minister for fourteen years.[2] Here's how the women of her church hired Vickie.

> The women from Northwest Bible Church put together a written proposal. They included quotations from well-known women about the need for a relevant ministry to women and quotations from women in their own church in response to the survey. They detailed plans they had in mind. They demonstrated their conviction that a woman was needed on staff to administer the program. Then they invited the elders and their wives for dinner and presented each elder with a folder containing the program laid out clearly. They answered their questions and discussed the subject thoroughly. This thorough approach and the evidence the women offered convinced the elders, and, consequently, a salary for a minister to women was included in the next year's budget.[3]

Chapter 4

BUILD YOUR TEAM

*O*ur goal is transforming women's lives. How does it happen? It trickles down from an inspired and passionate lead team!

We laughed until it hurt. We were celebrating the end of a fruitful year in women's ministries at our last board meeting. Our retreat chairperson arrived with a bright bag full of little wrapped boxes. Curiosity piqued, we asked, "What's in the boxes?" "You'll see," she teased. After our meeting, she instructed us to take off our shoes and socks. Then she handed each of us a little box. We tore them open to find a toe ring inside.

Through the year we had chided her about her toe rings. She loved casual shoes and her feet were always nicely pedicured, nails painted, sporting at least one toe ring. Somehow a woman in her late forties with toe rings made us laugh. We loved her young-at-heart attitude, her creativity, and her delight in exploring new ideas.

We slipped on our new toe rings and joined hands around the circle, women from twenty to sixty. We lifted our hearts in gratitude to a chorus of "I love you, Lord." God had done great things! He had used this team to bring women to faith, grow them in His Word, and challenge them to serve.

As the women chatted, hugged, and laughed afterward, I thought back a year and a half earlier to when we formed this team. Why had it worked? Certainly because God had blessed us. But there were also strategies that helped us connect and minister together. In this section, let's look at why teams are important (and biblical) and how to build an effective one.

Why Teams?

Jesus built a team. In His three-year ministry on earth, He invested heavily in the Twelve. He chose them carefully and spent His days living with them as He trained them. He sent them out to minister in pairs. He taught them to work in groups. He knew when He founded His church that we are more productive together and that we need each other. He modeled team building, and that's reason enough for us to build them too. But we have observed that many women resist teams.

Do You Resist Teams?

Let's find out! Do you agree or disagree with these statements? Be honest!

- If I want something done right, I'd better do it myself.
- I'll have to set up meetings, and they are a waste of time.
- Most people won't follow through and I'll have to do it all myself anyway.
- Teams ultimately mean conflict and I hate conflict.
- It takes more time to recruit a team than to do it all myself.
- I've had bad experiences with teams in the past.
- Teams are more trouble than they are worth.
- I don't want to be accountable for other people's mistakes.

- Why risk a team effort when I know I can meet the standards of excellence expected?
- I don't want to share the credit.

If you agreed with any of these statements, you may resist the team concept. We agree that, initially, building teams might take extra time. But if you refuse to invest in them, you'll pay a price. Teams are essential to the Transformation Model!

What's the Price?

When I observe a board member who won't delegate, I start looking for her replacement. I don't have to ask her to leave. She burns out.

Laura was dynamite at organizing our women's dinners. She transformed the room into a showplace reflecting the theme of the dinner. It became a Hawaiian beach or a garden gazebo. The women knew it was the best ten dollars they would spend all year. But Laura refused to take the time up front to organize committees and call women who were eager to help.

As a result, she spent the last week alone hanging decorations from the ceiling and haggling with the caterer. Exhausted, she bailed out of her two-year commitment. Her replacement immediately implemented teams to help. The dinners ran like a German train and the coordinator enjoyed the experience.

I grieved for Laura. God had given her extraordinary abilities to minister through these events. But her refusal to share the load took her down. You can carry the ministry by yourself for a while, but inevitably you'll burn out.

The Transformation Model Requires Teams

The Transformation Model is about transforming women into mature, productive, joyful daughters of the King. For a woman to be transformed, she must have opportunities to see how God can use her. She must know her gifts and step out in faith expecting God to work through her. When she does, she experiences profound pleasure and usually surprise.

The feelings we experience when God works through us to teach and minister to women can't be described—only experienced. God wants every believer to know that joy! God expects leaders to offer multiple opportunities for women to serve.

Offer Multiple Levels of Opportunity in Any Size Ministry

1. Offer Entry-Level Opportunities

No matter what size your church, new believers and newcomers need entry-level opportunities to serve. These jobs will not sink your ministry if neglected. They don't require training, maturity, or expertise. In an entry-level job, you aren't overseeing others. Every ministry should have the tasks divided in such a way that even new believers and women without experience can participate.

Are you providing service opportunities for women who have never volunteered before? Are you giving newcomers a chance to show you who they are and what they can do? Are they nurtured by trained coordinators who will shepherd and instruct them so that they will enjoy a positive experience?

From these entry-level opportunities will bubble up women with leadership gifts. Women will emerge who are diligent, punctual, gifted, and personable. You will identify those who work well with others, those you can count on, and those who love women. One day, these women will lead the ministry. One day, one of them will sit where you sit.

That's the plan. Begin by using volunteers for entry-level tasks, but recruit women you know to serve as sub-team managers and coordinators.

2. Offer Subteam Manager Positions

Once you have identified a woman who works well on a team and has the attitudes and gifts for overseeing others, you are wise to give her the chance. For example, if you chair an event, let her be your registration coordinator. Find a woman with computer expertise and the gift of administration. Let her register women, oversee making name tags and man the registration table. See how well she delegates. She might replace the coordinator next year.

In every area of ministry, these varied opportunity levels should be in place. The process of transformation cannot proceed without them.

3. Give Major Responsibilities to Tested Coordinators

The coordinator oversees the major facets of your ministry. She usually emerges by serving first at the entry and support levels. She has distinguished herself as a spiritually mature woman. She may be young in years but is well grounded and shows promise. She works well on a team. She is passionate about her ministry. She understands the Transformation Model and knows that her work is more than accomplishing a task, putting on an event, or serving in a support capacity. She is building leaders with you. She is sold out to transforming women one at a time.

Let's Examine Some Team-Building Principles

The Transformation Model is built on teams. To transform postmodern and modern women, we must embrace them one by one. You don't have enough arms or enough time to do that alone.

Refusing to work with others is often a sign that you fear losing control. Women's ministry is messy. It has been compared to herding cats! You may fear the conflict that might erupt when women work together. Maybe you've had a negative experience in the past and it is coloring your perspective. Maybe you think you can do it better yourself. If your only concern is decorating the stage or providing a delicious dinner, you may pull it off. But this is not a transforming women's ministry. To transform women requires multiple arms, hearts, and minds—and it's a lot more fun!

If teams scare you because you don't know how to build one, the following team-building principles should encourage you.

How Will You Structure Your Team?

You can call your key leaders a team, board, committee, or anything you want to. Make it fit your environment. It is important, however, that you give it a name—an identity. New millennium ministry may be characterized by *chaord,* but there is still order in *chaord* and you'll need it to accomplish your vision.

Structure in Small Churches

Since the majority of churches in America average less than two hundred members,[1] most women's ministries won't need a large leadership team. But you *will* need a team. Guard against the tendency to do it all yourself because it is more expedient. However few women you have, the Transformation Model is about providing them opportunities to get involved and to develop their own potential for leadership in God's family.

I (Kelley) serve on the women's leadership team at Creekside Bible Fellowship, now nine years old. The women's ministry averages about twenty regular participants at this time, although that number spikes at our annual retreat. Our leadership structure has fluctuated as well, but the most efficient team was made up of three, jokingly nicknamed "the Triumvirate." I offer it here as a solid, working illustration of women's ministry in a small church.

The director of women's ministry served on a volunteer basis since our church plant could not afford her salary. Having previous experience and seminary training, the director wrote and taught the Bible studies, counseled women, and guided the vision of the ministry. She attended staff meetings and kept the male leadership informed about what the women were doing.

Depending upon the gifts and training of your director, some of these responsibilities may be given to someone else under her management. For instance, she may recruit a teacher for the evening Bible study, a worship leader, someone to oversee childcare for the morning study, and someone to do hospitality. It is in the director's best interest to delegate as much of the detail work as possible to other women. In doing so, she creates a sense of ownership and excitement in them as they serve other women.

The second member of our team, "the administrator," managed the women's finances, publicity, annual retreat, and various other details. With so many day-to-day responsibilities, the administrator of a small church's women's ministry is in a perfect position to form a small subteam.

She might find someone who understands computer graphics to help with publicity. She would definitely want to recruit a retreat coordinator, hopefully someone who has experience with past retreats. With so few women involved, such helpers could make up the subteam level of leadership rather than making each one a board position.

The "shepherd" held the third board position. She was responsible for the care of the women's souls. This means practical as well as spiritual help. She saw that every hospitalized woman was visited, that meals were provided for new moms and the sick. She was there to disciple or coordinate others to disciple the women, so that each person would feel she had someone involved in her life that cared for her. It meant building relationships through the Bible study ministry so that she could more accurately assess where the women were spiritually. Although individual shepherding was already occurring, this board position provided some accountability. It was a very pastoral role.

The women's leadership team provided a means for serving the women at Creekside, challenging them to greater responsibility and spiritual maturity. It did not always work perfectly, but the basic structure remained in place to keep the women's ministry on track even when our director resigned. Your church will not always experience straight paths and smooth waters, either. Be flexible, pray constantly, and work together.

Structure in Large Churches

Working Teams and Advisory Teams

As a church grows, consider expanding your lead team into two groups: a working team and an advisory team. An advisory team gives long-term direction to the ministry. These are insightful women whose valuable expertise helps steer the ministry, especially in changing waters. If we compared these two teams to the structure of many churches, the working team would be the staff and the advisory team would be the elders.

IBC has both a working team and an advisory team. The advisory team comes out of the working team. Here's what happens. The working team serves a limited term. When they complete their commitment, they automatically roll over onto the advisory team. Why not take advantage of their experience? They are invited to meet with the working team at the end of the ministry year to help evaluate and determine next year's course. Their participation varies—some are active, many consider this merely an honorary position.

An advisory team is optional. A working team is not. If particular women in your church want to run the ministry from the sidelines but balk at serving, don't give in to their requests. You need a group of women who will roll up their sleeves and work!

The Makeup of a Working Team

What will your working team look like? Below, we will provide a thorough survey of your choices. Remember: depending upon your size and resources, some positions can be combined with others, some can be bypassed completely, and others can wait until the specific need arises. Take a look.

Team Leader

Someone must be in charge, whether she is paid staff or lay volunteer. The pastor to women or director of women's ministries (whatever you call her) is responsible for the overall ministry. Her duties may include overseeing the board, counseling, training women, and teaching the Bible study. She is also responsible for all events, the budget, and many other details. If you are blessed to have more than one woman on staff, there are many ways to divide up the responsibilities. Find a way that works for you.

Bible Study Coordinator

Design your working team to reflect the needs of your women. Begin with your ministry priorities. Remember: the Transformation Model is Bible study centered. Therefore your first team position will probably be a Bible study coordinator.

How many Bible study coordinators will you need? If you plan more than one class, find a coordinator for each. How will you decide? If most of your women work, begin with a weekly Bible class that meets at night or on the weekend.

If there are just as many women who could attend during the day and you have the resources, begin with a night class *and* a day class. For moms with young children, provide childcare—first for the day class but later for the night class too. Then your single moms can attend.

The Bible study coordinator runs the class. She recruits leaders and administrative teams to handle all the details. We will discuss

Bible studies and the class coordinator's role in detail in later chapters.

Prayer Coordinator

Prayer is the foundation of your ministry. Every leader should include prayer in her work not only personally but also as part of the way she leads her team. A prayer coordinator may oversee prayer chains, special days of prayer, or prayer workshops. Her role is to promote prayer in the entire ministry. She should be a woman of prayer and passionate to help others pray. Knowing that prayer undergirds our women and our ministry encourages us all. In addition we attribute any ministry fruit to the power of prayer. Every women's ministry needs a prayer coordinator.

Administrative Secretary

This woman is invaluable to the team leader. She takes care of details. For example, the secretary is the communication link between the team leader and the team. She notifies members of meetings, changes, and procedures. She keeps minutes and records. She can also oversee the logistics, food, and transportation for team retreats and annual events that edify the team.

Event Coordinators

Although according to the Transformation Model events are no longer central to women's ministry, women still love events. And they are valuable. A weekend away to focus on God and build relationships can have a profound effect on a woman's spiritual growth. These events often provide an entry point to propel women into other ongoing ministries. Events give women the chance to connect, relax, and laugh. Chapter 10 will show you how to create exciting events.

Identify events that benefit and appeal to women. Consider retreats, conferences for deep spiritual impact, light-hearted seminars, holiday dinners for fellowship and outreach, mother-daughter banquets, high teas, and whatever else your creative women dream up. You'll need a coordinator for each of your major events—like a weekend retreat. Some may be grouped depending on their complexity and timing.

The best event coordinators are strong administrators and encouragers. They sell their team on the vision of the event and then have fun getting prepared. Women who cannot commit to an ongoing ministry can often head up event teams.

Publicity Coordinator

Who is informing the women and the church about your ministry? Who knows how to package what you do so that others will be excited about getting involved? The publicity coordinator's role depends on how much staff publicity support you enjoy. It also depends on the size of your church. This job in a large church looks different from the job in a small church.

In small churches, she may simply write bulletin announcements and design flyers for the halls or restroom stall doors. Publicity may be mostly word of mouth as women interact. She might make the women's ministry brochure on her computer. With ready-to-order papers, attractive brochures can be produced that way.

However, in large churches, a brochure on ready-to-order paper might not fly. Other ministries produce four-color professional pieces and the women's ministry is under pressure to do the same. If your church has in-house capabilities or supplies the budget, your publicity coordinator has the resources she needs. It may help, however, if she has experience in graphic design, writing, or production. Again, adapt this position to your setting.

Financial Coordinator

Who will handle the budget? The women's ministry director at IBC is great with numbers, and I'm not. I'm delighted to delegate the budget to her. At my former church I recruited a young mother who was also a CPA. I am amazed at how many professional women in our churches are eager to use their accounting skills for the Lord.

Special Interests Coordinators

The larger your church the more of these you will need. As your ministry is settled and you begin to branch out, special interest needs will emerge. Mothers of young children want a mom's ministry. Single moms have unique needs.

Divorcees and widows often request their own ministries—but don't group them together. Their circumstances and struggles are different and they won't appreciate being linked. We will cover ministries for special groups in depth in chapter 11.

Missions Coordinator

Are you a missions-minded church? Do you want your women to enlarge their perspective and become global in their thinking? Are there opportunities for your women to actually take short-term mission trips? Can you find creative ways to encourage full-time missionaries sent out from your church?

A missions coordinator should be a woman with a heart for women all over the world and the ability to plan a ministry that will inspire others. The missions coordinator's goal is to promote a global perspective in all that your women do. We network with our missions pastor and deliberately choose our missions coordinator from women on the church-wide missions team. That way we are assured of working together. This position looks different depending on the way your church handles missions. Again, complement what already exists in the church.

At my former church, we labeled this position *outreach* and asked the coordinator to oversee both inner-city and world missions. We structured the position this way because missions were done through the denomination and there was limited access to full-time missionaries. Few short-term mission trips were planned through the church. Every church does missions differently. Assess yours and complement it.

Mercy Ministry Coordinator

Many women's ministries include some form of mercy ministry. This can take two forms: helping the needy within your church body, then perhaps reaching out to those outside the church. First, design a ministry to meet the needs in your own body. At IBC we call it *Many Hands.*

Many Hands volunteers take meals and clean homes of the sick, visit those in need of encouragement, do handyman jobs, provide transportation, and meet other special needs. It began in women's ministry and is now churchwide.

We also support a food pantry by collecting food monthly from our Bible studies. The coordinator recruits volunteers and stays abreast of the needs within the church congregation.

Affirmation Coordinator

Hebrews 3:13 commands us to "encourage one another daily." As the team leader, you won't have sufficient time and energy to show your appreciation to the board members and volunteers. Find a woman with the gift of encouragement, give her a budget, and unleash her.

Our affirmation coordinator makes sure everyone feels appreciated, and she plans a special dinner for the board in late spring. She hosts dinners for our Bible study leaders and coleaders twice a year. She finds unique ways to say thank you and models the gracious spirit of a grateful woman.

Hospitality Coordinator

If your board wants help with food, recruit a hospitality coordinator. Find a woman who knows food and caterers, who loves to oversee its preparation and make it look good, and who enjoys assisting others. She helps with dinners, lunches, and our team kickoff retreat. If it involves food, she's the resource.

Historian

We want our memories recorded. The method depends on your church. In one church we created a beautiful scrapbook and bulletin board. At IBC, where we use multimedia to enhance our ministry, a year-end video highlights events of the past year. This is fun for a creative woman. Equip her with a good camera and give her the budget she needs. Then enjoy the labor of her hands and heart.

Team Positions for Your Unique Needs

What distinguishes your church from other churches? You may want to create a team position that fits your special design. Here are two examples.

Arts Coordinator

Postmoderns relate to images and art. We use art whenever we can. IBC has a full-time arts pastor and our women's ministry arts coordinator is part-time paid staff. She leads our arts integration and production teams and oversees drama, worship, and related arts in our Bible studies and retreat. We'll talk more about using the arts in your ministry in chapter 9.

Elective Coordinator

If you use a Bible study with complementary electives format you will need an electives coordinator on your board. This format will be explained in the section on Bible studies.

What Positions Should You Include on Your Team?

Look over the list and choose what fits your vision and resources. There may be some not on this list or you may call them by different names. Make it work for you. If you are just getting started, keep it small. Small churches are wise to limit what they do to what they can do well. If you have four widows, don't organize a widow's ministry. They should be able to link up without it.

At a minimum, include a team leader and her assistant, and coordinators for Bible study, prayer, and events. Then perhaps choose a secretary, publicity coordinator, and financial coordinator, or find someone who can do all three tasks. If needed, others can be added in time.

Don't forget to add your Bible teachers to your team if they are not already involved. They are leaders in your ministry and should be included. In addition, they will be better teachers if they understand the heartbeat of the ministry and cooperate with you.

Which Are Support Positions?

As you recruit your team, consider that some of your leaders will need to recruit their own teams to carry out their ministry—but others won't. These are support positions and can usually be accomplished solo. As a result, the women who serve in support capacities won't need team-building skills. Support positions are secretary, publicity, finances, affirmation, historian, and hospitality. These women may get help but won't absolutely need it to do a good job.

See appendix A for a sample board structure.

How Long Should a Team Member Serve?

Term limits are mandatory with a few exceptions. If you don't limit the time board members serve, you will be perceived as clannish and cliquish. In the Transformation Model, you want to give as many women as possible the chance to develop their gifts and have the opportunity to experience God working through them.

The exceptions would be staff positions and unique ministries that are too extensive for a lay leader to be expected to tackle. For example, the standard of excellence at our retreat makes it unreasonable to ask a new volunteer to head it up. The same woman led IBC's retreat for twenty years and recently handed it off to her assistant. These women are lay volunteers but are so exceptional that we allow them to remain on the board. No one objects.

But under ordinary circumstances and for the health of your ministry, limit the time your team serves. We ask our women to commit to two years with a third year option. At the beginning of the third year, we discuss whether a third year is recommended. Three years is an especially good idea for women working with subteams. For example, our Bible study coordinators learn the job the first year, fine tune it the second, and train their replacement the third.

When considering the third year option, we look at personal circumstances, the health of the ministry, and the individual woman's desires. If she wants to serve a third year and it is good for her family and the ministry, we are delighted.

An ideal scenario has about half your board rolling off each year. The seasoned members set the tone for the year as they welcome and train newcomers. This has occurred naturally with the boards I have planted. Some women move away. Others won't delegate and burn out. Some take the two-year option because of personal circumstances.

How do you retain the women who roll off the board? They are treasures to our ministry and it is important not to lose them. We honor them by immediately putting them on our advisory board. In addition, we make sure each one is plugged in the next year.

For example, our daytime Bible study coordinator loved her work, which was heavily administrative. But she missed the personal one-on-one time with women. She took a spiritual mothering class the summer after she rolled off the board and spent the next year shepherding a small group and linking up with several needy women who needed spiritual mothering. After a break, she could be asked to serve again—although we would give preference to a promising newcomer.

How Do You Recruit Your Team?

First write clear job descriptions. See appendix A for samples. Ask each team member to rework these every year to reflect what she is actually doing.

Then meet with several women leaders or your entire team to pray and brainstorm possibilities. Your team members often know just the right women to replace them. Try to come up with several women for each open position.

Consider their gifts, age, and experience. Try to balance your board so that a variety of women bring differing perspectives. I try to have several young single women if possible. I want a young mom and some older women. Ideally the team should reflect the makeup of your ministry.

For key leadership positions choose women that you know well. One wrong choice can make a miserable year. Be selective. If God doesn't bring someone to mind, wait.

Recruiting Your First Board

Recruiting your first board is a bit different. You probably won't know the women that well. It is risky, but you move ahead anyway. The first year we put together a board at my former church, we made two or three terrible choices. We had no experience working with these women so we chose the ones who appeared to be most qualified. They weren't always the best choices, but we learned over time.

The Recruiting Process

The woman who oversees the entire ministry should do the recruiting. The team works for you and needs to know that from the start.

If you are just getting started or the board is small, you may want to meet face to face with each candidate. Otherwise phoning them is fine. Before you begin your calls, pray that God will give these women discernment. You don't want them to say "yes" unless they are led of God. You don't want overcommitted or status-seeking women. You want women who are passionate about serving women and glorifying God.

Next, examine your list. Which board position is most strategic to next year's ministry? Which suggestion is the strongest? Often the same woman may be suggested for several positions. Where do you need her most? Ask her about that position first.

When you reach her, tell her that you would like for her to pray about serving on the board next year. Ask her if this is a possibility. If she knows up front that she is moving or is already too busy, then you both save time. If she says she will consider it, then proceed.

Describe the position you have in mind and ask if she thinks this might be a fit for her gifts and passion. If that job is not a good fit, you might suggest another position. If she is open, explain the details.

A Suggested Checklist

- Send her the job description.
- Suggest that she dialogue with the outgoing team member.
- Inform her of everything else expected. Tell her when the board meetings are scheduled.
- Give her the date of the board's kickoff training retreat and explain that her attendance is mandatory.
- Explain that she will be working as part of a team and that her input and prayer support are vital to the overall success of the ministry.
- If your board is required to attend one of your weekly Bible studies, make sure she understands that requirement.
- Explain the two-year commitment with a possible third.

- Tell her she would be serving with an incredible team doing God's work in women's lives—and that she'll have fun!
- If she is still interested, ask her to pray for at least a week
  and discuss this with family members.

Then wait for her answer. Don't call someone else for this position until you hear from her, but continue down your list until you
have asked someone to fill each position. A week later, call each one
back. If she accepts, express your delight and explain when her term
begins. If she declines, thank her for wisdom in listening to God's
leading. Then call the next woman on the list for that position.

Recruiting goes in rounds and may take a couple of hours once
a week for several weeks. Begin to recruit several months before
your new board begins its term. Women usually plan their year in
advance and they are often already committed if you wait until
later. The longer your ministry is established and the more fruit it
produces, the easier it is to recruit your team. Women want to be
a part of an exciting women's ministry!

How Long Should a Lay Director Serve Without Pay?

If the church won't or can't pay you, how long should you serve
as director in a volunteer capacity? If the director only serves a
limited term of a couple of years, the ministry is adversely affected.
In most circumstances, asking a woman to work staff hours indefinitely without pay is unreasonable. Asking her to do the work
of the ministry without the benefit of networking with other staff
causes all the women to feel slighted.

Let's consider the issue. Women's ministry is one of the last ministry frontiers. As a result many churches do not understand the
value of having a woman on staff to shepherd their women. In
some churches tradition bars the door. In small churches the leaders may see the value but money is the limiting factor. But because
of Titus 2 and the fact that over half of most churches are female,

women need a female shepherd. Without consistent leadership, any ministry will flounder.

What can you do? Here are some options:

If Your Church Can Afford It, Ask Your Leaders for a Woman on Staff

In chapter 3, we told you about how the women of Northwest Bible Church sought approval for a women's minister on staff to lead them. They not only wrote a proposal, they served their leaders a delicious dinner. Then they presented them with a folder detailing their vision and hopes. They presented their request graciously, and also asked to be a part of the search process. The result was Vickie Kraft and fourteen years of a model ministry that has impacted other churches around the world. This is the best result for the health of the women's ministry.

Stay and Serve Without Pay

If you are financially able, you can stay and serve, hoping that in time the leadership will recognize the value of your work. I did this for seven years at a former church. We poured our hearts into the women and I loved it. I admit I longed to be a part of the staff, but the ministry was enough. However, I could have been more effective as a bona fide part of the team. In addition, the church would have benefited from a woman's perspective.

Sometimes it was humorous. Secretaries throughout the church would alert us when the church forgot us in a brochure or ministry fair. We would find a gracious way to remind the leadership that we existed. They didn't exclude us intentionally—we simply were not part of the tradition. Nevertheless it was hard to feel that women were really valued.

I delight in the knowledge that our efforts were not in vain: soon after my time there ended, the leadership did put a woman on staff as director of women's ministries.

Ask to Be Part of the Staff with Little or No Pay

If you know your church budget definitely can't afford you and you don't need the money, you might consider asking to serve on staff with very little or no pay. Maybe you could be half- or quarter-time. Of course you would probably log more hours, but at least you would be participating with the staff. As the church was able they could increase your pay.

This is not a very good option, but there are some advantages. You bring consistency to women's ministry by serving longer than two years. In my experience, replacing directors every few years brings trouble! Consistent vision and momentum is lost. It takes time for women to trust the leader.

Leave, Trusting God Has a Better Place

If you need the money or find you cannot work a staff member's hours as a volunteer with a good heart attitude, then you need to leave. Your anger or resentment will never honor God. Trust Him to lead you to the right place for you.

Your women's ministry will never flourish if you change directors like light bulbs. But church leaders are accountable to God for the spiritual health of their women. Do all you can without an angry heart or rebellious attitude. Then trust God—He is faithful.

Chapter 5

RALLY YOUR TEAM

And let us consider how we may spur one another on toward love and good deeds. Let us not give up meeting together, as some are in the habit of doing, but let us encourage one another—and all the more as you see the Day approaching. (Hebrews 10:24–25)

*T*he most effective churches today are the ones that are developing team-based leadership. This pattern will likely continue into the twenty-first century, both because Scripture emphasizes Spirit-led, Spirit-gifted, collaborative team fellowship and because today's culture is receptive to such leadership," writes team expert George Cladis.[1]

Why Should Your Team Meet?

If a woman questions the need for your team to meet periodically, you can bet she is not a team player. We meet because God's work benefits. We meet because we all benefit. When the team gathers, each member understands that she is a part of the whole of what God is doing. She is less likely to become territorial and shortsighted. Our gatherings produce energy and momentum as we hear what God is doing in other facets of the ministry. If we are discouraged, we pray for one another and help one another with new ideas. If we are fruitful, we rejoice together.

If you desire to minister to postmoderns as well as moderns, you will need them on your teams. Young women are not content to sit on the sidelines. Involve them or lose them.

How Often Should Your Team Meet?

Meetings are beneficial—but nobody likes unnecessary meetings. Women are busy. Don't meet when you don't need to. IBC's board meets seven times a year, including an end-of-the-year celebration supper and excluding a beginning-of-the-year weekend retreat. We plan these meetings a year in advance and get the dates on everyone's calendar early.

Can we accomplish our goals in so few meetings? Remember: the team has spent a weekend together bonding, training, and brainstorming to kick off the year. So, at the first meeting, they know one another. They also attend a weekly Bible study and many of them enhance their friendships there. We seem to accomplish our plans with just seven meetings. But choose what works for you.

We choose a regular meeting day and time—for example, the last Thursday of the month at 7 P.M. in the conference room. We meet during the evening because that allows working women to participate. The majority of the board would prefer daytime meetings, but they are willing to come in the evening because they understand the importance of including our single and working women.

Even when we plan a year ahead, last-minute emergencies and responsibilities keep our team from attending every meeting. This will happen no matter how much the women want to be there. Nevertheless it is your assignment to make the meetings something no one wants to miss.

How Do You Run a Team Meeting That No One Wants to Miss?

Make every minute meaningful! Make it informal, fun, and inspiring. Discard the stuffy parliamentary procedures of *Robert's Rules of Order*. This is the time to evaluate your ministry in light of your vision statement, encourage one another, and hear the great things God is doing. It is also time to get feedback and to come to the aid of anyone who is struggling. Establish some ground rules. Here are some guidelines:

- Limit your meeting length to two hours.

- Hand out a written agenda. (See appendix A for a sample.) The agenda shows you have a well-thought-out plan. Follow the agenda unless there is a good reason to be flexible. The flow of a typical meeting includes elements like prayer, a devotional, or an informative report about a new ministry. Give every leader an opportunity to communicate what's happening in her arena.

- No two-party business allowed.
  That means that we don't waste time discussing what could better be hammered out by the two people involved. Team meetings are not the time to discuss details anyway, and the leader should make that clear, in a gracious way of course.

- Don't do all the talking.
  Interaction adds interest. Encourage everyone to participate. Make your ministry relational, suggests George Cladis:

Relational ministry best sums up the ministry of Jesus. God did not send a committee or an organization to die on the cross for us. God sent the Son who loves us, teaches us, rebukes us, redeems us, and empowers us—all very relational dynamics! Ministry teams that are relational and network forming rather than bureaucratic have wonderful opportunities to grow and thrive in the postmodern world.[2]

- Challenge the team to grow.
  We usually begin our meetings with a devotional from one of the members. The first year women share their stories. Sometimes I assign a book to read and report on. Everyone gets a turn. Limit these devotionals to ten minutes. If a woman goes too long, don't scold her in front of the group. Instead have your board secretary reiterate the time restraints to the woman who will do the devotional at the next meeting.

  You may want to include a training section in each meeting, especially if your team is full of women new to ministry. Be creative and don't be afraid to ask your team to do reasonable assignments that will help them.

- Spend up to half your time on prayer requests and prayer.
  You can let your prayer coordinator oversee this part of the meeting. Always begin with a short prayer if you do business first. Prayer sets the tone and reminds everyone that we are about God's work. Personal and ministry prayer requests are appropriate.

  Connecting as people is just as important as doing business. We love one another and are anxious to hear what's going on in one another's life. Emphasize confidentiality. If time is limited we often pair off and pray for one another. Then everyone and their ministry are prayed over. Don't neglect prayer. You are modeling the principle that this is God's ministry!

- Listen respectfully to everyone's ideas.
  Provide a safe atmosphere where the team can suggest ideas
  and never fear humiliation. When you ask for input, you
  may occasionally get some unusual responses. While you
  would never consider implementing every suggestion, especially the unwise ones, neither do you want to discourage
  any woman from participating. Often as you brainstorm, a
  good idea grows out of a bad idea. Respectfully listen to
  even the newest and untrained member.

- Don't be negative or critical.
  When women are late or don't follow through, it is easy to
  be negative. If team members aren't faithful, you may feel
  like reprimanding them at the meeting. Don't! This is not
  the time. Do this privately and gently, assuring the women
  that you have their best interests in mind and that of the
  ministry as a priority. If board members are in conflict, address the issue privately as well.

  You set the tone for the meeting. If you are negative,
  they will be negative. And discouragement will take you all
  spiraling down. I am not saying that you don't discuss general problems. But do so with an upbeat attitude that shows
  you trust God to help and overcome.

- Set the atmosphere for maximum effect.
  Be sure the environment enhances your meeting. This is
  important wherever ministry happens. Consider how many
  people attend. At Creekside, we usually have about six. At
  IBC, we expect between ten and fifteen. I like to hold our
  meetings in a cozy, intimate room. We set up the tables in a
  U or a circle so everyone can see everyone else. Our secretary or hospitality coordinator provides goodies to snack
  on during the meeting. We dress casually. We laugh and

usually hang around afterward just because we enjoy being together. And we do our two-party business then.

Atmosphere matters! Cladis, in his book *Leading the Team-Based Church,* says,

> Years ago I was sent by my denomination to report to a session about the work of the denomination. The pastor and his clerk sat at a head table. The twenty-four elders present sat in chairs that faced the head table. . . . All eyes were on the pastor-moderator who led the discussion and answered most of the questions raised. He was set up as the authority and the one responsible for the organization, the one with all the answers. Configuration speaks volumes. Change it to reflect an enabling style. Meet in a circle. Although the moderator is certainly a principal player . . . spread out power and responsibility so that more and more people are the answer-tellers.[3]

Plan your team gatherings prayerfully and carefully. What happens there trickles down and impacts everything else you do! When your lead team enjoys encouragement, prayer support, financial resources, and training, they will partner with God to transform women's lives!

Pioneer Profile: Vickie Kraft

"A church without a vigorous, relevant women's ministry is like a home without a mother." So says Vickie Kraft, minister to women at Northwest Bible Church in Dallas for fourteen years and founder of Titus 2:4 Ministries. "Men and women can teach women," she says, "but only women can role-model godly womanhood."

Such focus on women mentoring women has been a hallmark of Vickie's ministry for the past thirty years. A missionary mother of five, she and her husband served with Child Evangelism Fellowship and later with Luis Palau. For fifteen years she taught a weekly Ladies Bible Study at Faith Bible Church in DeSoto, Texas, which also included women from churches in the neighboring communities. Vickie exhorted women to follow the biblical model of older women teaching younger women. This ministry became officially known as Titus 2:4 Ministries, Inc. in 1984.

Having graduated from Dallas Seminary in 1985, Vickie joined the staff of Northwest Bible Church as minister to women. "I started there part-time and eventually worked up to full-time," Vickie remembers. Her ministry centered around Bible study. She incorporated a variety of electives to follow the weekly studies, partly to give women interesting learning opportunities, and partly to encourage their leadership skills. "We were always developing leaders from these electives," says Vickie.

Older women were encouraged to pair up with younger women in mentoring relationships. As this ministry became more popular, it gained the name "Heart to Heart." "This was not meant to be a heavy counseling program, but a way to develop relationships," says Vickie. "The women commit to a one-year relationship in which they will meet once a month and talk on the phone and pray for each other weekly. They are free to arrange their meetings as they like—some go shopping, other meet for coffee, whatever they are comfortable with."

Heart to Heart is based on the premise that older women have life experience that they can pass along to younger women. Young marrieds can minister to singles, college girls to high schoolers . . . it doesn't matter what age, as long as the mentor is one step ahead in life. In 1991, an interview with Focus on the Family gave Vickie's ministry national exposure. She was invited to write her thoughts and studies in book form. This led to two books published in

1992: *Women Mentoring Women* by Moody, and *The Influential Woman* by Word. In 1996, Word published her third book, *Facing Your Feelings.*

Over the years, Vickie encountered a fair share of opposition, sometimes hostility, from her male counterparts in ministry. *Why are you, an older woman, at seminary? Why should you get paid as much as a male pastor at church? Women don't belong in public ministry.* How did Vickie react?

"I always considered myself a pacesetter. I chose my battles," she says. "Women don't want to be like men, we want to be free to be all the woman God intended us to be. We aren't trying to compete with men, we just want to be free to do all that we are supposed to do." On one occasion, while addressing a seminary class at the invitation of the professor, she told the men, "Women can teach and apply the Bible to women better than men." As the men struggled to understand her argument, she continued. "How many of you understand your wives completely?" No one responded. "How do you expect to understand half your church's population if you can't even understand your wife?" One student theorized, "Because I'm not a woman?" "Yes," replied Vickie. "Women are not in competition with men—we are complementary."

To women aspiring to join a church staff as a women's ministry director, Vickie advises, "Go in with a full sense of your own value to the staff. Attend meetings. Participate. Everyone will benefit from your input."

How Do You Transition from the Old Team to the New Team?

Each year about half our board are newcomers. Some don't know anyone on the board well. How do we help them feel included and unleash them for ministry? We need an extended time together to share the vision, to hear their story, to bond them with other members, and to equip them for their calling.

IBC's board takes two days away in early summer to transition in the new board. In addition, we need a block of time to evaluate the past year and to pray and plan for the year ahead. We get out of town to limit distractions. Church members lend us their lake or ranch houses for this concentrated weekend.

We used to call this our board *retreat* but it was so labor-intensive, the team teased me about false advertising. Now we call it *training camp* and we invite those who want time to actually relax to come a day before or stay after. There is so much to accomplish during those two days that we pack nearly every minute with stuff to do.

But don't forget to balance the intense times with times to relax and enjoy each other. Include an evening of informal games even for those who don't attend the extra day. If you are as task-oriented as I am, you need a reminder not to schedule every second. Down times are valuable too.

What do we do during training camp? Our staff women's ministry team chooses a theme for the weekend. We ask God to show us the board's greatest need for the year ahead. One year our Bible studies exploded with new women. A major emphasis that year was acclimating all those women. We wanted to sensitize our board and their teams to how it feels to be new.

Here's a schedule for that weekend:

Friday

8:30 A.M.	Leave the church
10:30 A.M.	Arrive, unpack
11:00 A.M.	Gather for preview of weekend

- Play "Bafa Bafa"—a game where the women divide up and create two different cultures with opportunities to interact as a newcomer to the other culture
- Discuss results

12:30 P.M.	Lunch and break
2:00 P.M.	Gather for story time

- The new women pass a three-minute egg timer and tell everything they can about themselves in three minutes

2:30 P.M.	Training on characteristics of postmodern women

- Discussion on how to include them and retain older women
- Ten-minute break at 3:30

4:30 P.M.	Tell more stories

- Returning members pass the egg timer

5:00 P.M.	Praise and worship

- Members share one-sentence blessings
- Praise songs led by our arts coordinator

5:30 P.M.	Prepare and eat dinner
7:00 P.M.	Games and fun

- If women don't know each other well, plan fun activities to bond them

Saturday

8:30 A.M.	Breakfast
9:30 A.M.	Team reports

- Each member reviews the year and shares vi-

> sion for the next year, handing out a one-page
> report that she prepared ahead
> • Ten-minute break at 10:30
>
> 11:00 A.M. Business (procedures, rosters, explain and sign
> conflict resolution contract, etc.)
>
> 11:30 A.M. Old board member meets with new board mem-
> ber to hand over materials and to discuss the
> ministry
>
> 12:30 P.M. Lunch
>
> 1:30 P.M. Gather to take prayer requests, both personal
> and ministry-related
>
> 3:00 P.M. Prayer, commissioning, communion
>
> 4:00 P.M. Pack and drive home

Make your training camp fit your ministry. Remember: these two days are invaluable! They equal the time you will spend in board meetings for the rest of the year. If you forfeit this initial time together, you probably will not experience the depth in relationships that fosters ministry success. If two days away won't work for you, find other blocks of time together before or early in the ministry year. The fruit you experience throughout every other facet of your ministry begins here.

How Do You Schedule a Last-Minute Meeting?

Here is an example of what *not* to do! Recently a woman called my husband to set up a meeting for two pastors and six lay leaders. She asked, "What times and days of the week can you meet? We are trying to find a time that will work for everyone."

Her boss had given her the task of finding out all the times and days these eight people could meet and then finding a time that would fit all their schedules. She did her best and called my husband several times during the process. She spent hours trying to set up this meeting.

The time they finally decided on was Sunday afternoon after church, but when they called to tell my husband, he informed them it was Mother's Day. "I'm taking my wife out to lunch." They had not bothered to look at the calendar. The process was so confusing and frustrating that they didn't meet at all. It doesn't have to be that way!

First, check your church calendar for conflicts. If it is a church-wide event, pay careful attention to competing events and meetings. Our church staff meets once a year to haggle over the calendar. We don't want too many church-wide events during the same month. If the gathering only affects a small group, check the calendar for holidays or other events that might hinder your group from gathering.

Next, search for times when weekly events and meetings aren't scheduled. For example, Wednesday nights and Monday nights are packed with activities and Bible studies at our church. That leaves Tuesday and Thursday nights open. I usually schedule a meeting on Thursday night because our women's activities are on Mondays and Tuesdays and I know our leaders are less rushed on Thursday.

Pick a day, two at most, and announce the meeting. If two-thirds can attend, nail it down. It's unlikely you'll ever find a time that everyone can be there—especially a last-minute meeting. This simple process saves time and frustration.

Build trust and have fun. Again we turn to Cladis.

> Leadership teams that build trust are teams that spend time together. There is no substitute for this time together. Trust is dependent upon a narrative of events that builds up the team's identity and confidence. Those events will be both serious and playful. The serious events will be the ones in which the team worked through crisis and brutally honest sharing. The playful events will be the ones in which the team learned about one another's gifts, personalities, and approaches to life.[4]

Invest and enjoy!

Chapter 6

CREATE YOUR OWN LIFE-CHANGING BIBLE STUDIES

Ashley clicked off her e-mail after a quick reply to her boss. Work followed her everywhere. Four-year-old Erin was pulling on her arm. "Can I have Stouffers mac and cheese for dinner—pleeeeeze?" Ashley poked holes in the plastic, popped the tray in the microwave, and pondered the evening's plans as she waited.

She had promised her coworker Susan that she'd go to church with her tonight. *Why did I do that?* She knew why. Susan was a real friend. She was the mom Ashley never had. And although some of Susan's ideas were strange, Susan was always there for her. She would go for Susan—just this once.

She felt guilty leaving Erin another night. But at least she'd kept Erin. Maybe Jerry would watch her tonight? Jerry arrived as Ashley finished putting on Erin's coat.

"Can she stay home with you? I rented a video. Couldn't you two just hang out?"

"Sorry, I've got too much work to do."

Oh well, she wasn't Jerry's kid anyway. Susan said they had stuff for kids to do. Maybe Erin would have fun. Susan honked and they piled in. They talked work on the way with Susan doing more talking than usual.

As they pulled into the parking lot, Ashley observed every kind of woman emerge from the cars—women in pant suits with briefcases, mothers towing toddlers, women in sweats, silver-haired grandmothers, and teenagers. Some were loud as they greeted each other from across the parking lot. Others hugged. *This could be really weird,* thought Ashley.

They walked briskly through doors held open by smiling women. One hugged Susan, then asked about her grown son Ben. After news about Ben, the woman reached out her hand to Ashley. "Who's this?" she asked. Susan introduced her. The woman looked in her eyes and said, "Good to meet you. Hope you enjoy yourself tonight." She seemed to mean it.

They left Erin with a buxom woman in "Kids Klub" and they were off again, swept along in a current of women. The room was bigger than any church Ashley had ever been in. It was full of round tables, spaced out into every nook. As they whisked by tables, she saw that some had lit candles and others had flowers floating in shallow vases. All had food—trays of vegetables, or chips and dips or sweets. They looked homemade.

There must have been twenty-five or thirty tables. As they passed a doorway, she noticed more tables outside in a foyer. And she smelled something delicious out there. Susan suggested that after they settled in she get them a latte or cappuccino from the coffee bar. *A coffee bar in a church! This is a strange place.*

When they reached their table, Susan introduced Ashley to their leader and the women chatting around the table. Two stopped their conversation and greeted her. Ashley sat down while Susan went for cappuccinos.

Then a frightening reality hit Ashley. In a few minutes, this table was going to fill with women. And when it did they would sit face to face. What did they expect from her?

They all had Bibles and notebooks. Ashley didn't own a Bible. What were they going to talk about—religious stuff? She would have nothing to say. Then again, she did watch Oprah when she was home sick.

Someone was talking over the mike. She looked up and on the stage was a little white-haired woman beaming. "Welcome. I'm Barb. Please find your seats and we will get started." She paused for a minute as women scurried to their places, and then she prayed, "Dear Father, we gather tonight to learn more about You and to encourage one another. Help us understand Your truth. Help us live it out. We love You. In Jesus' name. Amen."

Jackie, a curly headed woman in her thirties, bounded onto the platform and directed their attention to large screens, one on each side of the stage. On each screen was a painting of the ocean with giant waves catapulting against rock cliffs. "Tonight Philippians will teach us how to have joy in the midst of tough times. Look at this painting. Even though the waves swell to fifty feet on the surface, fifty feet underneath the ocean floor is peaceful and calm.

"The waves are the circumstances in our lives. We can't control them and often they toss us about until we think we will go under. But even as we are tossed about, deep within us, God can give us a peace that passes all understanding. Tonight we will learn about that peace and how to possess it."

Then her tone changed. She grinned, "I know some of you just came from a long day at work and you could use a back rub. So let's all turn to the person on our right and give each other a little massage. And then when you're done, look under your chair. If you find a green dot, you are the winner of a full body massage." After a short back rub, everyone scrambled. Soon the winner ran up front with the green dot on her finger to claim her prize. Ashley's brow lifted. *A church that gives away massages! Now I've seen everything.*

Then Mary, the worship leader, asked everyone to stand. Four women jumped on stage and grabbed mikes. Music with a hefty beat blared over the speakers and Mary began to sing about joy. The words of the song appeared on the screens. Then the other women joined in singing, and they went back and forth echoing each other and filling the room. They clapped at certain places in the song and clapped when they finished.

Mary sat down at the piano and led praise songs—one blended into the next, except when she stopped to pray. A few women raised their arms. Many closed their eyes. Ashley watched and sang off and on when she could. *Are these women for real?*

After worship, the women sat down around the tables. Ashley didn't pull her chair up close to the table like the other women—not until later. Susan introduced Ashley to the group, explaining that she often helped her on computer projects that were beyond her expertise. She praised Ashley's attempts to be a good mother to Erin. Susan seemed to understand and appreciate Ashley's desire to rebuild her life. Ashley felt warm inside.

Their leader asked the women if there were any prayer requests. They began to write them on note cards and hand them to the leader. A prayer request? What would she write? Then she remembered that Erin's day care was closing and she needed to find another caregiver while she worked. She wrote that on her card.

The leader read each request and a few women elaborated. They had real problems. One's marriage was in trouble. At least they were married. She wondered if Jerry would ever suggest marriage. Another's mom had cancer. Her mammogram had uncovered a lump and she was going for a biopsy tomorrow. One was trying to quit smoking.

The leader took the cards and laid them in the center of the table. Susan whispered to her that they use the cards to pray later, but no one would pressure her to pray out loud. *Good!*

The table leader led them in a discussion of Bible study questions they had answered at home. There were three levels of questions, so they could do as little or as much study as they wanted during the week. As Susan handed Ashley a Bible, the leader commented, "Don't feel any pressure to participate, Ashley. I know all this is new. Just sit back and enjoy." *Whew!* What followed was a respectful, honest, in-depth exchange of opinions and perspectives on the Bible passage. Ashley listened intently. The women didn't always agree, but they were kind to each other.

Susan looked up the passage in Philippians for Ashley to follow along as the group shared what the passage meant to them—and they talked personal stuff. She didn't know if she would ever have the courage to unmask herself that way.

That little white-haired Barb's voice came over the speakers again. Time to close down the discussion. Time to hear about opportunities to learn more and serve others. The leader passed out a paper listing the times, places, and people who needed this and that—inner-city ministry, a mission trip to Russia, an upcoming MOMs ministry meeting. They passed around a list to sign if you were interested in workplace ministry and another list if you could bring canned goods for the food pantry.

Suddenly the room darkened. Soft music swelled and then faded. The spotlight fell on two women sitting on a couch on the stage. In the drama, their father had died the night before and these two sisters were helping each other to cope with the tragedy.

Ashley identified with one of the sisters. She had felt that way when her father died six years earlier. Tears filled her eyes as she heard this woman articulate feelings she'd buried. She wiped them away quickly as the lights came up.

The spotlight shifted to Jackie, the teacher. The coleader passed out an outline of her message. Jackie talked about her years before Christ. She pointed to her hip and revealed that there was a little devil tattooed there. She related the heartache of those days—part of that she brought on herself. Then she talked about struggles now.

She said to expect these hard times—they were part of life. She drew principles out of the Bible passage they discussed at the table and showed how these principles could work in life today.

The outline in Ashley's hand was full of blanks, but the answers were displayed on the screens. She filled in the blanks and wrote out quotes and Bible verses she especially liked. The teacher used a movie clip to illustrate a truth. Ashley was familiar with the movie, and what the teacher said made sense. The teacher's voice was strong but full of love. Her words rang true. *Maybe the Bible isn't a book of myths and fairy tales.*

For her last illustration, the teacher explained that sometimes our joy must come from what is ahead. For the Christian that meant looking forward to being with Christ in eternity.

Jackie told the story of a woman who knew she was going to die. She invited her pastor to her home to plan her funeral.

"I want to be buried with a fork in my hand," the woman insisted.

When the pastor asked why, she explained, "At pot luck dinners, after we eat the main course, someone always says, 'Keep your fork.' That means that dessert is coming—chocolate velvet pie and lemon squares and brownies. That is always the best part. I want to be buried with a fork in my hand to let people know that the best is yet to come."

When Jackie finished her story, the coleaders passed around a plastic golden fork for everyone to take home. It was wrapped with a gold and silver bow and a card with Romans 8:28, "In all things God works for the good of those who love him." *Could that be true?* Ashley slipped the gold fork into her purse.

After the message, the table drew back together for a "concert of prayer." Women who wanted to pray aloud took a card from the requests in the center of the table. The leader again soothed Ashley's fears by telling the whole table there was no pressure to pray out loud. But most of them did.

Someone prayed for Erin. They prayed that God would lead Ashley to a caretaker where Erin would be safe and nurtured. Ashley could hear muffled voices from all over the room seeking God's best for their sisters.

Mary closed prayer time by playing softly on the piano, and then everyone joined in a chorus that centered on joy—a supernatural, abundant joy that comes only from God. Ashley sang along, a song that came from somewhere deep within her. A closing prayer. A room of laughter and conversation.

Susan and Ashley picked up a cheery Erin who had made a friend who wanted her to come over and play next Saturday. Ashley was quiet during the ride home. Her journey had begun.

Ashley's story represents the ideal. In reality the woman at the door may have forgotten to greet Ashley or a child may have hurt Erin's feelings in Kids Klub. But despite the occasional blunder, this format has worked at IBC. Our rolls have mushroomed from two hundred when we launched in 1998 to over seven hundred in 2002. Women come to faith and grow. Every year we tweak the study in an attempt to heighten our effectiveness.

What kind of a Bible study will transform the postmodern and modern women God sends you? This chapter will help you design and implement just the right Bible study for your women.

Why Is Bible Study the Priority?

What will change Ashley's life? What will transform her into a joyful woman of integrity and strength? Only one thing! She must experience an intimate relationship with Jesus. And that relationship begins and grows as she studies His Word.

After your leadership board is in place and operational, the next priority is Bible study. Remember: churches with flourishing women's ministries are Bible study centered. The size of a church or the number of women involved has no bearing on this principle. If we envision women's ministry as a wheel, the hub of the wheel is the study of God's Word. All other ministries are the spokes of the wheel.

The Scriptures are God's love letters to His children. They convey His heart and mind, and they are the primary way God communicates with us. God expects us to know His Word thoroughly and to apply it diligently. Through knowing His Word, we know Him. And when we know Him, we are transformed!

What happens behind the scenes to make possible such change in women's lives? How will you create an experience that will propel them deep into God's Word? Whether you minister in a large or small church, the goal is the same—to partner with God as He transforms your women.

Effective women's ministries must make the Bible their priority, but each will use different methods. How will you structure your study for maximum impact? What resources are available to you? Tailor your structure to the needs of your women. Investigate other women's ministries for ideas, but don't merely duplicate. What works for them may not work for you. Gather your team and pray. Then hammer out answers to the following questions.

Will You Study Books *of* the Bible or Books *on* the Bible?

First, you must decide *what* you will study. Will it be in-depth studies that guide your women through a book of the Bible like Genesis or the Gospel of Luke? Will you dig into studies with biblical themes like the covenants or the parables of Jesus? Or will you serve up lighter studies on topics like forgiveness and friendship or the hot best-seller on how to live for Christ? All are valuable—but which will transform your women with more power and impact? We recommend a steady diet of books of the Bible or biblical themes with sporadic snacks of topical studies. Why?

I know men; and I tell you that Jesus Christ is no mere man. Between Him and every other person in the world there is no comparison. Alexander, Caesar and Charlemagne and I myself founded empires, but upon what do these creations of our genius depend? Upon force. Jesus alone founded His empire on love; and to this very day millions of men would die for Him. [1]

—Napoleon Bonaparte

A person has deprived himself of the best there is in the world who has deprived himself of a knowledge of the Bible. . . . There are a good many problems before the American people today, and before me as president, but I expect to find the solutions of these problems in just the proportion that I am faithful in the study of God's Word. I beg you, read it. Find out for yourselves that the Bible is the Word of life. Read, not little snatches here and there, but long passages that will be the road to the heart of it. [2]

—Woodrow Wilson

The Bible contains sixty-six separate documents written over a period of more than fourteen hundred years by more than forty human authors from varied cultures. Yet it is a single unit. Each book is interwoven with the others, fitting together to produce the only literary work in history without error. God, inspiring and empowering human authors, gave us a living book with the power to transform us supernaturally from the inside out. Study it!

Topical studies of particular interest to women are great for a change of pace. You might offer topical studies in the summer for a lighter fare. Christian bookstores stock a variety of topical study booklets that are easy and fun.

But often the study instructs women to read pertinent Bible

verses, usually plucked out of context. Without understanding the context, we are more likely to misinterpret the meaning.

In their favor, these studies are easy to organize. Order a booklet for each participant, recruit a group leader, and enjoy digging into a topic together. For variety, choose a popular book to read and discuss.

However, your core curriculum will focus on books or themes in the Bible because they change lives. Studying the Bible itself, instead of books on the Bible, does require more effort on the part of the leaders. One of you must know the Bible in order to guide others. You must write or find a curriculum that fits your needs. Some passages are controversial and can stir up theological disagreements that you will need to research and address.

In addition, the Bible is not always easy to understand. It is ancient literature and its truths are often buried treasure. You need to know the historical and cultural background as well as geography. Untangling detailed passages will frustrate lazy women. As a result, some leaders are tempted to choose topical or book studies because they are simple to organize and manage. Don't!

It is worth the extra effort to bring your women deep into the heart of God's Word! IBC senior pastor Andy McQuitty offers some benefits.

> You can take virtually any book of the Bible, Old or New Testament, and teach through it expositionally and you will find occasion to teach on every felt need. . . . You've got to have confidence that God's Word is sufficient to touch the needs of your people and that *you* don't have to be the one who selectively pulls from God's Word to meet the needs you see in your people.
>
> It's important as teachers of God's Word that we are forced to deal with passages that we wouldn't necessarily choose. First, we need to not let our teaching ministry be

guided by our personal preferences. We're supposed to teach the whole counsel of God's Word. . . . The second benefit is for your students. They encounter passages that seem inconsistent, harsh or confusing. If their spiritual leaders are only teaching the popular, the passionate, the easy passages and are skirting around the difficult ones, it may create in the minds of students an insecurity that maybe there is no way to understand or reconcile the difficult passages. So we actually diminish our students' confidence in the Word of God because we don't deal with tough things. Expository teaching forces us to deal with issues that ultimately strengthen students.[3]

If you want to transform women, use the most powerful tool available. Study the Bible!

Will You Create Your Own Studies or Borrow from the "Experts"?

You can buy excellent Bible studies written by gifted scholars and teachers. Some have supplementary videos you can watch if you don't have a teacher. These made-to-order packages are useful to help you get started—especially if you are resource-poor.

But make it your goal to wean yourself from video studies as fast as you can. Find gifted women in your church to teach or write your curriculum. You may need to rely on experts for a while, but ask God to enable you to create your own studies in time.

Why Raise Up Your Own Teachers and Writers?

There are women with the gift of teaching in every church. If your goal is to transform women, then you must provide opportunities for them to stretch and grow. A key element in the transformation process is to let God work through women to accomplish what they could never do alone.

When a woman experiences writing a Bible lesson or teaching a Bible passage through the power of the Holy Spirit, she experiences God. She will never be the same. When God uses her labor to build His kingdom, she feels an indescribable and profound joy. By providing opportunities for each woman to use her gifts, you are cooperating with the Spirit's work in her life.

Postmoderns Insist

The postmodern woman wants to know her teacher personally. George Cladis asserts, "The postmodern world wants to know the heart of its leadership. Words like *authentic* and *genuine* are being used to describe effective and able leaders. The most important question for those who would follow a leader is no longer, Does she have the educational and professional requirements to fill this position? but rather, Is she trustworthy and will she listen to my concerns?"[4]

You may argue that the quality of the study will suffer. You don't have a woman in your church who will ever write or teach like the "experts." Maybe not—but you might! These "experts" all started somewhere. Even if you don't have a potential Kay Arthur, a living teacher who knows your women intimately will be a better fit in time.

It Is Necessary for Transformation

A teacher is available for counsel and mentoring. She is a real-life model they can hug. They can watch her live out the truths she teaches. And as women watch God use one of their own, they will begin to realize God can use them in significant ways also. Women will step out in faith and amazement as they understand that God desires to use them as part of His plan. Teams of ministers and armies of spiritual mothers will emerge. This process is ongoing in a healthy women's ministry. But the process requires that you equip your own women to be the experts in your church.

Sue's Experience

In the parachurch Bible study where I was trained, the leaders always wrote and taught their own lessons. I would never have tried to write my own lessons if the leaders had not expected it of me. But they did, and I am grateful. I began by observing lessons written by my teacher. She critiqued my work and ran it through a review committee before the lessons went out to the classes.

Helpful Resources

For a sample lesson, see appendix A. Our teachers write similar lessons that are reviewed for content before they are copied and bound for distribution.

If you need semester- or year-long series of lessons to begin the process of writing your own curriculum, see our Web site (www.newdoors.info). For a reasonable price you can order lessons to reproduce or change to fit your needs. Let your novice writers tweak them and in time they will learn to write their own from scratch.

We also suggest you try Logos's *Lesson Builder* or other software helps for writing studies. They give a general format, with broad questions to help get the writer started. Each lesson can then be created to meet your unique needs.

Remember: the Transformation Model is about finding the hidden gifts and talents among the women in your ministry and providing opportunities to use them to glorify God and minister to others.

Look for women who are talented in graphic and visual arts. Enlist their help in producing an attractive lesson and binder that is both functional and beautifully highlights your Bible study theme at the same time.

We hope this will jump-start the process in your church. Writing and teaching are skills that improve through the years. We all need a place to begin. Provide an opportunity for women to use their gifts and watch God work wonders!

Will You Offer Many Different Studies or Just One?

Think back to the story of postmodern Ashley at the beginning of this chapter. Remember her experience in a room filled with several hundred Christians worshiping, discussing the Bible, and praying together? She left desiring to know more about Jesus. Experiencing the entire Christian community together is a powerful evangelistic tool—and it energizes believers too!

The ideal is to offer one choice study on a book of the Bible that all your women can enjoy. And if you have the facilities, bring them together in a large room for worship, teaching, and arts elements like drama. But also be sure to divide them up into small groups for more intimate fellowship and prayer—within the large room if you can.

However, this format may not be optimum for you.

Consider These Issues

How large is your church? How many women participate in the study? If fewer than fifteen women attend, choose a book of the Bible that best meets the needs of that group, and study that book. But as your study grows, you will need to divide the women into small groups. Small group structures will be discussed in depth in chapter 8.

When deciding whether the groups will study the same material or whether you will offer choices, carefully consider your resources, especially the number of teachers you have and the size of your facility. If you have several teachers who want to develop their gifts, you could give your women the choice of different studies. If your facility won't hold everyone, offering several studies is an option. Women enjoy variety and giving them options is one way to provide it.

Create Excitement

Even if you offer multiple studies but want to create excitement and a sense of broader community, think about bringing the women together sometime during the study. This energizes the whole group.

During our Bible study sessions, our women meet in our sanctuary around tables. As our study has grown, we have moved some groups out of the large room and into smaller spaces.

Women who were distracted by the noise level join those groups for their discussion and then return to the main room for worship, fellowship, drama, announcements, service opportunities, teaching, and prayer. There is something wonderful about worshiping the Lord together. During the concert of prayer, I am often near tears as I listen to the sacred sounds of women praying in their small groups.

Create Connections

There are other advantages when everyone studies the same curriculum. Friends enjoy discussing the concepts they are studying even if they are not in the same small group. Our men's evening study meets at the same time we do and often they study the same material. Then couples interact over the material at home. If you have a children's program, it is fun if the kids study a scaled-down version of mom's study.

Create Continuity

Design your studies with long-term benefit in mind. For example, the first year I taught at IBC, I taught the Gospel of Luke. I wanted the women to know Jesus. The next year we studied Acts. I entitled the series "Acts of the Spirit" because the study focused on the work of the Holy Spirit in the first-century church and in our lives today.

The third year I taught "Love Letters from Paul: A Study of Five Epistles." This study built on the founding of the churches in Acts. As we dissected the letters Paul wrote to those churches, we learned key doctrines necessary for living the Christian life. Over these three years, the women came to know Jesus, the Holy Spirit, and key Christian doctrines. The fourth year we studied the covenants to give women an understanding of God's panoramic promises from Genesis to Revelation.

We laid a solid foundation for the myriads of new believers coming into our church. But the material was also challenging for women who had walked with the Lord for many years.

Plan a curriculum that aligns with your purpose, find a format that works for you, and tackle it with passion. Remember: women are transformed through an intimate relationship with Jesus, and you are the matchmaker.

What Kinds of Curriculum Keep Women in the Word?

A Curriculum That Requires Homework

The most important part of your Bible study occurs *before* the women gather. The best lessons require homework. This format encourages your women to find a quiet place where they can reflect on the passage and commune with God. The lesson you provide is merely the tool God uses to deepen the relationship.

A Curriculum That Offers Choices

A Bible study that transforms lives brings women of different ages and life stages together. Titus 2 mandates that older women mentor younger women. Often the older women have studied the Bible longer. How will you keep your older women challenged while not overwhelming those new to Bible study? You give the women choices.

I write studies with several levels. Again, see appendix A for a sample lesson with multiple levels.

Here are three levels I usually include in each lesson.

1. Core-Level Questions

I always write a core level for new believers and busy women. I have also learned that some women won't spend as much time on their lesson as others. This doesn't always mean the studious women are more mature. Often it reflects the woman's gifts.

For example, a woman with the gift of pastoring or encouragement focuses on relationships. She wants to be with people. However, a woman with the gift of teaching can sit for hours at her desk lost in study. This is God's design. Provide options for the great variety of women God creates.

The core-level questions require one or two hours of study time weekly and provide a basic understanding of the text. The core level consists of at least three kinds of questions:

1. *Observation Questions*

   These questions force the student to look carefully at what the passage says. Most observation questions can be answered from the text.

2. *Interpretation Questions*

   These questions ask the student to decide what the passage means—first for the original audience, then for us today. Often these questions cause the student to think critically about the way God works in the world and what He wants for His children.

3. *Application Questions*

   These questions challenge the students to examine their own lives in light of the truths they are studying and to adjust their thoughts, actions, and attitudes. Small groups often spend more time on application questions because most women love to share their lives with others and because life change results. But don't skip the observation and interpretation questions, which lead you to correct applications. This is the pitfall of many Bible studies and small group discussions.

We cover most of the core-level questions in the small group discussion. If a woman is faithful every week in her study of the core questions, she'll be amazed how much she will learn over several years. I encourage the new and busy women not to be intimidated by women who have more time to study or who have different gifts.

2. Digging-Deeper-Level Questions

Some women want to learn more about the passage. The digging-deeper-level questions suggest parallel passages to compare and contrast. They require outside resources such as an atlas, Bible dictionary, or concordance. They challenge the students to learn more about history, culture, and geography.

3. Summit-Level Questions

These questions are for women who want to probe the text even more. These questions ask women to grapple with complex theological issues and differing views. Women are encouraged to use an interlinear Greek-English or Hebrew-English text and *Vine's Expository Dictionary* on their own. These questions ask the student to create charts, outlines, and character studies in seminary-style, open-ended assignments. Women with teaching gifts and an interest in advanced academics enjoy exploring the summit.

Due to time restrictions, the digging-deeper- and summit-level questions may not be covered in the discussion groups. Nevertheless, women who want more depth in their study have the option. Because it is critical not to discourage new women, and at the same time to provide challenge for mature women, offer choices.

Once you have chosen your Bible study curriculum, you are ready to shape your study.

Chapter 7

SHAPE YOUR STUDY

*O*ur goal is to unleash women into the world to change it for Christ. Does Bible study *really* equip them? Consider the ripple effect of Bible study in this true-life example.

Every Monday night, Creusa and Sofia were faithful to attend Bible study. But I wasn't aware of their involvement in a local inner-city ministry until I read the ministry's weekly report sent out by its executive director.

> My heart has been breaking over the Hispanic ministry— we needed someone to replace Reverend Martinez to lead the Spanish Bible study. His duties at church would not allow him to continue. For two weeks, I tried the best I could with my tourist Spanish and a Spanish/English Bible to teach the faithful.
>
> Saturday two new volunteers, Creusa and Sofia answered the call. Our faithful Hispanic neighbors walked in the rain—some twelve blocks with only a towel to keep dry— to hear the Word. We hugged them and introduced them to Creusa and Sofia.

What a joy to hear Creusa ask me, "We have three who want to pray to receive Jesus. Do you want to join us for prayer?" Tears of intercession turned to tears of joy as Mr. Pedro, an older gentleman, little nine-year-old Erendida, who has a hole in her heart, and her older brother, each prayed to receive Christ.

Two days later I received this e-mail from the director:

> Sue, I am so excited about the way Creusa and Sofia have stepped up to the plate to organize the Hispanic Bible study at Metro-Link . . . one plants, another waters, another harvests . . . you have part of that harvest from what you have planted in their lives in your Bible studies!

We don't know whether the women we teach and train will minister to other women or to children, youth, family, neighbors, or the world. And we really don't care. We simply want them to get out there and make a difference—like Creusa and Sofia! How will we shape a Bible study that turns out an army of unstoppable women?

Keep in Mind Your Size

The most common characteristic of dynamic women's ministries around the country is the content of their study—the Bible. Churches of any and every size can implement these foundational truths in the lives of their women. The differences lie in the details. How does such a ministry get started? What does a church need to consider?

The answers to these and other questions we will raise in this chapter depend upon the size of each church and the number of resources available to it. If you minister in a small church with few resources and a small group of women, your organizational concerns will be few. Ministry will be fairly simple.

The larger your church is, the more complicated becomes the task of providing quality, exciting ministry. Conversely, a church with many resources has the ability to offer multiple ministries and diverse opportunities. The potential is virtually limitless.

We encourage each of you to read this chapter with an eye to your own circumstances. Much of what is said here may not be necessary (or even possible) for small, newly formed ministries. Take what you can use and apply it passionately. Larger, more established ministries can benefit from the topics we cover. We wanted to include every possibility, so that no matter the size of your ministry, your women will be involved in a well-organized, well-planned means to spiritual growth.

Who Will Run the Bible Study?

Ask God for a woman with the gift of administration and a love of His Word and women. Find a woman with experience in managing a ministry, a family, an organization, or the secular equivalent. Look for a woman with an eye for detail, a shepherd's heart, and the willingness to both delegate and lead. If a woman with these gifts or experience is not available, find a woman who is teachable.

Three Gifted, Teachable Women

Linda and Barb served on our board as the morning and evening Bible class coordinators. Neither had ever overseen an organization the size of our studies. Last year our night class enrolled about four hundred and our morning class about two hundred. Both Linda and Barb were overwhelmed. After the first board meeting, they expressed concern that they were "square pegs in a round hole."

Linda

Linda was terrified of speaking in front of such a large group. Each week to begin the study she had to lead the group in prayer;

later in the morning she would announce a page of ministry high-lights and opportunities to serve. She was diabetic, and I was concerned that the stress would affect her blood sugar. For the first few weeks I watched her quietly, praying that she would overcome her fear and hoping she wouldn't pass out.

Linda completed her term as A.M. class administrator last spring. The last day of class not only did she pray and make the announcements. She also shared a ten-minute testimony! She stood on the stage in front of the microphone and spoke to several hundred women with God's confidence.

Her words warmed my heart:

> When Sue first approached me and asked me to take this job, I couldn't believe she was asking *me*—I was honored, yet scared out of my mind. Again my past haunted me, and I had no confidence in myself. Sue stretched me and challenged me beyond what I ever thought I could accomplish. We are very fortunate to have a women's pastor who stands alongside our heavenly Father to enable Him to complete the work He has begun in us.
>
> I am thankful that God has allowed me this opportunity to serve Him and you. It has been a very rewarding job. Just think, if there had been nobody to refresh my spirit or no one who expected something great out of me, I would still be sitting outside the Bible study group afraid to speak up for the Lord and wondering what my purpose is here on earth.

When Linda retired from the active board and onto the advisory board, she didn't leave women's ministry. She serves as a spiritual mother to women with acute needs. She teaches workshops at our retreats and in seminars. Linda would say her life was transformed by the experience. It is just beginning.

Tracy

Tracy is taking over the morning class. She is a mother and an experienced critical care nurse. She's organized and committed, and loves the Lord—but she's just as unsure as Linda was. I know God will give her everything she needs. I look forward to the day she expresses wonder at what God has done to transform her life as she has ministered to others. Is there any greater joy than watching God work this way? I don't think so!

Barb

Barb is the mother of six and the wife of a pilot. She organized a busy household, raised a family, and supported her husband as the military moved them many times. This and years in a parachurch Bible study prepared her for the position of evening Bible study coordinator.

But she was unaware of the value of her experience and the way God had gifted her to oversee the class. A few times she expressed concern that this ministry was too much and that she wasn't the right person to oversee it. I knew differently, and I was right.

She recruits her leaders early, delegates well, and has each class planned out in detail. The study runs like a rich bride's wedding. And Barb's life has been transformed as she has been instrumental in transforming others.

Pray diligently for God to show you the woman He wants to oversee the Bible class. Because the Bible study is the place women fall in love with Jesus and connect intimately with Him, the leader is crucial. Invest in her and unleash her. Then stand back and watch God work.

Who Will Teach the Bible Study?

There are women in your church with the gift of teaching! You may not know who they are and they may not know God has given them this gift. But He equips every church with the resources needed to teach His Word. Your challenge is to find these Bible teachers and then train them.

How do you discover Bible teachers? You provide opportunities for them to teach. You ask women to share a short devotional at board meetings or a short testimony at the retreat. You observe the process and watch for a supernatural connection with the students.

A woman with the gift of teaching loves to study. She delights in finding ways to help her students learn. She invests hours and hours reading and chewing on concepts God leads her to teach. But just because she is gifted does not mean she won't be nervous initially. If you encourage her, the fear will ultimately subside for the joy of doing what she loves—teaching!

Sue's Experience

My spiritual mother, Kathy Hyde, was like a bird dog tracking teachers. She planted six Bible classes and needed teachers for her team. She recruited leaders in each class and insisted they attend a leader's meeting each week after the class was dismissed.

For me, the leader's meeting was the highlight of the morning. We practiced leading the lesson for the next week. We prayed for our groups and for each other. And every leader was required to give at least one minilecture a year. Some leaders were so frightened by this assignment, they threatened to quit—but none ever did.

Kathy assigned a minilecture topic and asked each leader to speak for about ten minutes. New leaders had the choice of giving their testimony or speaking on the assigned topic. Often the topics would coordinate with the Bible study for that semester.

For example, if we studied Ephesians, we would choose a related topic such as grace or unity. We taught a Bible verse because she wanted us to teach the Bible rather than present a topical message. She showed us how to create a simple outline that helped us develop our message. She taught us how to find illustrations and stories that brought the message alive. Out of that simple assignment emerged Bible teachers who continue to teach the Scriptures in a variety of churches and Bible classes.

Is Seminary an Option?

As you discover a woman with a teaching gift, equip her or find someone who can. Encourage her to attend seminary if possible. I taught the Bible for ten years before I went to seminary. I studied tirelessly to prepare for my lectures and God used those messages to bless women. A teacher can train herself and some of the finest Bible teachers have done so.

However, I was amazed at the resources I could draw on after seminary. In addition, doors opened that probably would not have opened otherwise. Not everyone can attend seminary, but if you can, go for it!

If seminary isn't possible, read books on teaching. Listen to skilled teachers. Attend workshops and seminars. Pray for God's enabling because teaching is far too overwhelming to do in your own strength. Then teach. It's a skill, and like any skill requires years to do well.

Occasionally small churches cannot initially identify a teacher. If you find yourself in this situation, consider asking a seasoned teacher to help your church get off to a good start.

Susan McKenzie, a gifted Bible teacher in Dallas, Texas, agreed to teach in two small churches for two years with the stipulation that they would do their best to be ready the next year with women from their own church. Susan is skilled at recognizing women with teaching gifts and was able to help them stand on their own quickly. That's the goal, because developing your own teachers sets the precedent that God wants ordinary people to do His extraordinary work. And that's an important part of transforming women!

Where Will Your Study Meet?

You can meet in a home, church, recreation center, or any other facility that is centrally located and comfortable. If your ministry consists of one or two small groups, a home atmosphere is intimate. However as you begin to grow you will need more space. In addition, you need to set up childcare facilities as soon as possible for moms.

Most studies end up in a church where there is little expense if any and childcare facilities are close by. As you add small groups that unite for a portion of the study, you will need a large room where you can spread out your tables.

Circles—Not Rows

Why round tables? Because they facilitate interaction. They give the women a place to put their Bibles, their coffee, and their muffins. There is a sense that we are united as we gather in a circle to share what God is doing in our lives. As women meet face to face around a circle, they connect.

Classroom-style seating in rows says the emphasis is on the woman up front. In the Transformation Model we don't want to spotlight the leaders. We want to spotlight relationships—first with Jesus and then with others. The focus is what's going on internally in the women's hearts and minds.

Provide Comfort

Whether your groups meet in a large room together, in small rooms individually, or in some combination, be sure there is adequate lighting and the temperature is comfortable. Consider the needs of the elderly and those with chronic pain when you choose rooms and seating.

Welcome Newcomers

If you have multiple groups, you will need to set up a registration table each week for newcomers. Place it where a new woman can see it easily from the entrance. Have friendly greeters and a system in place to quickly integrate newcomers. Our registration and greeters team stocks the table with registration forms, childcare registration forms, study guides, and temporary name tags.

The class coordinator is there with group lists that show which groups have openings. If the newcomer arrives with a friend or requests a particular group, we try to accommodate her. After a woman registers, one of the greeters walks her to her table and introduces her to the leader. First impressions are important!

Will You Need Special Equipment for Arts Elements?

If you use drama or ceremony in your format, you will want to find a room that you can totally darken. If resources are available to raise and lower lights or sound, use them. If not, there are ways to improvise.

Give your location serious consideration. The atmosphere of the study sets the scene where God transforms lives.

When Will You Meet?

Who are your women? All moms work, but do some work for a paycheck? Do single women attend your church? Are there stay-at-home moms who would prefer to gather during the day? Consider all the women's needs as you plan when to meet. Women's ministry should be inclusive—postmoderns and moderns. I tell the women there are two prerequisites for involvement: you must be a woman and you must show up. Pick a time that everyone can participate.

If you have the resources, consider two classes—one in the evening and one in the morning. Our evening and daytime classes are identical except the evening class is fifteen minutes shorter to accommodate children's bedtimes.

Does your church serve an evening meal during the week to complement a variety of activities? You might consider piggybacking on what's already in place. Otherwise find a time that does not conflict with other activities and block out that time in the church calendar for a year. Soon everyone will know that this is Bible study time and they will plan their activities around yours.

How Long Will You Meet?

Women's time is precious, so make every minute meaningful. You must allow enough time to incorporate all the elements of a transforming experience without wasting time. Consider how the length of your study affects the women and their families or work. For example, how soon can your women get there from work? When do children need to be in bed? Will mothers need to leave to pick up kindergartners?

Consider the pace of your community. In large cities, I suggest you meet for two to three hours. In rural areas, the women may want to gather longer. Women in morning classes may want to linger while those in evening classes need to get home and prepare for the next day. Think through what will work in your particular setting.

Listen to women of all ages and stages and make decisions accordingly. Be willing to adjust your start time if you notice that a majority of your women are arriving late or leaving early.

What Format Will You Choose?

The old, trite saying, "There's more than one way to skin a cat," is perhaps offensive to cat lovers, but true enough. There are many ways to accomplish your objectives. And there are many Bible study formats that transform women. However, there are elements that all formats should include:

- Bible study
- community
- prayer

- opportunities to worship
- opportunities to use what you learn
- opportunities to serve
- variety

You Can't Please Everyone!

How you weave the basic elements into a meaningful whole is your choice. Whatever you choose, you won't make everyone happy. Task-oriented, bottom-line women who are there for Bible study would prefer less time on relationship-building activities, prayer, and sharing. Often women who are attending primarily for community get restless discussing details of the Bible lesson and theology. Neither is wrong. Each must guard against extremes and both can benefit from the other's perspectives.

What if we put all the task-oriented women in one group and those there for community in another? What if we adjusted the format to make each group happy? They would like it—but it would not be good for them.

If they are married, their spouses are probably more like the other group. If they have children or work, they live and work with people in the other group every day. We all need to appreciate and enjoy the differences.

Those of us who are task-oriented need to loosen up and value relationships. Those who are more interested in community need to redeem time and accomplish something! It's healthy for us to study the Bible together and learn from one another.

Although I love women, I am task-oriented. When I began serving women more than twenty-five years ago, I didn't understand women who were more interested in community. I thought everyone should be like me. As a result, my studies were highly structured with little time for sharing, prayer, or fellowship. I was there to teach the Bible, and they needed to learn it!

But God has opened my eyes to the importance of relationships more and more through the years. I surround myself with women who keep me balanced and sensitive to the value of different approaches and perspectives. Know yourself and guard against the mistakes I made.

As you decide on a format, be open to change. Do year-end evaluations and tweak your format in response. But don't overreact to each comment. You will never please everyone. As a leader you aren't there to be popular. You are there to transform women. By God's grace, you will earn their respect. So do what you can to give each group what they need, and help each group understand why they need balance.

Sample Formats

Your format is like a fine quilt, a variety of pieces precisely stitched together. The end result is something splendid. Let's look at ways leaders all over the nation structure their studies. Examine these models and extract elements that will work for you.

Altogether Separate Format

In this format women meet together for parts of the study and meet separately in small groups for others. The choice is yours. Usually you include the same elements in the format each week. You achieve variety by changing the order of the elements or by adding special emphasis days when you offer workshops or something totally different. Here are options within this format:

All Altogether

Everyone studies the same curriculum and the women do not travel during the study. They meet around tables in small groups in a large room. The room must allow the tables to be spread apart far enough that women can hear as they meet separately in their small groups. With each format there are advantages and disadvantages.

Advantages are:
- There is excitement generated by being together!
- Time isn't wasted moving from place to place.
- Worship that fills the room is a powerful witness to nonbelievers and energizes everyone.
- You can incorporate drama into the teaching.

Disadvantages are:
- Some women find it hard to hear during times focused around the table.
- Women at tables located far from the front may feel disconnected from the action during together times. If many of your women are elderly, this format may not work. However, one way to solve the problem is to adopt the next option.

Altogether Some

Some of the groups can remain in the large room while others travel to self-contained spaces for table time. Then these groups can join the large group either at tables or in chairs in rows around the large room. Or all the small groups can meet in separate rooms and come together for teaching, worship, and other communal elements of the format.

Hardly Together

If you offer multiple studies, those studying the same curriculum will need to meet together for small groups, prayer, and teaching. But you can still join together for worship, announcements, and service opportunities.

Electives Format

This format originated at Northwest Bible Church under Vickie Kraft. She wrote homework questions to accompany her teaching.

First women gathered to worship, hear the Bible teacher, and listen to announcements. Then they divided up into small groups.

For their small group, women could choose an elective class instead of discussing the Bible study lesson.

Advantages are:

- Variety is built in! Elective classes range from developing spiritual and practical skills to support groups.

  Here is a sampling of elective classes: quilting, calligraphy, flower arranging, Christmas crafts, finishing touch (women bring their own projects to complete), stock market, evangelism training, prayer workshop, fundamentals of biblical counseling, how to study the Bible, nutrition, aerobics, time management, parenting teens, weight management, Christian dating, parenting adult children, and guiding your children's sexual values.

  The topics are endless. Vickie always included a group called "Bible Study Follow Up" for women who wanted to discuss the Bible lesson.

- The idea that "all of life is ministry" is taught. Women understand that in whatever they are doing, they can honor God. All of life is sacred!

- Many women have the opportunity to teach what they know. Women who will never teach the Bible can teach their areas of expertise. Professional women can share from their experience, homemakers can teach how to manage a home, and seasoned mothers can teach child rearing. More women develop leadership skills as they teach and shepherd a small group.

- Hands-on service opportunities help women put their faith into practice. For example, an elective called *Vacation Bible School Workshop* helps undergird VBS by planning, praying, and making name tags and decorations. A group interested in inner-city ministry might leave the church for several hours to tutor students or pray with the elderly.

Disadvantages are:

- If women do not discuss the Bible lesson in a small group, they may not be as diligent in their homework. Discussing the Bible lesson with others adds accountability. It also deepens women's understanding of the Scriptures. They hear different views and learn from one another. For many women, especially those without Bible training—including most postmodern women—this element is crucial to their transformation.
- If the elective teacher monopolizes the time by instructing rather than letting the women participate, community and prayer suffer. Women starving to connect need blocks of time to interact. Time must be set aside to verbalize needs and pray together. This can be overcome through teacher training. The elective teacher must understand that community and prayer are just as important as the content of her lesson.

Half In/Half Out Format

You don't have to use the same format each week. If your women like change, another way to add variety is to change your format from semester to semester or even week to week.

At Elmbrook Church located in Brookfield, Wisconsin, Laurie McIntyre's lead team has experimented with all kinds of creative formats. For example, one semester the women spent the majority of time in small groups while the next semester focused on Bible teaching. For more examples, see her book *Designing Effective Women's Ministries.*

The down side of using different formats is that they are

confusing to administer and confusing to women who don't attend regularly. As long as you keep your format simple, most class coordinators can keep the agenda straight. But if you begin to add multiple elements on top of an inconsistent format, it can be overwhelming.

If a woman misses a few weeks, she may be confused about what to expect the day she returns. Calendars and clear communication help. In addition some women love chaos while others enjoy routine. Keep both in mind as you plan your format.

Shape your study with prayer considering the needs of the women God sends you. Remember: its form and features will either attract or repel women who want to know God and His Word. You will never design the perfect structure for everyone—it doesn't exist! But you can organize a study that woos women to God's Word, and if they persevere, their lives will be transformed.

Chapter 8

FEATURE SMALL GROUPS

*M*ack says me and the kids have to move out by May 1. He owns the house and we have to leave. Do I need a lawyer? How will I pay one?" asked Jessie. Her eyes were swollen and she spoke in a monotone. She described their four-year marriage, a second for both. Her three children, now nine, eleven, and sixteen, had never bonded with Mack and Mack had not spoken to them in over a month.

He had never hit her, although a year earlier he had thrown her against a wall, frightening her so much she called 911. But Mack told the police she was lying, and because there were no physical signs of abuse, the police simply filed a report, warning them that if there were a second offense, someone would go to jail. Since then he no longer raged. Now he was silent and mean.

Mack began attending another church, where he joined a divorce recovery class—even though he wasn't divorced. When Jessie found out, she showed up at the class and embarrassed him. Her response added to his anger.

Jessie did not move out May 1, but she did retain a lawyer to look after their interests. Because there was no physical abuse, the lawyer suggested that she stay in the home. Often the best course of action is no action, giving God time to work. The lawyer also told her that if he filed for divorce later, she would be better off financially if she stayed.

Over the next two years, I (Sue) worked with Jessie as she transitioned from a wife to a single parent. Mack refused to make any effort to heal their marriage, but Jessie continued to hope—until one August night.

Mack continued to demand they leave—with greater and greater insistence. We later learned that he was pursuing another woman who didn't know he was married. On August 14, Jessie dropped the kids off at church for AWANA, shopped for groceries, and drove home. As she approached the driveway, she saw her daughter's puppy dead in the street.

Nine-year-old Mandy named him Fudsie because his chocolate brown coat was sprinkled with tan, which Mandy said were the nuts. Now his coat was stained red, but not from an automobile. His little neck was twisted and blood spotted his face and neck. Jessie was grateful Mandy was not with her. She ran into the house.

"What happened to Fudsie?" she demanded.

"Oh, he got out," answered Mack, but his sneer was evident. She knew he would never admit the truth. She walked into the bedroom to try to clear her head. Mack followed her. Suddenly he was in her face. He began to rage and rail with obscenities. He knew her vulnerabilities and used them as he followed her from room to room. Jessie began to cry. Then she felt a hot anger burning from within and she gave into it. When he grabbed her arm, she slapped him. He smiled.

This time Mack called 911. When the police arrived, Jessie was still angry. She tried to explain what he had done to her daughter's puppy. But Mack had a different story and they believed him.

As a friend rounded the corner bringing the children home, they saw their mom being handcuffed and put into a police car. Fudsie still lay dead in the street.

Hope was gone. Jessie was released, but the judge required that she attend an anger management class and was put on probation for a year. She moved out immediately and began a journey to rebuild her life and help her children rebound. Mack's girlfriend wised up, and he tried to see Jessie several times over the next year.

She agonized over whether or not his advances were genuine. They went to a professional counselor, but in the end Mack resisted the work assigned and filed for divorce.

This is real women's ministry. It's messy and often heartbreaking. True, this is an extreme example, but it is not uncommon. What can we do as leaders to help women like Jessie? We need more than programs and parties. We must provide systematic support from God's Word and God's people. Only through intimacy with Christ and authentic community can a woman like Jessie find the inner strength to rebuild her life.

I met with Jessie periodically, but my ministry partner was her small group. Jessie's leader had the experience and the heart to help her. In addition to weekly calls, her leader planned a weekend retreat at a lake house for her small group. They popped corn in their pajamas, talking late into the night. Jessie's small group was the community God used to keep her close to Him, to enable her to overcome her circumstances, and to teach her how to respond to them biblically.

Why Small Groups?

So far we have been discussing how to organize the overall study. Did you notice that we assume you will incorporate small groups into your ministry? Small groups are not an option. Why?

In part 1 we saw that postmodern women are starving for relationships. This was evident from the panel Sue attended at Multnomah, where the young women kept wishing for a "home." Their voices trembled as they pleaded with women leaders to remember their need to connect. Small groups serve as "home" in your study.

Most modern women love fellowship too. God created women to be relational as a reflection of His triune character. Women should never be ashamed of enjoying relationships. Building relationships—first with Jesus and then with each other—is the second pillar of the Transformation Model, second only to centering on Scripture. Small groups are the means to relationship and thus transformation.

Therefore you are wise to invest prayer, time, and resources into building your small groups. It is a key priority. Let's analyze the small group process.

What's the Ideal Makeup of a Small Group?

The best small groups are mixed in age, spiritual maturity, and life-stage experiences. Because of the biblical mandate in Titus 2, God desires that we put women of different ages together. In my experience, if we teach the younger women to take the initiative, natural Titus 2 mentoring friendships emerge out of the mixed small group. In addition, it is healthy for women to come in contact with all kinds of women. However, that does not mean we draw their names out of a hat when we divide up the groups.

How to Construct a Small Group

The process of group selection is prayer-based, time-consuming, and critical to women's transformation. Here are some guidelines:

Recruit a Team

Every group needs two leaders—a discussion leader and a co-leader. You can call these leaders shepherds, spiritual mothers, or anything else you want.

Limit the Size

The optimum size of a small group is eight to twelve. That's how many you want participating each week. A more intimate group of four to six works well if there is a high commitment level.

But in most church studies, you attract both responsible women and those who give up easily.

The goal here is to make the group large enough to create interesting discussions but small enough for intimate sharing, individual participation, and effective facilitation by the small group leader. Expect that your attendance will fluctuate during the semester so that some weeks you may have more than ten and others considerably less. Our goal is for each group to connect, minister to one another, and experience true community.

Pray, Pray, Pray

Build each group carefully and prayerfully! Preregister as many women as possible so you will have an estimate of how many to expect.

Shortly before the semester starts, we gather a small team consisting of the class administrator, the women's pastor and/or director, and anyone else who knows the women well. We commit our task to God in prayer as we begin.

Match Up the Leader and Coleader First

We begin by matching up the leadership teams. Identify their giftedness and pair women who complement one another. Categorize these leadership teams according to the women to whom they will most likely connect. Pair empty nesters with new or single moms, working women with others who share their experience.

Begin by Placing Women You Know

Then we begin the task of organizing the small discussion groups. The registration forms tell us the woman's age, church, marital status, address, if she works, children's ages, if she requests to be with a friend or in a particular group, and other pertinent information.

Then, using the information provided on the cards and our

personal knowledge of the women, we begin to assign participants to groups. Remember: mix older women with younger, talkers with quiet ones, and think critically about the leaders to whom you assign nonbelievers, women from different churches/denominations, and women with special circumstances. And be sure to assign strong-willed, opinionated women to experienced leaders.

Next, Place New Women

After we have placed all the women we know, we place new women. We examine their registration forms to learn all we can. Then we place them based on what we know.

Take a Final Look

After all women are in groups, we evaluate the particular makeup of each group. We try to visualize this group interacting. Is there a good mix? Does the group fit with its leaders? Are there too many talkers? needs? potential problems?

We ask God to show us if these are His choices. Building groups is a bit like building families. We want them to love and respect each other. We want them to learn from one another. We want meaningful friendships formed that will last a lifetime.

Think of how complex a family of four can be. We are building families of twelve! We build with finite understanding, including women we have never even met. It's a wonder any of them work! But they do. Not all, but many. And when they do, we celebrate. When they don't, we know we did the best we could.

We try to leave several openings in each group for women who have not registered and for neighbors who decide at the last minute they will come with friends. If we don't have enough openings, we know we need to recruit new leaders. We entrust the groups to God and work hard to find a good mix. God uses our efforts to transform lives. It is worth every minute.

How Long Should a Small Group Meet Together?

Small groups should not meet indefinitely. If they do, they become ingrown and impenetrable. In time, members know one another's history and bond tightly. As a result, a newcomer can't break in. Close relationships are beneficial but not if groups become exclusive.

Our goal is to create a place where women fall in love with Jesus. Then He transforms them from the inside out. If our groups no longer welcome women who want to know Him, we have lost sight of why we exist.

How long should the groups remain together? That's up to you. Ours meet for a year. That works well because most of our new women join us at the kickoff of a new study.

There are always groups who beg to remain together another year. They have a reason why they are the exception. As the women's pastor, I'm the "bad guy" who says "No" whether they understand my reasoning or not. I stand firm because God has entrusted me with keeping us on target. I am responsible for remembering what we are about—transforming lives!

How Do You Choose Small Group Leaders?

Look for spiritually mature women who love God, His Word, and other women. Look for passionate women who have worked through their emotional baggage and are able to invest in others. Find women who will persevere through challenges and are eager to make a difference. In addition, you want women who are teachable and humble. You want women willing to work within your parameters and sold out to your vision. You probably won't find women that meet all these criteria, but at least find women who desire to become this way.

Generally, draw from women you have observed in the study. Occasionally a woman will join who has extensive experience in another church. Recruit her only after careful analysis. Try to find someone who has worked with her. It only takes one difficult leader to make your life miserable and do harm to the study.

Recruit leaders using an adapted version of the process for recruiting a lead team (in chapter 4). Consider recruiting one or two more than you think you will need in case your numbers swell. Ask them to be on call if they are needed.

What Are the Different Roles of the Leader and Coleader?

Generally the leader directs the discussion. She is in charge. The coleader assists her and oversees the group's administrative details. See appendix B for the small group leaders manual. You will find the roles clearly defined there. This manual was hammered out in Bible Discussion Groups, Inc. Adapt the manual to your study if you find it useful.

You can change the job descriptions of the leader and coleader to fit your purposes. However, we suggest that they do not share leading the discussion. A group grows used to a particular leader's style and finds a change every week confusing.

Some women's temperaments and gifts make them better leaders and others better coleaders. Don't insist that everyone make it her goal to be the leader. Just as everyone in the church is equally valuable to God, let your coleaders know that they are equally valuable to you.

How Will You Equip Your Leaders and Coleaders?

Gather them together periodically for in-depth times of training and interaction. Design a training manual so that they understand what you expect. Again, refer to the sample manual in appendix B. Give each leader a copy and find creative ways to teach them how to use it. Help them understand that leading small groups is a skill and will take time to master.

Our leaders meet for training at least a week before the class kickoff. Set aside at least four hours. Here is a typical agenda for the morning training:

9:00 A.M.	Icebreaker games and goodies as women arrive • Seat leaders and coleaders together
9:20 A.M.	Introduce each leader briefly
9:30 A.M.	Hand out manuals and teach small group leading techniques and strategies • Use drama, games, role-play, and other creative teaching tools • Let experienced leaders help as the group interacts • Break midway and again at the end.
11:00 A.M.	Class administrator explains how the class operates and hands out her expectations in writing • Hand out group rosters if they are ready • Explain and sign conflict resolution covenants, Q and A
11:20 A.M.	Break for quick box lunch and fellowship
11:45 A.M.	Gather in a circle for mock lesson led by instructor • The leaders bring a completed lesson 1 to go over as a model
12:30 P.M.	Prayer (as a group or as leader teams) for groups, kickoff, teacher, etc.
1:15 P.M.	Dismiss, extend nursery so leader teams can meet until 1:30 • Trainer stays around to answer questions

Build on this initial training all year. If you meet periodically as leaders, take ten minutes and review a leading principle. Create a humorous pop quiz to see what your leaders remember. Ask your leaders to share actual situations they have encountered. Enlist everyone's input on how to handle the issue. However, protect confidentiality by asking leaders not to mention names.

Once you learn the skill of leading a small group, you will find many other opportunities to use it. I (Sue) was active in my children's high school, both as band club and PTA president. Once after a meeting a woman who chaired a local political party complemented me: "That's the best run meeting I ever sat through." I smiled. I was just using the skills I learned leading small groups for Bible study.

We have examined many decisions you need to consider as you plan your Bible study. Use the ideas that work for you. If you are overseeing women's ministry in a small church, the process is simpler. Enjoy a less complex ministry, but understand that God may expand your influence. When women's lives are transformed, often others will follow.

However, growth depends on a variety of factors—the overall growth and health of your church, the support you receive from your leadership, and the experience of your team. We will address these issues in later chapters. For now, work hard and depend completely on the Lord. He is responsible for the results.

Chapter 9

ROMANCE THE
POSTMODERN WOMAN

Sarah was a twenty-six-year-old newlywed. Five months earlier she and Bryan made a covenant to love and honor each other until death separated them—and they promised to include God in their marriage. But Bryan lost his job right after they returned from their honeymoon. And sex had been extremely painful for Sarah—so much that they still had not had intercourse. Their dream honeymoon bombed and they were both discouraged and disappointed.

Losing his job and feeling rejected by his bride, Bryan stopped talking. Finally when he did communicate, he yelled at Sarah, "Any God that would let this happen is a God I don't want to know." He refused to attend church and dropped out of men's Bible study. Bryan's anger only made Sarah more distant physically.

Their marriage spiraled down toward destruction and if they didn't turn it around, they would soon be another statistic. As a women's pastor, what can you offer Sarah? Biblical counseling, of course. But more than that.

Ministering to Postmodern Sarah

Sarah will need a woman who has walked through her circumstances and come out on the other side intact. She will need God's Word to help her view her marriage from God's perspective. She will need women friends so that she will not expect Bryan to meet all her relational needs. She will need prayer from sisters who want her marriage to succeed and are willing to invest in her life to make that a reality. She will need God and an army of His women.

She will find these resources in a Bible study designed to transform lives. But it has to be a Bible study where Sarah, as a postmodern woman, feels loved and accepted. It has to be a place where leaders understand postmodernism and are willing to employ methods that work for them.

If we count the hours Sarah will spend at home on her lesson and attending the study, she will invest three to five hours each week. How can we design these hours for maximum impact in Sarah's life—as well as the lives of the modern women needed to mentor her?

Make It an Experience!

For all women—but especially for the postmodern women—it must be more than an intellectual exercise. It must be an experience! As women go deep into God's Word, witness the powerful impact of faith in others' lives, and take in images of eternal truths through a variety of media, the experience colors the rest of their week. In time, as they cooperate with God, they are transformed!

We saw in chapter 1, *Who Is the Postmodern Woman?*, that many young women demand more than propositional truth. They want to see Jesus lived out in His followers. They want to know if the experience is real.

Please don't misunderstand. I'm not advocating that you put boxes of tissues on the tables every week. Our goal is *not* hysteria so women will make decisions based on emotion. Don't stop teaching the truths of Scripture through sound, solid reasoning. Just add elements that will move these truths from head to heart.

Why? Because our relationship with Christ involves more than our minds. Yes, it begins there. And we want lessons and teaching that take us deep into the complexities of life and theology. But relationships touch the heart also. We want women to *love* Jesus and to *love* His Word. His love has the power to make us overcomers. His love fills the holes in our hearts and we are made new. Women yearn to be loved. How do we connect them with the love that Jesus yearns to lavish upon them?

Live Out His Love

We feel loved when others care for us and respect us. We feel loved when others make it clear that they will not withdraw their affection if we let them down. We feel loved when they have our best interests at heart. We feel loved when others care enough to tell us the truth gently.

We show these women love by the way we treat them from the moment they walk in the door. Leaders express love when they create an atmosphere of unconditional acceptance in the groups. We love them when we give them our best.

We all feel loved when caring is expressed in tender ways— through music, praise, special words, and images that travel through our senses and connect us to our loved One. God created us this way. Let's make it our goal to express the love of Jesus to women during the study. How? What are some practical ways to create experience in your study? Here are some ideas that work for us.

Add Art

The Bible is full of powerful stories, songs, poetry, symbols, and images that shout His love for us. Why not incorporate them into the experience? Add art to your format. It is a powerful communicator. By touching the senses, art can often reveal truth in unique ways.

"The arts matter," says IBC Fine Arts Pastor, Arthur Morton, "because they help us move into our hearts. God crafted us beautifully. He not only gave us a mind, but emotion, imagination, and heart: that part of us Scripture calls the center of man (Proverbs 4:23). The arts engage this center and enable us to offer those deeper parts of ourselves to each other, and more importantly, to God. Then we are able to worship Him with all our humanity—fully alive."

For centuries art revolved around Christian themes. Visit the great museums and cathedrals around the world and you will see the Bible illustrated in moving masterpieces. Does music influence our world? Every teenager's ear is glued to a CD player. How persuasive are images? Think about the impact of advertising, TV, and film. With images they direct the course of our culture. Often pop culture opposes God and takes people deeper into degradation.

But these media are not evil. Their influence comes from the heart behind the art. God is the great Creator and He gave us creativity. Yet we have abandoned these tools of communication to the world. Let's take them back for God's glory. I realize the world spends millions of dollars on art to make money, and we can't compete with the music, film, and TV industries. But we don't have to. Some of the world's art still communicates great biblical messages. Borrow from them, with their permission of course.

Churches like Willow Creek write insightful drama that you can buy. Christian music is available for the price of the print music and a CD. There are creative ways to use art. When we illustrate our Bible teaching with art, we find that our impact soars. Let's experience God in both our minds and hearts!

IBC employs a full-time arts pastor and also uses music, drama, PowerPoint, and handout sheets in its services. "During the message, the PowerPoint slides are coming out on the screen as I give them," says Andy McQuitty, IBC senior pastor. "We pass out notes with fill-in blanks so that people are motivated to watch the screen, fill in blanks, and follow along. It's well known that the more sensory gates through which you can bring information, the better they will retain it."

Our church invests in the technology to exhibit all kinds of art. For example, we have two large screens on each side of the sanctuary to display outlines, quotes, maps, song lyrics, movie clips, and paintings. We have an art gallery in our church where we display local artists' works. So it is natural for us to use art in our Bible studies.

I incorporated art in my teaching when I taught in a traditional church. I had few resources. Nevertheless, I handed out outlines decorated with clip art, used visual aids, and displayed paintings on easels if they expressed the theme of my message. I dressed in a band uniform, wore silly hats, and delivered the message in a British droll to make my point. When God called me to a church that used art, I was delirious with the new resources. Use what you have.

I love art, but not all teachers do. If not, God has women in your church with artistic abilities that would love to use them to honor Him. Look for scriptwriters, actors, singers, musicians, dancers, designers, and technicians. Find women who majored in music or drama in school. Find women who love the arts and recruit them to help you.

God gifted many women with angelic voices. Others play instruments. Others dance or paint. Locate them and give them opportunities to use their talents and complement the Scriptures at the same time. These media can drive the Bible message deep into the hearts of the women.

Center the Experience on a Theme

The theme is the main idea of the Bible passage you are studying that week. There may be several themes in the passage, so ask your teacher which theme she plans to emphasize in her message.

Who will design the Bible study experience around the theme? Enlist a team. Include the teacher, the worship leader, and other creative women in your church. We call these creative women our arts integration team, and our worship leader leads the team. Her job is to oversee music, art, and drama as well as all the technical elements of the Bible studies.

The Process

How does the arts integration team generate ideas? They meet with the teacher to brainstorm ideas for the whole series at least a month before the kickoff. Producing the team's ideas takes time. This requires that your teachers work ahead on their lessons and lectures. It helps if teachers create a rough manuscript draft of their messages. Unleash creative women with these manuscripts and stand back for an idea explosion.

Teachers who won't work ahead hinder the process. Of course, teachers can make last-minute changes to their lectures, but they must know the main ideas early because the theme begins with them.

You know the week's theme. The team is meeting to find creative ways to illustrate it. What kinds of ideas do they generate?

Illustrating the Theme

Here are some questions to prime the pump:

- What worship songs complement the theme?
- Can you find a related painting or picture to display on the screens or an easel during the study? Remember: you must have the artists' permission. Find their Web sites and ask. Most artists are delighted to comply.
- Can someone write or find a short drama to illustrate the theme? If not, there are many quality dramas available both in Christian bookstores and online. Some IBC

dramas are published and can be downloaded from www.churchideas.com. There is a minimal charge for these scripts. See appendix C for the drama used to introduce Sue's Covenant Study.

- Is there a film clip to illustrate the theme or a point in the message? You can buy a license covering many major producers from Christian Video Licensing International for $150–$200 annually. See www.cvli.org or call 888-771-CVLI. For permission to use videos and films in their entirety or clips not covered by the CVLI license, contact the production companies directly. CVLI will give you the contact information if needed.

- What about a special song that illustrates the theme? Should a group sing it or would it be more effective as a solo or maybe an ensemble of instruments?

- Would a woman signing the words add meaning? We have a woman who signs for the deaf. She blesses us with gracious sweeping movements that take us into the meaning of the music in a powerful way.

- At the tables, is there a game to play, a question to answer, or a case study to ponder that would complement the theme?

- Is there a ceremony that would be meaningful? Could you serve communion, light candles, or nail prayer requests to a cross?

- Are there sound effects that would enhance the experience? During a lesson on the Rainbow covenant, we played the sound of rain in the background.

- Is there a special food that would complement the theme? During the lesson on the Holy Spirit, the teacher treated us to *Dove* chocolate bars.

- Are there visual aids to enhance the experience? During the lesson on the Armor of God, we spotlighted a life-size suit of armor standing on a draped platform. We bought the armor at Garden Ridge. To enhance a theme on our value to God, we gave out pretend million dollar bills.

- Is there a story that fits? Can a woman share a related testimony?
- Are there special books on the theme you want to give away? We give away a related gift weekly at the beginning to encourage punctuality.
- Is there a poem, story, or piece of art to make into a bookmark or picture for the women to take home? Are there other mementos you could make?
- Is there a costume the teacher could wear to illustrate her message?
- Should we all wear something significant to the message? We wore party hats to celebrate God's work in our lives and jogging suits when the theme was spiritual health.
- Is there a magic trick to illustrate the theme? Once I used chemicals to illustrate forgiveness. I poured black water into a glass pitcher. Then I added a red solution and the water instantly turned clear.
- Could a dance be choreographed to illustrate your message?

* * *

Remember: honor all copyrights and obtain permission before using arts elements that are not original. It's an integrity issue!

* * *

What other ideas come to mind? Use them as tools to enhance the experience. However, be careful not to use too many at one time. Too much can overwhelm the senses. Our worship always complements the theme. We normally display some kind of art that announces the theme as soon as the women walk in. But the other elements are used sparingly. We use drama about once a month. Choose the strongest elements for that theme and do them with excellence. Yes, it's work, but the results are worth it!

Teach Messages That Emphasize Application

In seminary we learned to think theologically. We studied every book of the Bible as well as a variety of views on almost every theological subject. We learned to think propositionally, to reason carefully, and to apply biblical truth to everyday life. Our training was invaluable and provided resources for teaching that help us constantly.

Most women (and for that matter most seminarians!) don't care about the difference between supra- and superlapsarianism. That is especially true of postmodern women. The mothers and grand-mothers of today's generation come to church asking, "Who is preaching and what's their subject?" Today postmoderns ask, "Who will be there, and will they accept me?" They want to know if they can find a *home* and they want to see if we are real.

Therefore, our main idea needs to be practical. Our message outline points need to relate to real life with words like *you* and *us*. And our message should be full of illustrations and stories that bring theoretical truths alive. This has always been good teaching. But it is even more critical today because postmodern women aren't impressed merely with our scholarship. They want to see if our faith works.

Teach Women to Connect

That may sound ridiculous. Don't women know how to connect? Yes and no. Most women are eager for friendships, but many live in isolation because they are bound by fear. They have never lived in a functioning family. People, especially their parents, let them down. They are desperate to connect but suspicious that you will wound them.

Americans are taught to be independent. According to census data released in May 2001, "the number of Americans living alone grew rapidly in the 1990s—for the first time surpassing the num-ber of married couples with children."[1] We live next door and across the street—yet we remain strangers. Our calendars are so full of activity that there's little time for relationships. We work long hours, play hard, and are entertainment junkies. Friendships are often not a priority.

Teachers can help women connect. Last year at IBC I taught Titus so I could hammer home God's mandate to older and younger women. I shared the way my spiritual mother nurtured me and I challenged them to nurture each other.

I instructed the younger women to take the initiative if they wanted to be mentored by an older woman. I helped them understand that an older woman was not going to approach them with words like, "I've learned some things I think would help you, dear. Would you like to get together?"

We want mentoring relationships to occur naturally as a by-product of women spending a year together in Bible study. And they do. But often women need encouragement and training. We offered a class on spiritual mothering in the summer and over fifty women signed up. Women want to minister to one another. Teach them.

Provide Time for Women to Connect

What good is teaching women to connect if we never give them time? I would love to have an hour each week to teach. But I take thirty-five to forty-five minutes, although I often feel rushed. I have learned that time spent interacting in the groups is just as important as time spent listening to me. For some, it's more important.

Our first session of the year, we set aside a block of time for women to get acquainted. Monthly we extend our time of fellowship around a meal. We encourage our leaders to take their groups on an overnight retreat during the first semester. Leaders plan several gatherings outside of class.

Leaders and coleaders split the roster and connect with the women by phone regularly. They write notes. They sing to women on their birthdays. They bring flowers, candles, and snacks to brighten up their tables. I am often overwhelmed by the creative ways they express love to the women in their groups. It's all part of the experience!

Pioneer Profile: Dianne Miller

Dianne Miller was Baptist to the bone. But the first time she worshiped in The Church of the Apostles, an evangelical Anglican church in Atlanta, the experience was so moving that she wept. Less than two years later she joined their staff as women's ministry director.

"When you have a personal relationship with the living God, the liturgy nurtures your soul, refreshes your faith, and reminds you of your First Love," says Dianne. "The sacraments and symbols reawakened worship in me in a new and different way. I loved praying on my knees and the weekly focused emphasis on the communion table. I often cried as I witnessed the community of faith affirming the essentials of why we remember Him.

"The church calendar helped us visually experience our faith, and the emphasis on the lives of believers through the ages connected me with my Christian heritage as never before."

She learned a new vocabulary from the rector, Michael Youseff. The governing board is the vestry, and heading the vestry is the rector's warden. Originally, when the rector took home the collection for safekeeping, he needed a bodyguard—the warden—and the name stuck. Dianne, a history buff, loved the church's rich heritage dating back five hundred years to the time of Henry VIII.

But there were also similarities that made her feel right at home. Each week Rector Youseff preached a rousing sermon from the

Scriptures. And his heart for missions gave the church a global flavor. In addition, Rector Youseff gave Dianne "a blank check" to invest in the women. The church licensed her as a deaconess in the Anglican Church and unleashed her.

During her first year she built the infrastructure by enlisting a women's board. They enjoyed their first retreat and widow's ministry, and they hosted a Heart to Heart conference with Vickie Kraft. Dianne loved shepherding the women, and it broke her heart to leave them.

But within a year her husband's job moved them back to Dallas. Returning home to the city where she taught Bible Study Fellowship and earned a degree at Dallas Theological Seminary was a blessing—but Dianne misses the dear women at The Church of the Apostles. God filled that void, however, with new ministry opportunities at Northwest Bible Church.

Dianne learned there are many ways to worship God! A Baptist lady found wonder and delight in what she calls "ancient future," where she drew close to God in a new way. This experience enriched her faith and impacts how she ministers to women today. With many postmoderns hungry for symbols, sacred experience, and transcendent beauty, these lessons were priceless. Dianne learned that the church is a many-faceted diamond, and sometimes its beauty sparkles from an unexpected angle. What a great lesson for us all!

Teach Women to Pray and Give Them Time to Pray

We wait for several weeks before we pray together in the groups. Why? Because many are terrified to pray out loud! A few quit the class when they learn we pray together.

Carol came to us three years ago from another church. In her tradition, they did not study the Bible and they only prayed rote prayers. The thought of talking to God in her own words in front of others made her sick. But she didn't give in to her fears and in time she conquered them. She moved away last year. On the last day of class she gave me a big bear hug and whispered in my ear, "Thank you for teaching me to pray. It has made all the difference."

We usually end our study with a concert of prayer. God loves the beautiful sounds that echo through the room as the women bow their heads around their tables. Because it is at the end, prayer is easily neglected. Don't let this become a habit. Prayer is a priority! But it won't matter how much time we allot if women don't pray.

How do we teach women to pray? We ease them into it. For the first three weeks of class, we just take prayer requests. Each table has the freedom to handle prayer requests however they want. The last page of each lesson is a prayer journal where the women can record celebrations and concerns. Some groups use that page to write down each other's requests.

However, most groups pass out 3 x 5 cards. When the women arrive they write down their prayer requests. The leader takes up the cards and reads the requests. This method seems to take less time than if every woman verbalized her own request. For the first three weeks we pass out the cards and ask the women to pray for each other at home. We use the extra time building community.

On the fourth week, we streamline the format to allow me time to teach a short workshop on how to pray together. This is a great time for a short testimony from an overcomer. I lay down parameters for conversational prayer. I teach them about "popcorn" prayers—short, simple bursts of words to God.

I give them freedom not to pray out loud but I insist that they join others silently in their hearts. I gently chide returning women who still aren't praying aloud. I talk about the amazing promises and benefits of intercessory prayer. Then we pray for about five minutes.

The leader opens with short words of praise and then the women pray for each other's needs. The leader has passed out the cards so nervous women can simply pray the request right off the card. I close from the front and then the worship leader directs us in a simple chorus. The next week, we extend the prayer time to about ten minutes, sometimes more depending on that week's schedule.

A group member often volunteers to e-mail the weekly requests. Some groups ask a prayer captain to keep a prayer journal of requests as well as answered prayer. What fun to read back over the requests and praise God for the way He's worked!

We don't brow beat women who don't pray. We model prayer in everything we do. We thank God for the awesome privilege of prayer. We find that our women become prayer warriors not out of compulsion but because they can't help it. Prayer works wonders. Teach women to pray and give them time to practice.

Employ Surprise and Variety!

It's a sin to bore people with the Bible—or with Bible study! Don't lock yourself into the same format every week. Our Bible study lead team meets after each study to plan the format for the next week. We ask God to reveal ways to drive His Word deep into the women's hearts with surprise and variety.

We don't change it every week—only if there is a good reason. But if there is, we don't hesitate. This is our usual format:

- Welcome and opening prayer
- Give-away incentive to be on time
- Worship (ten minutes)
- Small group time: take prayer requests, go over the lesson (forty-five to fifty-five minutes)

- Announcements and service opportunities (five to ten minutes)
- Lecture (thirty-five to forty-five minutes)
- Concert of prayer (ten minutes)
- Closing chorus

We begin on time and end on time—almost without exception. It's an integrity issue. We have scores of children waiting in the nursery, and we appreciate the Kids Klub's ministry. Dismissing on time keeps us on good terms with our kids and their caregivers.

But within our time parameters, we have fun. When we add drama, we may shorten worship and the teaching. We insert the drama wherever it is most effective. Sometimes it is in the lecture, if it illustrates a particular point. Other times it sets up the lecture.

We may place a special song or ceremony at the end. Occasionally we shorten the discussion time and tack on a question the women haven't seen to discuss after the lecture. A testimony might fit within the lecture or come at the beginning of the study to set up the theme.

On our last day of the year, we usually throw out the format and celebrate. We fill the time with all kinds of interesting surprises. We thank our leaders, eat, pray over summer requests, and introduce the next year's study. We may do that with a drama. We may have testimonies—either planned or spontaneous as we reach another milestone in our lives.

Have fun with the format and don't be afraid to try something new. It may bomb and then you won't do it again. But often it will be a special reminder to the women of how dear they are to you. Each week is another opportunity to enjoy an experience with Jesus.

Plan Tight, But Don't Appear Structured

I love structure! I like things where I can find them, and I like to know what's next. I like people who are on time, and I like things to go precisely as planned. I'm typical of many women of my generation. If you are like me, what I am about to say may seem silly, but hear me out. If you aren't attracting postmodern women, this could be why.

My daughters prefer a more relaxed approach and so do most of their friends. The postmodern women who lead and attend our studies want us to make every minute meaningful, but they don't like to feel rushed. They want to know that if there's a good reason to make a spontaneous change, we will.

Remember the bell? Women hated it! For my first two years at IBC, we rang the bell. We rang it to let women know they had ten minutes left in their group time. I rang it when I was switching subjects as I led the concert of prayer from up front. I let them know they could wrap up what they were praying before we moved to another subject. I thought I was being considerate. They were annoyed.

In time they communicated their disdain for the bell. We threw it out. We do begin and end on time. And normally we follow the schedule. But if they need a few more minutes in the group that day, we make a quick adjustment. And we don't make an issue of time. It rolls along on schedule, but we don't announce, "Five more minutes in your groups." Instead we say something like, "It looks like most of you are wrapping up. We'll get started on our announcements in a few minutes."

Actually it is still highly structured. But we don't make a big deal of it. And we will flex if we need to. Women appreciate a more relaxed atmosphere—even though every minute is planned for maximum effect. It's just another way to make the experience pleasant in a 24/7 world.

Will any of these suggestions fit your ministry? If so, give them a try. The experience you create each week is a powerful tool to transform women. Not all women will be faithful. Studying the Scriptures is hard work. But for those who do, a great reward awaits them—an intimate relationship with Jesus, the great Lover of their souls. Knowing that you had a part in bringing them together is one of life's greatest joys!

Chapter 10

OFFER EXCITING EVENTS

A transforming women's ministry provides consistent opportunities for women to gather and grow spiritually, which is why it centers around regular study of God's Word. You will find, however, that women sometimes need to feel special, cared for, pampered. Periodic events provide a change of pace and opportunities for relationship and community, and can be powerful tools to complement your ongoing ministries.

Wendi's Experience

Wendi was a successful lawyer, but her evenings were increasingly spent in front of a big screen TV with a rum and coke—make that, rum and cokes. Her husband of six years had encouraged her to take the promotion and move from their New England home to Dallas. His salary as an auto mechanic was a fraction of hers, but he liked his work and decided to stay until she was sure she liked the new job. The spark was flickering anyway.

The new job was challenging but internal conflict in the firm made the days tense. *Why all this competition?* Weekends she worked at home or sat on the couch missing her cat, Honey. *I'll send for her soon.*

Her neighbors Bonnie and Phil helped her hang a ceiling fan and made her a pie the day she moved in—a coconut cream pie. "Best pie I've had in years," she told Bonnie, and it was true. *But who cooks anymore?* Nevertheless, the sense of being mothered lingered for months.

"A retreat—what's a retreat?" Wendi asked in response to Bonnie's invitation. "This one's just for women," explained Bonnie. "We get out of the city and into nature and just kick back for a couple days. You can ride horses, water ski, karaoke, or just relax with a good book. It would give you a chance to meet my friends. And we have a great speaker. I've heard her before. I'd love it if you'd come with me."

"I'll think about it," replied Wendi. She checked her calendar for that weekend. As usual, nothing. She liked Bonnie—a little weird, but genuine. *What could it hurt? I'll take my own car so I can escape if necessary.*

Wendi arrived late but Bonnie had been watching for her. At check-in she received a cloth-quilted name tag and a tote bag loaded with folders and goodies like earplugs, lotion, and chocolate. On the tote bag were the words, "Patterns of Our Lives." *What's the pattern of my life? No, I'm not here to think. I'm here to relax.*

The registration room fed into a huge room full of chairs— maybe four hundred. Around the walls hung dozens of quilts, and next to each quilt hung the story of the quilt and the woman whose hands had delicately stitched each piece of fabric to make a beautiful whole. Interwoven in the words were legacies of wise women devoted to family, friends, and faith. Their stories intrigued her.

Off to the dining hall to meet Bonnie's friends. Introductions, smiles, laughter. Wendi was so engrossed in their interaction she forgot the bland cafeteria food. She noticed a few other women like herself sitting in silence observing others, but most were caught up in stories and fun. Faint memories of Christy, her childhood friend. *We used to laugh like that. What happened?*

Four hundred women streamed into the quilt room, flopping down on red, yellow, or blue chair cushions. The first third of the room was red, the middle, yellow, and the back, blue. Wendi and Bonnie found two blue cushions. Being late had a price. But Linda, the emcee, introduced herself and asked each woman to sit on a different colored cushion each session. *Good, Bonnie and I will get to sit closer tomorrow.*

In the middle of Linda's announcements, Rachmaninoff's "Flight of the Bumble Bees" filled the room and four women in brightly colored bumblebee suits buzzed out of a twelve-foot hive on the stage. Linda pretended to be surprised. They introduced themselves as Queen Bee, Quilting Bee, Spelling Bee, and Busy Bee.

Queen Bee was obviously the leader. After a few minutes of clever slapstick humor the four buzzed off down the aisle to the roar of laughter. *Silly but clever.*

Linda introduced the worship leader and the speaker—both women belonged to Bonnie's church. Wendi wondered what church was like. She had never been in a church except for weddings and her grandfather's funeral.

Worship was an experience. Four hundred voices filled the room with praise. Bonnie showed her the words in her folder and she joined in as best she could. Why were these women singing with such intensity? Soon she too was lost in melody and rhythm. But who was this God they were praising?

The speaker opened with a prayer that sounded like a conversation—no big words, no flowery language—just simple affection. For the next forty-five minutes, Wendi listened to her describe a sacred romance between herself and God.

The speaker was introduced to Christ in her twenties by her fiancé, and they both had decided to follow Him. Within two years, they wearied of the corporate lifestyle and a marriage already on the rocks, so they left their jobs and traveled in a van for six months to focus on what God wanted for their lives.

They ended up in seminary, and now fifteen years later she was a Bible teacher. Jackie spoke of a new joy and a transformed life. *Did they orchestrate this just for me? No, of course not. There are four hundred women in this room. Still. . . .*

The women split up into small groups all over the camp. Bonnie and Wendi were in the same group but everyone else was a stranger. They spent half an hour getting to know one another—two moms, a grandmother, three single women, one a paralegal.

Wendi connected with the paralegal, Susan, immediately. Although Susan worked for a law firm downtown and Wendi's firm was north of the city, her apartment was close to Wendi's rented house. Susan and Wendi talked for an hour after the small group while Bonnie visited with friends.

At the end of small group time, their leader gave each one a T-shirt—that fit each woman perfectly—with the same "patterns of life" logo as on her tote.

Snacks, games, loud music, karaoke in the barn, talking into the night. Wendi and Bonnie sat on their beds balancing plates of homemade chocolate chip cookies and cups of suisse mocha coffee.

They connected that night, and it was evident that Bonnie really enjoyed Wendi's sharp mind and sense of humor. Wendi opened up about her marriage, her drinking, and her restlessness. Bonnie listened intently but did not offer advice. Instead she told Wendi about her rebellious years and the way she wounded her Christian parents.

"How did you get over it?" asked Wendi.

"I fell in love with Jesus," answered Bonnie.

Restless sleep. Leisurely breakfast of pancakes and sausage. Back to the quilt room, now on the red cushions. The bumblebees buzzed. More worship. More Bible teaching. The Bible—*it's an ancient book,* thought Wendi—but this teacher brings it alive. Her words pierced Wendi's heart. *She's talking about me again.*

In the small group, the leader asked questions relating to the message. They grappled with tough issues—like why would God allow Susan's dad to die of cancer and what was the point of praying if God already knows what's going to happen. Wendi had never participated in a spiritual discussion before. The ideas about God and life fascinated her. Susan recommended a good book.

The afternoon was a smorgasbord. Softball brought back memories of family reunions when mom and dad were together. Sweat, dirt, and ribbing the losers. After a shower, Bonnie suggested they attend a workshop on how to study the Bible. After years of undergraduate and law school Wendi knew how to study, but Bible study? How hard could it be? The class wasn't as easy as she thought, but she loved a challenge. And the teacher made it fun.

Saturday night several friends joined Wendi and Bonnie in their room. They rehashed the message and talked about their lives. Wendi listened. After lights out, she lay awake most of the night reflecting. These women loved life. They saw it as an adventure with God—a God who was their Father and guide. And they loved each other. She observed over and over how they included everyone—even the *unlovable* women.

She wondered what they thought about her. Her ideas and life were so different from many of them—yet although she was among four hundred strangers, she felt somehow at home. They called themselves Christians, but they weren't the somber, judgmental Christians she'd seen portrayed in the media. Having Bonnie next door comforted Wendi, almost like a family member—the family she'd longed for but never experienced.

Bonnie had invited her to church and Bible study several times. *I think I'll go with her next time and see what kind of a church turns out people like this.*

If Wendi had been the only woman attending the retreat, it would have been worth the hundreds of hours spent planning and preparing. What was the purpose of this retreat? There were many.

The Purpose for Nonbelievers

First, this event was an opportunity for the Wendis of the world to be exposed to a community of real Christians. For many postmodern women, an "in your face" kind of evangelism is counterproductive. Believers must overcome stereotyping from so much bad press. But living in the midst of authentic community for several days is a powerful tool to combat the bad press and cause women to reflect on God, their lives, and choices.

On Sunday morning at the retreat, the speaker presented the gospel and Wendi probably took her first communion among new family and friends. If not, she probably will after attending church and Bible study with Bonnie. Her marriage, her husband back home, her work, her extended family, maybe even future children—all will be affected by this event.

And Wendi is only one of four hundred.

The Purpose for Believers

Of course, the majority of women attending are already believers. What's the purpose of the retreat for them? It is different for every woman. Some just need a weekend away from busy households and jobs to relax. Most have crises of some kind and interaction with the Word of God and concerned friends is invaluable.

Working moms and single parents, exhausted from overwhelming responsibilities, need a schedule change and a chance to spend a few hours relaxing by a lake.

Women seldom take time for themselves. Many are so busy taking care of others that they've never sang karaoke style or participated in an impromptu skit. Women normally in bed at ten find the energy to play games, laugh, and talk into the morning. They leave physically tired but surprised at their newfound zeal for life.

And most important, women do business with God. They make "fork in the road" decisions. They heal from wounds that have shackled them all their lives. They return determined to work on their marriages and conflicts. They go home passionate to serve God and encouraged to stretch in spite of their fears.

Was this event worth the hours invested? What do you think? And how would you create an event as welcoming and life-changing as this retreat? Let's look at the variety of events happening in women's ministries all over the country and then let's explore how to make it happen!

Pioneer Profile: Elizabeth Inrig

"The church of Jesus Christ needs women who not only are smart but who have SMARTS (Spiritual, Mature, Able, Responsible, Teachable, Sensitive). Those women will live godly lives, will care more about developing their character than their charisma, will love God more than they love their own lives, and will boast not in their own power but the Master's."

As national director of women's ministry for the Evangelical Free Church of America, Elizabeth Inrig seeks such women to join her in serving the next generation of Christian women. Her ministry centers on the Word of God and is designed to help women understand their identity and attain their potential in Christ. "The church needs women," she says, "who love women, and who love God's Word."

Elizabeth's journey began when she was a young girl in Vancouver, Canada. Raised in a family that loved Christ, she learned early the value of having a woman of God in her life. "As a little girl, I watched my mother use her skill in making and baking shortbread to build relationships with many younger women. Together, my mother and the woman who had come to see her rolled out the dough, cut it into shapes, and popped it in the oven. Then they would sit on the sofa and 'have a read.' That was when my mother opened the Bible and read a text to answer the young woman's questions. Although she didn't know what it was called, she was mentoring."

Elizabeth never intended to work with women. She earned her degree in education and became a schoolteacher. But despite her vows never to marry a preacher ("I wasn't sure what they did with their time!"), Gary Inrig brought her as his young bride in 1966 to Dallas, Texas, where he was enrolled in seminary. There she sat under the teaching of the professors' wives, women like Jeanne Hendricks, Geraldine Walvoord, Doris Witmer, and others. "They were important women in my life," remembers Elizabeth. Years later she returned to DTS to earn her own master's degree.

It was on their return to Canada that Elizabeth first learned to lead small group Bible studies. Her perspective on ministry began to change, due much to Gary's influence. "Gary encouraged me to use my gifts in the context of the local church for the good of women, for the health of the local church, and for the glory of God. He urged me to see these open doors as entrustments from God rather than intrusions."

The young mother of three soon found herself moving beyond the safe confines of home and family, into the church—teaching and leading women into deeper relationships with the Lord. "I like to teach women how to handle the Bible," says Elizabeth. Getting women from this resistant, skeptical culture into the Word of God became the focus of her ministry.

In 1997, the Evangelical Free Church of America invited Elizabeth to be their national director of women's ministries. Drawing on her experiences in the local church, she has developed training tools for women to use while starting and maintaining their own women's ministries. Recently her national leadership team has begun to teach "Equipping Celebrations," a national EFCA initiative in which Elizabeth and women involved in local church ministries equip local women in essentials for a healthy women's ministry.

What is unique about Elizabeth's perspective? "I'm a team builder," she says, pointing to the team of nearly a hundred women who serve with her in the women's ministry at Trinity Evangelical Free Church, where she and her husband minister now. "Together we minister to over five hundred women on a weekly basis in Bible studies and outreaches."

She recently designed an internship program at Trinity, in which a small group of committed women take a ten-day program of intense study and teaching. They learn Bible, theology, and practical strategies in order to be better equipped to start or sustain a local women's ministry. "This is how I reproduce myself," says Elizabeth.

To those considering women's ministry in the church, Elizabeth advises, "Volunteer to work with the women in your church, even if it isn't a job. Get to know some older godly women who are doing women's ministry in their church. The greatest advocate for a young woman wanting to serve God is an older woman who recognizes a teachable spirit within her. And rejoice in your God-given responsibility of ministering to women."

Kinds of Events

- Retreats—a day or two away at a camp or hotel for the women of the church and their friends.
- Specialized retreats—for particular groups such as singles, working women, or moms.
- Or on particular subjects such as prayer, community, worship, or solitude.
- Theme events around food—(breakfasts, brunches, luncheons, teas, dinners, desserts).

- Choose a fun theme such as South Pacific, a cruise (secretly Noah's Ark), or a 1950s party. Have fun decorating, making favors, and coordinating the food.
- Dinner theater—Are there women in your church interested or experienced in drama or music? Let them use their gifts to entertain and inspire.
- Craft fair—Raise money for women who work outside the home and offer affordable gifts.
- Faith-lift—Offer a day of workshops on various topics of interest to women.
- Training days—Do you need to train Bible teachers or small group leaders? Enlist a teacher to help equip leaders.
- Welcome event—Invite new women for a time of orientation to women's ministries and connecting with other newcomers.
- Mercy event—Sponsor a day ministering at a school, nursing home, hospital, or soup kitchen.

Any ideas to share not on the list? Send them to www.newdoors.info so we can share them with others.

How to Make It Happen!

Determine Your Purpose

Why are you investing in this event? Who is your target audience? Does your event meet their needs? Don't continue an event that is no longer effective just because the women expect it. Surprise them with something new!

Include Variety

Does your ministry sponsor a healthy balance of different kinds of events? For example, does your event calendar include outreach, growth and development, and opportunities to serve? Are some events light and fun while others concentrate on serious spiritual issues? You don't necessarily need all these kinds of events every year, but don't overload the year with fun when the women need serious spiritual direction, and vice versa.

Recruit the Right Leader

A leader has influence and followers. She builds a team and inspires them to do the details. She needs vision to keep the big picture in mind and she needs administrative gifts to delegate the details. The larger the event, the more critical her ability to give away the ministry.

Some women are sprinters, not distance runners. Use your distance leaders to head up ongoing ministries like Bible studies and prayer chains. Enlist your sprinters for events. Women who travel periodically or have seasonal stresses can't always commit to weekly responsibilities. But they make great event coordinators.

Set the Budget

Retreats are expensive. Will you need to cover your costs or can your church help out? Will women give scholarships to those who can't pay? What kinds of accommodations will your women expect? Can you provide a variety of accommodations to allow *all* women to participate? Are there wealthy women in your church who might underwrite the cost? Nail down your resources and let your team know how much they have to spend.

A word to the smaller churches: bigger is not necessarily better. You have an advantage over the large churches—intimacy. Much of what goes into a large women's retreat is an attempt to develop and maintain the intimacy that a small group inherently has. Be encouraged. You do not need a large budget, or a large number of women, to have a successful retreat. Do what you can with what you have. Some of the meticulous planning that goes into a large retreat like we described earlier probably won't be necessary for a smaller group of women.

Decide How Much You Can Pay and Choose Your Speaker

Speakers can be expensive and there is no standard. Whom should you choose? God has someone for you—often someone in your church or neighborhood. And she will be easier on your budget than will a "big name" speaker. Expect to pay a local speaker about $500 for a weekend, depending on her experience and credentials. If she speaks for just one session, $100 is adequate. And a woman from within your own church should not be paid at all, although a gift is appropriate. This is her contribution to her church.

Even local and in-house speakers should be booked a year ahead. Most limit their retreats due to family or ministry obligations. Don't forget to make her experience memorable by providing a hostess, asking her how the team can pray, and thinking of special ways to express your appreciation.

She invests numerous hours preparing ahead and internalizing three or four messages during the weekend. When she's not reviewing the upcoming message, she's with your women—and often she will never see them again. You can be sure she goes home exhausted—so do all you can to assist and support her.

You also have the option of seeking a well-known author or speaker. These are often paid thousands of dollars as well as airfare and expenses. A few ask for a percentage while others won't quote a fee. They usually will take a love offering or allow you to decide on the amount.

Can you afford a big name speaker? Is it worth what it will cost you? Can you get on her waiting list (which she is sure to have)? If you really want this speaker, expect a challenge; but patience and perseverance often pay off.

Decide How to Register the Women

A systematic, fair registration procedure squelches conflict and confusion. And the larger you are, the greater the necessity. At

IBC, we only register by mail. The brochures contain clear instructions and a tear-out form. Each woman sends in one form to one place with all the necessary information included as well as her payment. She lists her roommates, the requested accommodations, her T-shirt size, and desired activities. Rooms are assigned on a first come, first served basis.

Train Your Team to Be Ministry-Minded

Teach your team that their specific task is only a small part of their calling. Ask them to complete the task ahead so they will be free to focus on their real role—to lavish the women with love and to make sure no one feels left out.

Why did Wendi feel special? The little things speak volumes. Her T-shirt fit. The extra effort to make the surroundings beautiful and comfortable said they cared. A wrapped gift under her chair each session and a chocolate on her pillow each night repeated the message. Women strategically placed to initiate conversation—especially to those alone—helped Wendi feel accepted.

However, teach the leaders to back off if they sense that a woman needs alone time. Help her feel safe participating but just as free to observe from the sidelines. Acquaint the women with the various activities available and then let them choose how they want to spend their time.

What's amazing is that caring is contagious. This retreat we've described is twenty-one years old, and now not only is the team ministry-minded, but so are the participants. They've learned to model what their leaders do, and as the retreat has grown from forty to four hundred, it's a good thing!

Plan Ahead

Why did the retreat impact Wendi? What happened in the year prior to the retreat to make it so meaningful? Why did she feel included and cherished? Here's the calendar and the methodology for the retreat that changed Wendi's life. Extract and adapt it to your events.

Two Years Before the Retreat:
- Book camp or hotel
- Decide on speaker and get on her calendar

April
- Second week: retreat occurs
- Third week: debriefing by retreat team and begin brain-storming next year's theme
- Follow up with needy women at the retreat

May
- Recruit next year's retreat team (list core team leaders—entertainment, registration, decorations, hospitality, notebooks)
- Distribute prayer calendar

October
- Overnight team gathering with speaker who presents overview of messages
- Finalize theme, coordinate with speaker's messages, and brainstorm creative uses
- Keep the theme a secret to add suspense

November
- Create brochure
- Begin ongoing communication with camp or hotel

January
- Define, create, and/or build decorations

- Determine a theme-related gift for each woman at each session and enlist a team to purchase or make them

February

- Mail out brochures and assign rooms
- Retreat team dinner (status reports, worship, prayer, and great food)
- Make or order tote bags, name tags, T-shirts
- Recruit actors for drama
- Locate sound system and technician to work the retreat

March

- Finalize schedules and details
- Recruit emcees for each session
- Practice entertainment and dramas
- Create notebooks
- Wrap all gifts
- Send out postcards with room assignments and other information

A Week Before the Retreat (If Possible)

- Relocate to the retreat site with core leaders
- Decorate, bond, practice, pray, and play

Friday Morning

- Set up last-minute details
- Check sound system
- Prep greeters
- An hour before women arrive—team prayer time with all women's leaders and speakers

As Women Arrive

- Position all leaders at registration and later at dinner, relaxed and available to interact and welcome women
- Women at registration table alert and ready to identify a woman who is alone, informally assign a caretaker
- Dorm mothers in each dorm also alert to help women connect with others

During the Retreat

- Don't miss opportunities to connect
- Execute your task
- Help work out the kinks

After the Retreat

- Clean up, break camp, and praise God!

Creative, innovative events add zest to your year and give women entry points into your ministry. Often after a positive experience at an event, a woman will join your ongoing ministries—and they often build on the event. In addition, events break the routine with special times that women write on their calendars with anticipation. Make your events worthy and use them to transform lives.

Chapter 11

ADD OTHER
MINISTRIES WISELY

After your Bible study is established, how do you add other ministries? Let's look at the process and then at a list of potential ministries to consider.

The Process

Amanda Ware is the wife of IBC's worship pastor and the mother of five children. The leaders loved her insight in leader's group. Her answers inspired us and made us think. But her real passion was ministry to moms. How do I know? Here's what happened.

Many young families attend our church. As a mother, I know the stress during those first years. I know moms need training and encouragement. After our Bible study was established, I began to pray for a mom's ministry. Notice that I did not run out and start one. My calling was to cast vision, recruit, equip, train, teach, and lead. Somewhere in our church was a woman burning with a desire to minister to moms.

During Bible study I often join table discussions to connect with women. That morning I *just happened* to sit at Amanda's table. One of the application questions asked, "If you could do any significant work for Christ in your church, family, or community, what would that work be? What can make your dream a reality?"

The women shared their dreams and then Amanda added, "I have always wanted to start a ministry to moms." She explained why, and her words were pregnant with excitement. I shot up a word of gratitude to God. And after the study I was on her like cops on Krispy Kreams.

I never thought of asking her because of her other responsibilities. I knew she was capable but I wasn't sure the timing was right. God knew my heart and hers, and He made His choice clear. She prayed for God's direction and He confirmed that He wanted her to lead this ministry.

We met and prayed as she researched other mom's ministries. She advertised it as a ministry to mothers of young children rather than "young mothers of children" in sensitivity to new moms in their thirties and forties. She devised a structure and built a team of four, delegating each arm of the ministry to one of them. I asked them to pick a meeting time that would not compete with Bible study. They chose to gather once a month in the evening when dads were available to watch kids. The church provides a limited nursery for single moms and special circumstances.

Within several months, Amanda had her calendar and speakers in place. The ministry exceeded my expectations. I attended the first three months and now I attend sporadically. They don't need me. I go for my own enjoyment when I can. When invited to speak, I accept with pleasure. Watching these women birth and nurture this ministry to our moms delights me.

I knew we would lose Amanda as a Bible study leader, but she still attends faithfully. The mom's ministry was her calling. Even when she became pregnant with her fifth child, the leadership was so strong that they kept it going during her leave of absence.

Are new ministries always birthed with such ease? No, but they can be, when you follow some simple guidelines.

Discern a Leader's Readiness (or How to Turn Someone Down Graciously!)

God won't always plop the leader in your lap like He did with Amanda. But often He will make His choice clear. As women are transformed through the Bible study, they hear God calling them to serve. I challenge them constantly to step out and stretch. When they do, they take giant leaps in their spiritual growth.

As a result, a woman comes to see me. She sits in my office and tells me that God wants her to start a new ministry. Often, He does—but sometimes she isn't ready. I must discern which. And if she isn't ready, I want to help her see this for herself. My goal—and yours—is not to push my agenda on her, but to love her. We must let our women know that *they* matter to us more than our plans and schedules do.

When a woman expresses her desire to start a new ministry, I ask her to explain her vision. As she does, I am asking God for wisdom. If she is active in women's ministry, I have had the opportunity to observe her. If not, I'm at a disadvantage.

Question to Consider

I ask God to show me whether she is mature enough to lead others, to handle conflict, and to follow through. If she isn't, guess who gets to step in? And guess who doesn't have the time?

I also consider whether this is a ministry women need right now. Does it fall under the umbrella of our women's ministry vision? Or should I send her to another pastor where her idea is a better fit? Is this where we want to use our resources?

I gently ask her why she believes God is leading her. I try to identify her motives. Is she starving for attention and thinks by leading a ministry others will admire her? Is there a tragedy or abuse in her own life that she still has not dealt with? Or is her primary motivation to minister to others and bring glory to God?

I also probe to learn if she has any experience leading. Has she organized a home, managed a business, or overseen a grocery co-op? Can she delegate and lead others? Does she have any idea how to make the ministry happen?

What Next?

If I sense this is God's doing, I will communicate my support and ask her to bring me a proposal to submit to the women's board. We will talk generalities of how and when. And we pray for God's direction and enablement. This is how ministries are birthed and it's an honor to be part of the process.

If I am unsure, I won't communicate my support of the project, but neither will I tell her I have doubts. I affirm her personally and pray for her. I also ask her to bring me a proposal. I find that if she is not ready, it becomes clear when she tries to write the proposal. Either I never hear from her again or she returns realizing that this is not the time.

If she returns with a well-written proposal, we talk about details such as calendar and team building. I ask God for red flags. Is she willing to work with others, or is she a one-woman show? We don't need mavericks. If it still looks good, I will take the proposal to the next board meeting for approval. If the board confirms the idea, I will often ask her to attend the next board meeting as my guest. There she can share her vision and answer questions.

I watch to see how she interacts with other board members. Does she seem excited about their ministries? Does she understand that her ministry would be part of a bigger picture? Or is she restless when the attention is on others? Clues emerge as I observe her with the board members. These clues help me know if she is God's choice to oversee His work.

Notice that because the board meets monthly, we have now

considered this project for several months. This is intentional. I want to know if her passion is just a flash in the pan or a desire that will continue to burn over time. We've met several times. I've seen her in different situations to assess her character and background. We believe God wants this ministry as part of what we offer women. If she is still excited about the project and so are we, we get serious.

Undergird Her with Resources

What does she need to make it happen? money? leaders? a place to meet? publicity? Whatever it is, I am ready to help all I can. Don't ask someone to join your ministry and then fail to give her what she needs.

Usually a new ministry launches before we can put it in the budget. But part of enlisting support is getting the approval of our male lead pastors. I have talked with them and usually they provide whatever resources they can, including money. But I don't go to them until we have taken the steps that I just described.

If the resources are not available, we adjust our kickoff accordingly. We know it was not God's timing and we wait. But when it all comes together, we move ahead.

Don't Micromanage, but Monitor Progress

There's an art to knowing how much to help. Each leader needs something different.

Amanda

Amanda was gifted and capable, but young. She didn't have extensive experience. So I met with her several times as she began. I asked her to report her findings on other ministries. I attended the first leader's dinner meeting in her home.

As I worked with her, it became evident that she didn't need help. She was organized, efficient, and wise beyond her years. I stepped back in awe, and told her often that she was doing a great job! After one gathering I told her she could lead a full-blown women's ministry one day—and I meant it! If she wants to, she will. However, even though she was capable, I didn't know that initially. So I followed from a distance for a while, until I was sure I could let her go.

Andi

My assistance to Andi was different. She and I worked together in Bible studies before either of us came to IBC. She was wise and godly, and I knew if she tackled a project, it would be done well. I had seen her work. When she consented to build a mercy ministry for us, I knew that she knew how.

We met once. She returned with a proposal that would jump-start a small company. I went to work on the resources. In a month, she had five cocaptains and teams under them in process. She divided the ministry into meals for the sick, house-cleaning, hospital visitation, special needs, and handyman help. The first year she enlisted four hundred volunteers and the ministry went church-wide.

I know that Andi will inform me of any imperative issues. I did not need to walk beside her at the beginning. I didn't even follow from a distance. There was no need.

Celeste

Celeste felt led of God to start a widow's ministry in my former church. There was a definite need. Many widows attended the church but there was nothing to bring them together or serve them. Celeste had a heart for widows, but she was terrified. She had never led anything and lacked confidence.

I walked with her every step of the way for two years. I showed her how to organize the ministry. I took her to the secretary and showed her how to get an event on the church calendar. At first I led the planning meetings and attended every event.

But gradually, I gave over the reins of the ministry to her. She would lead part of the meetings and I would lead the other part. Then later I would attend but she would lead. Finally she did it all herself. What a blessing to see her grow! She became a gracious leader who brought joy into many widows' lives. It was worth the investment.

Always count the cost. Be sure you can make an investment without neglecting your other responsibilities.

Supervise each woman depending on her experience and abilities. Your goal is to hand off the ministry as soon as possible. Seldom involve yourself in the details. Women with this kind of vision will name their ministry, build their own teams, and supervise the details—with the exception of a Celeste at first. They dream their own dreams and then entrust those dreams to God.

Your role is to encourage and guide. If their creative ideas fizzle, you are there to help get them back on their feet. If they veer from your vision, direct them back. When the ministry flourishes, they receive credit—which they will learn to give back to God.

When you refuse to micromanage, the ministry becomes theirs. Give them the responsibility and the authority. Of course, you are ultimately accountable. Therefore, be careful not to put a woman in leadership before she is ready. And monitor everyone's progress as best you can.

There is risk in unleashing passionate women to do ministry that will reflect on you. But it's worth the risk. Because it is the way women learn what God can do through them. One day you will die or retire, and one of them will continue the work. Praise God! Isn't that what ministry is all about anyway?

Team Building

By now you recognize our passion for doing ministry as a team. The leaders of your added ministries will also need to know how to build their own teams. Insist on it! Even if your church is small, your new leaders will need teammates (perhaps just one or two at the beginning) to share the load. They should also know how to recognize a possible replacement. And it is your job to show them how. For more information on team building, see chapter 4.

Potential Ministries to Consider

Don't be pressured into adding new ministries—especially if you are a small church. Add them if it fits and the time is right. If a woman wanted to start a widow's ministry at IBC, I probably would decline right now.

Do I believe widows aren't worthy of a ministry? Not at all! But there are only a handful of widows in our church. There are simpler ways to support them than to create a full-blown ministry just for them. However, in my former church, there were many widows. Not only did I encourage Celeste to plant the ministry, I invested many hours myself.

If a woman asked to begin a ministry to single moms, I probably would also decline. And we do have many single moms in our church. Many of them are active in our Bible studies. Why would I resist beginning a single moms' ministry? Because Bob, our adult education pastor, sponsors a dynamic single parents class that, once a month, organizes a single parents' night out and treats the kids to fun, food, and fellowship at the church. If a woman came to me with a passion to minister to single moms, I would send her to Bob. Cooperate—don't compete!

A stellar women's ministry is not about programs. It's about people. If the people are engaged in a transforming relationship with Jesus and are learning His Word, then think about adding other ministries as the Lord leads. Remember: the hub of the wheel is Bible study. All other ministries are the spokes.

There is one exception—prayer. Prayer is a pillar of the Bible study, but I recommend you develop a more extensive prayer ministry. See the end of this chapter for suggestions on how to build a prayer ministry to undergird everything you do.

Here is a list of other options:

Ministry to Specific Groups

Moms, widows, single moms, working women, abortion recovery, divorce recovery, moms of children with special needs, infertility, blended families, families fighting drugs, cancer survivors, nursing home

Service Opportunities

Meals for new moms and the sick, hospital visitation, prison ministry, financial counseling, crisis pregnancy, inner-city missions, world missions, car ministry, food pantry, clothes closet, welcoming new women, office assistance, tutoring

Events

Retreats, conferences, workshops, dinners, lunches, brunches, teas, intramural sports, aerobics, out of town trips, museums, art galleries, theater

It may sound like we are against beginning new ministries. That isn't true. We support all kinds of ministries. We are simply cautioning you to be wise with your resources—especially if you are a small church. You can't do everything well.

But if a passionate woman wants to plant a ministry that you and your board believe is needed, go for it! Over time women will ask to start all kinds of ministries. Most will enrich your women's lives and give them places to use their gifts. They will meet a felt need and fit within the scope of your vision. As you expand your borders, more and more women will benefit.

How Do You Set Up a Prayer Chain?

Prayer is the foundation of your ministry. Put systems in place that facilitate prayer. Women in all levels of leadership need to know that others are interceding on their behalf. Women in the church are comforted when they know others are lifting up their needs.

There are two mediums to connect women to pray—e-mail and the telephone. In this postmodern world, you will need to use both of them.

First, set up a phone number and an e-mail address that women can contact with their requests. Then, designate one woman to monitor the requests and send them out. Our prayer board coordinator has two captains—one for the e-mail chain and one for the telephone chain. She edits the prayer request for brevity and confidentiality, then sends it to her captains, who relay the requests to the women who have volunteered to pray. About 90 percent receive the request by e-mail. However, some older women don't use e-mail. To honor them, we use the telephone to send them requests.

The benefit of e-mail is its speed and convenience. You can send it night or day without concern. The written request isn't subject to distortion. And you can quickly inform the chain of answered prayer.

But caution! Respect confidentiality. Ask women making requests to inform you if any part of the request is confidential. Then script those facts in general, unrecognizable terms. God knows the details and we want to be known for our integrity.

Chapter 12

PREPARE FOR AND SURVIVE CONFLICT

I'm *so sorry,* but I must ask you to step down from the board until we sort all this out." I (Sue) spoke gently, but still Sylvia's blue eyes brimmed with tears. Then she forced them back and declared, "No, I'll resign. I've had it! Ministry isn't supposed to be like this."

You're right, I agreed silently. It sure isn't.

Serving as women's ministry director was usually my life's delight—but on that day it was anything but delightful. I had dreaded our meeting, especially as I remembered Sylvia's two years of wholehearted service.

But her outspoken disagreement with several staff members and her continuous, public undercutting of authority made this day inevitable. Sylvia and her family left the church. What a waste. What a loss.

It's More Common Than You Think

Stay in ministry long enough and you will encounter conflict. It's my least favorite part of the job. But it's reality. Fortunately I would not describe my ministry years as full of conflict, but often—too often—conflicts have arisen. Many have been minor, but others have threatened the life of the ministry. Here's what happened to me in the early 1990s.

"You are holding women's hands to hell."

Margaret glared at me across the table. She accused me of false teaching before the executive pastor and several other staff members. We were teachers of unrelated Bible studies in the same church, and many of her former students were in my classes.

"You teach women *cheap grace*," she accused. "You must be stopped."

For almost two years she attempted to destroy my ministry and reputation. After multiple meetings with pastors, in which I was forced to defend my theology, the pastor dismissed the accusation as untrue and asked us to coexist in harmony.

However, factions were birthed. One of her followers repeatedly slandered me. Margaret also paid a high price. Month after month, the mud slinging continued. The executive pastor's gag order mandated that I not defend myself. So I learned to trust God as my advocate. But I wondered if my integrity would ever be restored.

As word of the conflict seeped out over those two years, women went on the offensive for both of us. Some were deeply wounded and others left the church without ever understanding what really happened. During those dark days, we witnessed the results of out-of-control conflict.

My accuser continued to say, "This isn't personal." But if it involves people, it's personal! Conflict handled badly damages people! I recall days of weeping, and I'm sure other women do too.

But I also experienced God's faithfulness. And I learned to focus on pleasing God instead of people. These were valuable lessons that equipped me for future ministry. We all made mistakes. There were no winners—and God was dishonored. Mine is an extreme example, but all leaders will face conflict in some form. Learn from my experience!

Be Intentional

I promised God that if I ever had the privilege of serving Him again, I would study how to resolve conflict biblically, and I would protect women who served with me. In my current positions, I've kept that promise.

Women on my team are required to sign a covenant promising to deal with disputes according to Matthew 18:15–17 (see appendix C for Conflict Resolution Covenant). I attended *Peacemaker Ministries* training and encourage my leaders to acquire the training or read their materials.[1]

If a woman says, "I am so angry about the way Jane treated me at the meeting," I look her in the eye and ask, "Have you talked to Jane about this?" Then I explain that Jesus gave us directives to help us work through hurts and disagreements. And I strongly suggest that she work this out with Jane instead of talking to me.

Whether you mediate a dispute or are a party to the conflict, you'll never forget the tense, exhausting hours of resolving conflict—especially if the problem is mishandled initially.

Here are examples:

- One member of a leadership team, which was formed to improve a particular ministry, didn't like some of the proposed changes and met secretly with the pastor, maligning the ministry. The leadership team felt betrayed, and the ministry was temporarily sidetracked.
- A Bible study planning committee could not agree on next year's curriculum, expressing its foundational differences in constant, petty skirmishes. The next year, many of the leaders resigned.
- In a Bible class, two people embroiled in a theological dis-

cussion over the sovereignty of God and free will ended their debate by taking swings at each other. Imagine trying to explain that to visitors!

Causes and Complexity

Conflicts vary in complexity. Some are between those who serve and those being served. At other times those serving together as leaders cannot agree. Then there may be friction between ministries within a church.

Conflicts may stem from doctrinal differences, personality clashes, or different ministry philosophies, styles, and traditions. Typically, each party is sure it is on a mission from God and that He is on their side.

Can Conflict Be Prevented?

Sometimes I see disagreements resolved graciously and the parties grow from the experience. Just as often, it ends like Sylvia's case or mine—in disaster! The wounded limp away, often never to serve again. The world hears one more account of how Christians "just can't get along." It's time to get serious about managing conflict *before* it's out of control. We need to recognize the early warning signs of conflict and understand how to address it when it erupts. Certain biblical principles should be a part of our basic training.

What Jesus Says

One of the most familiar passages on resolving conflict is Matthew 18:15–17. Jesus prepared His disciples and us with these words, which are hard to obey, but we often ignore them to our peril. Verse 15 says, "If your brother sins against you, go and show him his fault, just between the two of you. If he listens to you, you have won your brother over."

Step One: Go and Show

First, note that there are two parties in the conflict: the offender and the offended. Both are assumed to be Christians, as indicated by the term *brother*. Jesus instructs the offended to be the initiator in the peace process. If you are wounded, *you* are to go to the one who hurt you.

Notice also that the offense is termed a sin. What constitutes a sin? Sins listed in the Bible include sexual immorality, debauchery, coarse joking, theft, drunkenness, idolatry, witchcraft, hatred, discord, jealousy, rage, anger, selfish ambition, envy, bitterness, slander, gossip, quarreling, and pride (cf. Galatians 5:19–21; Ephesians 4:31; 2 Corinthians 12:20). Is the offense truly a sin, or could it lead to sin? Are you evaluating an action you have observed or a heart attitude you suspect?

Also, you must decide if you can overlook this offense. "A man's wisdom gives him patience; it is to his glory to overlook an offense" (Proverbs 19:11). Ask yourself, "Can I chalk this up to a bad day? Can I interact with my offender without this offense coloring our relationship?" If you can, forget it! If you can't, you should initiate a meeting with your offender to offset problems later.

Many people would prefer to resign from their commitments rather than discuss the conflict openly with their offender. The thought of expressing the hurt face to face is ranked with having a root canal or giving a political speech to an audience of opponents—no one looks forward to the experience. There is a possibility of greater misunderstanding and even rejection. But with prayer and Christlike love, you may leave the meeting with a more intimate, authentic friend than before.

The Principle of Containment

"Just between the two of you . . ."

Jesus limits the first meeting to the two parties—and no one else should know about the conflict. When I am hurt, the first thing I want to do is call my closest friends or corner my spouse and unload. I may try to fool myself into believing that I am doing this to gain wisdom or convince myself I need a sounding board. Sometimes that is true, but more often, I want to give my listener the gift of carrying the offense with me. Unfortunately, if the conflict is resolved, my listener, who was not privy to the peace process, may continue to carry the offense long after my offender and I have laid it down.

Step Two: Take Witnesses

> But if he will not listen, take one or two others along, so that "every matter may be established by the testimony of two or three witnesses." (Matthew 18:16)

Jesus says that if the first meeting is unfruitful, the offended party is responsible to call a second meeting and invite witnesses. Who are these witnesses? In this verse, Jesus quotes Deuteronomy 19:15. According to Mosaic Law, when an accusation was made, witnesses were to tell any related truth. A witness is there to testify to the truth or falsehood of the offender's account, and to help the two parties see the conflict honestly. Jesus is asking those who may have insight concerning the offense to join the parties and help sort out relevant details.

I am astounded at how differently Christians view events, actions, attitudes, and even the Christian life. Witnesses can serve as catalysts to bring about truth and a joyful resolution. But there are no guarantees!

Step Three: Take It to the Church

> If he refuses to listen to them, tell it to the church. (Matthew 18:17)

If Jesus' instructions have been followed, there are still no more than five people aware of the conflict. Now they are told to "tell it to the church." What does Jesus mean?

Two hardworking, respected women were unable to settle their dispute in the church at Philippi, and Paul placed the issue squarely in the laps of the leadership. "I plead with Euodia and I plead with Syntyche to agree with each other in the Lord. Yes, and I ask you, loyal yokefellow, help these women who have contended at my side in the cause of the gospel . . ." (Philippians 4:2–3).

Whomever God has placed in authority over you in the church is now in charge. Courtesy dictates that all parties are heard at the same time, and godly people follow the directives of their leaders. Then we can rest in the assurance that the outcome will ultimately be God's best for us.

What blessings can we experience as we learn the skill and art of peacemaking? Through conflict, we can see God at work in issues and relationships; we can learn more about His character and faithfulness as well as more about ourselves. Conflict resolution can mature and equip us. It can prepare us to minister in the real world. Although we often tend to view conflict negatively, Jesus said, "Blessed are the peacemakers, for they will be called sons of God" (Matthew 5:9).

Chapter 13

MINISTERING WITH MEN

The staff of Ridgeway Community Church sat in senior pastor Chip's office in silence. A tiny tear rolled down Nancy's cheek, and although the four men pretended not to notice, they all saw it and their conversation quit cold as a result.

All four men had welcomed Nancy as women's ministry director a year earlier. They valued her insight and appreciated her stellar program. They saw the results in the lives of their wives and were grateful.

Nancy sat quietly through most of the staff meetings, speaking up occasionally when the conversation concerned her ministry. The men had become accustomed to her presence, carrying on with their usual bantering and almost forgetting she was there. But now this—a tear.

They were in the midst of hammering out next year's calendar. Nancy had reserved the second Thursday in December almost a year before for the annual women's Christmas dinner. The date aligned with their sought-after speaker's calendar, and the women were ecstatic. They had been trying to bring her in for three years.

But Greg, the missions pastor, had scheduled that weekend for the missions conference, forgetting to inform Chip's assistant, the keeper of the calendar. Greg vied for the calendar date as if he were out to win a competitive tennis match. He raised his voice in a strong, heated tone, used sarcasm, and pounded the table once with his fist.

Greg often reacted this way, and the other men joined in the game. They jostled each other, joked, and jeered to make their point—and then went out to lunch together. But Nancy wouldn't compete. The result—a tear in staff meeting! The men were dismayed and perplexed.

How Will Women Change the Staff?

John Gray writes in his best-seller *Men Are from Mars, Women Are from Venus,* "men and women differ in all areas of their lives. Not only do men and women communicate differently but they think, feel, perceive, react, respond, love, need, and appreciate differently. They almost seem to be from different planets, speaking different languages and needing different nourishment."[1]

Women are joining formerly all-male staffs, and most men welcome them. But when someone "from a different planet" joins the staff, everyone must adjust. The dynamic of staff interaction is affected.

Whether one woman or ten participate on staff, they bring change—and often a presence and a tone that benefits the church. After all, churches are full of females. A woman's influence in the inner workings of staff most often results in decisions that woo women to Christ and make the environment more favorable to her flourishing.

How will a woman's presence affect the staff meeting? What adjustments should men make? We observed that the men on staff at Ridgeway Community Church continued to interact the way they always had before Nancy joined them. How was Nancy feeling during their meetings?

She seldom participated because their interaction was decidedly male. Their teasing sometimes bordered on ridicule. Their playful, competitive bantering made her uncomfortable. She set a softer, gentler tone in her women's board meetings. Should the men change the way they relate to each other because a woman joined the team? Yes and no.

Both Need to Adapt

Certainly Greg was insensitive toward Nancy in his attempts to win the calendar war. But neither can Nancy expect Greg to interact with her the way most women would. When men and women are working together for the good of the church and God's glory, both must adapt!

Nancy must learn to assert herself in the meetings when she believes she needs to speak up. Please don't misunderstand. Her tone should be gracious. She would be wise to think through her requests beforehand and present them clearly. She must be careful not to overreact or take personally the men's comments when no offense was intended. Whining, excessive talking, and crying is counterproductive.

On the other hand, men should remember that a woman is among them, respect her presence, and make appropriate changes. Competitive bantering and shoulder punching may be out of place. Give and take on both sides will result in a united staff that supports and trusts each other. The church will benefit as the congregation observes a beautiful picture of men and women serving God together in harmony. Marriages will be strengthened and gender issues addressed.

Most Men Welcome Women on Staff, But . . .

We serve in churches where men welcome women on staff and work hard to accommodate and value them. Steve Roese, IBC's executive pastor, asks Sue regularly if there is anything that she needs to fulfill her call as women's pastor. His door is always open when she needs direction or even a listening ear. He hired a graphic artist to upgrade the study guide she wrote for the Bible classes. Working with Steve and men like him is a joy.

And in the majority of churches where women serve, men support them wholeheartedly. But some men resist the changes women bring when they join staff. For a variety of reasons we'll examine, they don't want you ministering with them. What do you do if you believe God is calling you to serve with resistant men?

Survive Men Who Don't Value You

Darlene's Story

"I'll never have a woman on my staff," stated the senior pastor. Actually there were women secretaries and the financial officer was a woman. But Darlene knew what he meant—he would never hire her in a pastoral role.

The comment cut because she had been serving in a pastoral role for five years. She taught the women's Bible study and directed the women's ministry. She counseled women daily. She was one of the founders and loved the women dearly. However, she wasn't on staff, nor was she compensated financially although some weeks she worked over fifty hours. Darlene had never attended a staff meeting. She simply wasn't included in the inner workings of the church.

She prayed from the beginning that the church leaders would value her efforts so that women's ministry could earn enough credibility to be included as part of the staff. Darlene did not expect that she would be the woman they brought on staff—although she would have loved to join the team. But she knew from the pastor's comment that it would never happen.

However, Darlene also knew God had called her to love, teach, and train the women. She ministered there for seven years until

God removed her and sent her to a church where she enjoys staff support and is well paid. The year Darlene left, God withdrew several influential women from the church, women's ministries floundered, and within a year there was a paid director of women's ministries. God was working!

It's Part of Pioneering!

Is Darlene the only woman ever wounded by a man in ministry? No! And if you serve with men long enough, you may get hurt! I (Sue) often hear from women with similar stories.

A children's ministry director sat in my office bewildered. The all-male staff excluded her from staff meetings and the yearly staff retreat. She asked if she was overreacting and if not, how to convince them to involve her for the sake of her ministry and the church at large.

Why are some men against partnering with women in ministry? And if God calls you into a setting where you are not valued, how should you respond? Let's explore these questions.

Why Do Some Men Resist Women in Ministry?

Imagine working with a sixty-eight-year-old pastor who believed that 1 Timothy 2 prohibited women from all leadership positions in the church, thought that the working mother was a disgrace to God, and labeled all women as untrustworthy gossips because he remembered one who forty years ago had criticized one of his sermons. Sound like the ideal boss?

Thankfully, this fellow is fictitious! We created him to highlight the four obstacles that often prevent some men from accepting women as partners in ministry: tradition, their view of what the Scriptures teach regarding women's roles in the church, irrational fears, and the possibility of negative experiences from the past. Any or all of these issues may color a male pastor's perspective on working with women.

Tradition

Thirty years ago, a female staff member on the church payroll was likely to be the secretary or the organist. Pastoral positions were traditionally reserved for men. However, since the 1980s, women's ministry positions are common on large church staffs. And in more small churches, women are added as finances allow.

The change is evident in the seminaries as well. Dallas Theological Seminary, one of the most theologically conservative schools in the United States, began allowing women to study for a degree in 1976. When Sue attended from 1985 to 1989, women made up 12 percent of the student body. At the time, women were discouraged from pursuing a master of theology (Th.M.), the four-year program designed to train pastors. Yet when Kelley began her studies in 1994, she was encouraged to earn her Th.M. because its coursework aligned with her goals better than any of the two-year programs did. And by the time she graduated in 2000, women constituted over 25 percent of the student body. These numbers reflect an administration willing to adapt to the changing times by acknowledging the growing need for and benefit of training women to do the work of ministry.

Unfortunately, many men who lead *traditional* churches refuse to change. There is a "good ole boys network" where a woman doesn't fit. Some male pastors don't want to include women and probably never will. Women whom God calls to minister there must face that fact and choose to serve without resentment. They will need a right heart attitude that will honor God and help them survive.

However difficult, personal bias is not the primary obstacle women face. Most pastors think their opinions reflect God's will as revealed in Scripture.

Scripture

Why are some people so opposed to women serving on pastoral staffs? Ask most of them, and they'll point to a Bible passage or two to support their position. What *does* the Bible teach about the role of women in ministry? Bible scholars disagree. Three primary views have emerged from the ongoing debate.[2]

The Traditional View

Proponents of this view hold that women cannot serve in any role of authority within the church. They believe that although God considers men and women equal in His sight, He placed men in authority over women; therefore, any teaching or elder position is off limits to women. They hold that Adam named Eve, a sign of dominance, and that women therefore are under men's authority. First Corinthians 11 and 14, in which Paul discusses proper worship formats, are generally used to support this view. Traditionalists also point to 1 Timothy 2:12, "I do not permit a woman to teach or to have authority over a man; she must be silent."

Some traditionalists believe this hierarchy extends from the church and home into the workplace—government, business, anything. In their minds, women were not meant to hold leadership positions over men in any arena. Some even would claim that women aren't capable of true leadership because they are more gullible than men (after all, Eve was deceived, but Adam knew what he was doing!).[3] This view obviously imposes the most restrictive limits on women's participation in church life.

The Complementarian View

Complementarians believe that, though equal in being (Genesis 1:28) and having equal access to God (Galatians 3:28), woman was created as a complement to man, that together they make a unified whole (Genesis 2). This complementary nature of men and women leads to different roles within marriage and the church. The Council for Biblical Manhood and Womanhood describes the implications of this view:

We are persuaded that the Bible teaches that only men should be pastors and elders. That is, men should bear primary responsibility for Christlike leadership and teaching in the church. So it is unbiblical, we believe, and therefore detrimental, for women to assume this role.

. . . There are levels and kinds of leadership for which women may and often should take responsibility. There are kinds of teaching, administration, organization, ministry, influence, and initiative that wives should undertake at home and women should undertake at church. Male headship at home and eldership at church mean that men bear the responsibility for the overall pattern of life. Headship does not prescribe the details of who does precisely what activity.[4]

The complementarian view strikes a balance between the restrictive traditionalist view and the wide-open egalitarian view. In summary, equality in being does not negate differing roles for men and women.

The Egalitarian View

Finally, some hold the view that the Bible does not restrict women in any way from serving in the church. Men and women, they believe, are equal in every way and must be encouraged to use their God-given gifts, even if they are preaching and teaching, to edify the church. Christians for Biblical Equality (CBE), an egalitarian counter-movement to the CBMW, posts their beliefs:

The Bible, properly interpreted, teaches the fundamental equality of believers of all racial and ethnic groups, all economic classes, and all age groups, based on the teachings of scripture as reflected in Galatians 3:28.

We believe the Bible teaches the equality of women and

men. We believe that God has given each person gifts to be used for the good of Christ's kingdom. We believe that Christians are to develop and exercise their God-given gifts in home, church, and society.[5]

Want to raise blood pressure? Start a conversation on women's role in the dining hall or classroom at many seminaries or churches. See what happens! It is, unfortunately, one of the most divisive issues in the evangelical church today.

So what is clear in the Bible regarding women in ministry? Titus 2:3–5 presents irrefutable evidence that the Bible allows women— even more, it commands them—to minister to other women and children.

Elizabeth Inrig, in her book *Release Your Potential,* offers this reminder to the women and men in church leadership.

> Women committed to becoming fully developed Christ followers in the spirit of Titus 2:3–5 hold in their hands and hearts an enormous amount of spiritual power. It is a privilege denied men. It is the power to convince a watching world that God's purposes for men and women to function together in the church reflect the glorious interdependence of the Holy Trinity. The power does not come in exchanging roles but in celebrating harmony. The power comes when women take up the task of teaching the next generation of women to know and obey God's Word (Titus 2:3–5). The spiritual power comes when women take hold of God's mandate for women in the church and get on with the job.[6]

Harmony. It's the sound produced when each instrument in an orchestra performs its intended role, the notes coming together to create a harmonious blend of music. So it should be in the church.

God's Word makes it clear that He wishes women to minister primarily to women. Men should respect that command; women should heed it.

But how will this look in an individual church? Will the woman coordinating or directing such woman-to-woman ministry be acknowledged and supported by the church leadership? Will she be invited to join the staff in an official capacity? Each church must decide how much value they place on women's ministry.

Such change is difficult for some. It is made all the harder when unfounded fears and false assumptions about women obscure some men's minds.

Fear

Why are some men afraid to include women? Here are three common misconceptions that can affect some men's attitudes:

Some Men Believe Women Should Not Work Outside the Home

The modern generation of men (over thirty) includes some that cling to the "ideal" family of the 1950s. They truly believe that working women are responsible for the disintegration of the family. So they resist women working on a church staff. But in fairness we must ask, does every working woman contribute to the breakdown of the American home?

Some women choose to work even after they have children. Some families have found themselves trapped in a two-income lifestyle. It will take sacrifice to lower their standard of living so that the wife can stay home. Some women buy the lie that their value lies in what they do rather than who they are. They hear women say, "I'm *only* a mom," and they fear a loss of identity if they stay home with children. But a church that builds a dynamic women's ministry fights these lies.

Single mothers must work to pay the bills. In doing so, they contribute not to the delinquency but to the provision and nurture of their family. No one should sit in judgment over them. And those wives who need a little extra cash to make ends meet can benefit from a part-time position in a church that values family.

As women study the Scriptures, they learn to think biblically. Female Bible teachers wield heavy influence as they share their stories and wisdom from life experience. Instead of destroying the family, healthy women's ministries build the family unit and teach women to enjoy the part they play. Every year women in Sue's ministry choose to leave the workforce and spend more time with family.

The irrational fear that women should not work on a church staff because working women are destroying the family is simply that—irrational. There is room for the right woman in the right stage of life to serve her church as paid staff. And aren't women more likely to make family a priority if they are influenced by women pastors who teach and model biblical truth?

Some Men Fear Women in Ministry Will Lead to Moral Failure

Men who struggle with sexual temptation feel more comfortable in an all-male working environment. They view working with women as a distraction. However, we would argue that women working in churches would actually protect against moral failure.

The vast majority of female ministers are mature believers. The women's ministry workers are *not* most likely to cause men leaders problems. Needy women in the church are the primary culprits.

The majority of moral failures begin in counseling sessions, when male pastors spend long hours ministering to hurting women. Unfortunately, women in miserable marriages are often looking for a "spiritual" man who will listen to them. The counseling session can become a setup for moral disaster. This is a foolish tradition! Why place our male pastors in harm's way?

It is wiser to have a woman pastor counsel the needy women. This lightens the men's counseling load and prevents such potentially devastating situations. When a male staff member does interact with a woman member and senses a red flag, he should call on a woman pastor to work with them. The dynamics of the session completely change when another woman is in the room.

Paul instructed Titus to delegate women's ministry to women—and this is a key reason. It just makes good sense! Men who fear to work on staff with women should consider this benefit.

Some Men Believe Women Are Inferior

Although they would never admit it, some men still believe women are oversensitive, driven by emotion, and incapable of making bottom-line decisions. They see women as the weaker sex in more ways than just physical strength. This is a form of prejudice—a sin that can ensnare us all. Certainly it is out of fashion today—nevertheless some men in ministry still believe women aren't fit to serve in leadership. If that is a man's entrenched opinion, he isn't likely to trust her with ministry.

Previous Experience

The feminist movement has inoculated some men against women. If he had a bad experience with women in the past, that experience colors future interaction. You may reap what other women have sown. What can you do? Your task is to convince him that you are different from the women he worked with in the past. If he is reasonable, in time he will be persuaded. Your response is critical. Examine the next section carefully and ask God to help you respond with maturity and godliness.

How Do You Respond When You Aren't Valued?

Respond with Grace

We all need God's grace! We all have blind spots. Men who don't value women are sinners. Prejudice against any people group is a sin (see James 2:9). But women who respond with animosity are sinners too. If we understand the source of the sin, we are more inclined to give grace.

There are many reasons men resent women. Some men who fear or dislike women have unresolved issues rooted deep in past experiences. Some cling to traditions passed on from men they respected growing up.

Particular personality types gravitate to power. These men naturally hold theological positions that feed their desire to dominate. They find it difficult to change unless they are challenged to examine their views—usually by other men. Their sin against women is no worse than our sin of resenting them for it.

So respond with grace to men who don't like you. Jesus did!

Respond with Patience

At Sue's former church, we prayed for many years for the male leaders to value our work. From the beginning this request was on our lips. It was a request that would try our patience.

As the years passed without success, I once verbalized our prayer to a pastor. He responded, "Women's ministry is one of the best ministries in our church—if it ain't broke, don't fix it!" I wanted to shout, "It will break soon if things don't change!" I didn't. As I sent up a "flare" prayer, the Holy Spirit directed me to be quiet.

My concern for the welfare of the ministry was well founded. After four years of healthy, vibrant growth, the ministry faltered. Here's what happened.

Every two years, a new lay director led the ministry. Four years into the ministry, the job had grown so large no one wanted to serve. Besides, the director often clocked forty-hour weeks—sometimes even sixty! We couldn't find a lay leader called, equipped, and willing to put in those hours for no pay.

Our solution was to divide the job into three parts, giving an inexperienced woman the lead. She had the authority but little expertise. Everyone was frustrated. The original vision was side-tracked and the ministry suffered.

In addition, a catastrophic conflict erupted within women's ministries. The women's ministry leaders did not have the backing that staff members enjoyed. The conflict lasted almost two years and crippled the ministry.

The leadership crisis and this conflict discouraged us all. With my joy waning and my zeal extinguished, I was tired. We had waited years and our patience was thin—but we didn't dishonor God as we waited. And I'm grateful because God was in the process of working.

Whatever your situation, wait on God. He sees and He knows. Give Him time to work on your behalf. Remember: He is still a God of miracles!

Respond with Submission

We define submission as respect for leaders with God-given authority. God wants us to honor the leaders in authority over us. We are called to respect them whether they value our work or not.

Keep the men you report to in the loop—especially if you make changes. If they do suggest a change, listen. If you don't agree, explain your reasons respectfully—but if they still insist, comply. Don't complain or slander them. God will always honor your submission to their guidance.

Do the best you can with the resources available, knowing that God holds your leaders ultimately responsible for the ministry. If you are shackled, they will one day answer to God for the roadblocks they erected. Our calling is to honor God, whatever the circumstances. The rest is up to Him.

Respond with Strength

Because we respond with grace, patience, and submission does not mean we are silent and weak. Vickie Kraft, minister to women at Northwest Bible Church in Dallas for fourteen years, modeled Christlike courage when she worked on staff with men. She expected her church to pay her what a male pastor in a similar position earned. She asked for it graciously and they agreed.

During a staff meeting, one of the men argued that God exhibited only male attributes. Vickie countered with Bible verses where Paul described God in feminine terms. He resisted until finally Vickie suggested they talk later with another pastor present. Vickie never expressed anger or lost her composure. Neither did she back down.

Choose your battles carefully. Exhibit the fruit of the Spirit. Be a team player, not focused solely on your own agenda. Consider the cost. Don't nitpick. Study the previous section on conflict resolution and consult others before you proceed. But if God leads you to stand your ground, do so with dignity and backbone. Pioneering is dirty work, but someone has to pave the way for others.

Respond with Excellence

Stand firm. Let nothing move you. *Always give yourselves fully to the work of the Lord,* because you know that your labor in the Lord is not in vain. (1 Corinthians 15:58, emphasis added)

Strive for excellence in all you do. Don't focus on men who don't value you. Instead, focus on the Lord and the women He has called you to shepherd. He values you and He will sustain you. Don't obsess about the resources you lack. Be grateful for the resources God provides. Work hard and leave the results to Him.

Respond with Faith

I had served in a church where women's ministry wasn't valued; God then removed me (Sue) and opened up two new opportunities—both on staff with pay and both serving with men who valued women! The two offers arrived within a month. For a woman who had ministered to women over twenty years and never attended a staff meeting or been paid a penny, it was "a good measure, pressed down, shaken together and running over" (Luke 6:38). I still pinch myself!

The first position is adviser to women students at Dallas Theological Seminary, where I trained in the 1980s. I love the stimulating academic atmosphere and working with women students.

I also serve as pastor to women at Irving Bible Church, located in a suburb of Dallas. IBC is cutting-edge, Bible-based, and reaching out to both moderns and postmoderns. It's a perfect fit.

At IBC, there are four women pastors and eighteen women on support staff. I have four paid positions on my women's ministry staff—a director, an assistant director, and a fine arts coordinator in addition to myself. Once I was ministry poor and now my cup runs over!

I remember wondering if my days serving Him were running out. I longed to be part of a team and enjoy the support of the leadership. Would God answer my prayer? I had no guarantees and neither do you. But God "acts on behalf of those who wait for him" (Isaiah 64:4). Respond with faith, for He is your advocate. You never know what He is up to! At age fifty-five I can testify that His plan is good! Have faith, stick around, and watch.

PART 3

TAKING THE TRANSFORMATION MODEL TO THE CAMPUS

Chapter 14

WHO NEEDS A CAMPUS MINISTRY?

very fall women students all over the nation sit in orientation, many feeling overwhelmed and facing tremendous adjustments. Many are still unpacking boxes in unfamiliar apartments with new roommates in a busy city far from home. Some have flown across oceans, others have relocated from across the country, and others simply came from across town.

As adviser to women students at DTS, I (Sue) have the privilege of walking with women like these during their graduate studies. I meet with each one for an entrance interview, and for those who need it, I serve as a sounding board, prayer partner, cheerleader, and mentor.

Melissa's Story

Melissa needed it. I noticed her slip in late while I was welcoming the new women students at the orientation lunch. They sat around long tables decorated with red bandannas and Texas bluebonnets in cowboy boot vases, munching on tasty box lunches from a local deli. In four days they would walk into their first class at Dallas Theological Seminary.

Melissa grew up in a small Midwest town and attended a state college a hundred miles from home. She came to faith through friends in her dorm who then nurtured her in their collegiate ministry on campus. As a result, she left behind her drinking buddies and focused on knowing her newfound Love, Jesus. Although she graduated with honors, in her senior year she spent more time studying the Bible than the math textbooks required for her accounting degree. She was twenty-three years old and a baby believer—but God called her to serve Him. So she flew across the country to study at DTS.

Ten days into the semester, she collapsed in my office weeping. Her mother called the night before to inform her that she and her dad were divorcing. *The marriage has been a sham for years.* Melissa was stunned. Her world rocked, she came to unload and pray for God's direction. Should she continue her studies or go home? As we talked, other questions surfaced. So many fellow students it seemed to her had grown up in Christian homes and been to Bible college. Could she compete? She was thinking of changing her track from counseling to women's ministries or maybe even missions. What was *really* out there for women her age after graduation?

Melissa's life was at a critical juncture—just as mine had been when I was her age. I was not on a campus, but our needs were similar. We both needed an encourager who would show us how to rely on God in the midst of uncertainty and heartache. I found what I needed in a church's women's ministry. And she would be required to plug into a church during her Dallas stay. But due to time constraints and a different emphasis, she wasn't likely to become involved in the women's ministry in her church. She needed a women's ministry on campus. She found one, and a year later she was loving her studies, serving on the Women Students Fellowship Board, and processing her grief at her parents' split.

Do You See the Need on Your Campus?

Are you a student surrounded by women who need the support, encouragement, and inspiration that a women's ministry can provide? Maybe you are a professor or on staff and have observed this need for years. Or maybe you are a mother who wants these resources for your daughter and others who come behind her. You could be serving in a collegiate ministry that needs to get serious about meeting the needs of women students.

Can the Transformation Model be adapted to your campus setting? What would need to be changed? How would you get started? What's going on at other campuses? Could they serve as models that you might draw on? Who should lead a campus ministry? How will you maintain excellence and consistency when students are cycling in and out?

If you hear God's call to begin a campus women's ministry or you want to improve an existing one, read this section first. We will answer these and other related questions. We'll show you flourishing campus ministries and some just getting started. We'll supply resources and contacts to help you. After you've spent time digesting "how to's" specific to the campus, read part 2, *Taking the Transformation Model to the Church,* with the idea of adapting those principles to your campus.

When God Went Ahead of Us

Let's begin with two remarkable examples of the way God planted campus ministries—first on a seminary campus and then on a secular campus.

Women's Ministry at DTS

Lisa Samra grew up on the DTS campus. Her dad is a professor and administrator, and her mom serves on staff. After earning her undergraduate degree at the University of Texas, she returned to

DTS, this time as a student. A gifted leader, Lisa saw the needs of women students and responded. When I was hired in 1998, God had already worked in Lisa's heart to begin the foundational preparation for the Women Students Fellowship Board. These would be the student leaders in this new venture.

God linked Lisa, a postmodern woman, and myself, a modern woman, because He knew the ministry needed input and direction from both of us. The campus had changed in the eight years since I had graduated. Besides, campus ministry is much more effective if it is student-led.

When I attended Dallas from 1985 to 1989, most women students, like myself, were experienced in ministry. DTS opened its doors to women in 1976 and by the late 1980s we made up about 12 percent of the student body. In contrast, today women account for a quarter of the student population, and many come right out of college with little ministry experience.

When I attended, DTS had the feel of a man's campus, and it was two years before I mustered the courage to ask a question in class. Please don't misunderstand. Women were welcomed and treated with respect. I was simply in awe. Dallas turns out great Bible teachers and leaders and I felt honored to be there. But I allowed my timidity and reverence for the school to hinder my involvement. Although the campus had changed in many ways, many women students were still acting and feeling like I did as a student. God had done a great work in my life helping me overcome my apprehension and I wanted that for them. So did Lisa.

With Lisa as the first chairman, Women Students Fellowship Board launched my first semester at DTS. God's timing is amazing! My work in academia and in the ministry trenches at IBC benefits both realms. And my twenty-five years experience in women's ministry was a valuable resource to Lisa.

It's Made a Tremendous Difference!

When I meet with incoming women students for a "get acquainted" interview, I ask them about their adjustment. The responses last semester differed greatly from those I heard when I first arrived, thanks to a women's ministry on campus!

"I feel right at home," answered Susan when I asked about her first semester. "I connected with several women at the orientation lunch and the brunch the next day. We went out over the weekend and when I walked into my first class, I already had friends."

Her comments are typical.

Wherever women gather, there is the potential for a women's ministry. On more and more campuses—both secular and Christian—women are adapting the Transformation Model.

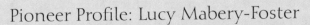

Pioneer Profile: Lucy Mabery-Foster

"You have a gift," the superintendent of Sunday school told her. "You have to use it." The teenager Lucy never forgot the admonition to use the teaching ability that God had given her. Having become a believer at a young age, raised in a conservative Christian home, she taught Bible to children in the Sunday school program at her church in her hometown of Dallas, Texas. She later became a schoolteacher.

Lucy married Trevor Mabery, a young surgeon, in 1959. As a young mother, she began teaching a "Through the Bible" course for women at Scofield Memorial Church. Moody Bible Institute sponsored the curriculum, giving college credit to the students for many years.

"The first time I taught the class, it took me seven years to get through the Bible," Lucy laughs. "When I started over again, I managed to speed up a little." She taught three classes of one-hundred-plus women per week for twenty years. She also counseled women regularly.

After teaching a Bible study to the wives of Dallas Cowboy football players, Lucy was encouraged to earn her master's degree at Dallas Seminary. "You need the credentials," her husband told her. So Lucy enrolled in the two-year master of arts in biblical studies program, then the only degree open to women at DTS, in 1983.

Upon her graduation in 1985, Trevor encouraged her to earn her Th.M. One year into her new studies, Trevor was killed—with three other men—in a private plane crash in Tennessee. The loss of her husband shifted Lucy's ministry goals. With her youngest child a freshman in college, she devoted all of her time to school, graduating in 1988. As God's plan would have it, the seminary was then discussing the option of inviting a woman to become a full-time faculty member. They approached Lucy with the offer, and she opened up a new door in women's ministry at Dallas Seminary in the fall of 1990, becoming the first woman faculty member.

"What did they want me to do immediately?" she shakes her head with a laugh. "Get a Ph.D.!" In a speedy two-and-a-half years, she completed a degree in counseling at nearby Texas Women's University.

How does the lone woman professor in a conservative seminary face the inevitable criticism? "I didn't take it personally," she says. That is her advice to women who find themselves in churches and academic institutions that traditionally aren't accustomed to having women on staff. "Whatever you do, glorifying God must be your primary focus." Sometimes that means ignoring unfair criticism. Other times it can relate to one's attitude. Fighting for recognition—official titles, salaries, positions in church leadership, for example—can backfire in some cases, she says. Women must understand their motivations. "Be willing to fit within the confines of the church in which you serve," she advises her students.

"Leave if you are uncomfortable, but do not split the church. Choose your battles wisely, making sure that your goal is to elevate Christ, not yourself."

Lucy serves in the Pastoral Ministries Department, splitting her time between counseling and ministry-related courses. Her primary ministry-related classes are Expository Teaching and The Role of Women in Ministry.

"Women in ministry need to know how to put together a conference, since most of them will one day lead other women through speaking engagements. I teach them how to put together a central theme, with four talks that should last for an hour each."

Lucy speaks—and teaches—from experience. Since the death of her husband in 1987, she has traveled extensively, speaking at women's retreats and conferences around the country almost every weekend. In 1997, she cut back on that schedule to make room for her new husband, C. L. Foster, a local businessman. They now travel the country together, sometimes for her conferences, other times for his business.

Her new life as Lucy Mabery-Foster continues to be full. In 1999 she published her first book, *Women in the Church,* one of the Swindoll Leadership Library collection. Her next book, *Spiritual Gifts in the Hands of a Woman,* is due out in 2003. She shines as an example to all women called to ministry—one who did not pursue an agenda but waited for God to open the doors He intended to have her walk through. Patience and endurance mark her walk with God.

Lucy went to be with the Lord on May 20, 2002, as this book was going to press.

Women's Ministry at Texas Tech University and Texas A&M

We always rented a trailer to take our children to college rather than my driving a second car. Why? Because I knew tears would hinder me driving back home. For both parents and their grown children, college is an enormous adjustment—and one that is often overlooked.

For Parents

For parents, it is knowing your offspring may never eat another vegetable. They can choose to stay out all night with people you will never meet. Will they find a church? Will it be your kind of church? Christian parents soon learn whether their son or daughter owns his or her faith.

For Students

For the college student, it is being completely in charge of your own life for the first time. Those who move far away from home must construct their social life all over again. They must navigate a new city and decipher a new campus. Vulnerable and sometimes naïve, freshmen especially risk making choices that sidetrack their progress and their faith. Those years of formal training are a vital bridge to adult life.

Sue's Story

Driving home after leaving my daughters, Heather and Rachel, at college was gut wrenching. At the time, I was studying 1 Peter and found comfort in the second chapter. Christ was alone, but He entrusted Himself to God (1 Peter 2:23). All the way home I prayed silently, "Lord, I entrust them to You. Lord, I entrust them to You."

God answered my prayers through Patricia Hogan and Bonnie Turner. These young women were not students at my daughters' schools, but God gave them a vision to begin a women's ministry on their own campus, and it spread to other schools—including my daughters'.

They planted a Christian sorority at University of Texas in 1988 called Sigma Phi Lambda (Sisters for the Lord) and chapters had spread to Texas Tech and Texas A&M by the time my daughters enrolled.

It Made a Tremendous Difference There Too!

Through "Phi Lamb," Christian women develop meaningful friendships, pray, and study the Bible together, and best of all, the organization is open to anyone. Their vision made the difference in my daughter's lives and answered the prayers of a mother they never met.

My daughter Heather writes: "Phi Lamb was probably one of the greatest, positive spiritual influences during my college years. The accountability, fellowship, and lifelong friendships created between us were essential to my growth in Christ. The small prayer groups and prayer partners encouraged me. I learned to be vulnerable and honest with fellow sisters who lifted up my needs to the Lord.

"Having friends to hang out with that were positive, spiritual influences helped provide alternatives to the typical negative peer pressure faced by college students. I had many opportunities to serve Christ through leading small groups, playing my guitar for worship, and mentoring younger sisters. I've been gone eight years, but I still keep in contact with many of my Phi Lamb sisters. I thank God for this incredible gift of true friendships that continue to spur me on in my relationship with God." (So does her mom!)

How would you plant a campus women's ministry with this kind of impact? Read on.

Chapter 15

CREATE YOUR OWN CAMPUS WOMEN'S MINISTRY

*H*ow will you begin? Here's a plan that works on both Christian and secular campuses.

Evaluate Your Campus Atmosphere

What Are Their Ages and Stages?

Who are the women on your campus? Is this their first time away from home, or have they had several years to adjust to living on their own at other schools? Are you at an undergraduate or graduate school? If you at are a medical school, your women's ministry will look different than if you are at a community college.

What are their ages? Are they mostly the same age—or do women from different ages and stages attend your school?

Are They Single or Married?

The social needs of single women are not the same as those of married women. Singles usually have more time to participate in a campus ministry and are more likely to volunteer to help. If you plan a Saturday night outing, don't expect many married women to attend. Older married women may have established themselves in a profession, or they may have family responsibilities that limit their time.

At DTS 60 percent of women students are single, and they primarily lead the ministry. Occasionally married women will join the board, but most of the time their hectic lives hinder them. Find out who needs your ministry and mold it to their needs.

Are there many married men on campus? If so, do you want to include their wives in your ministry? At DTS we realize that wives will be partnering with their husbands in the pastorate, mission field, and other ministries. Even though these women are not attending seminary, their training is often crucial to their husbands' success. A women's ministry can prepare these wives.

However, at DTS the needs of student wives and women students are radically different. Student wives need Bible training and mentoring, but women seminary students already receive this training in their classes. Long before Lisa dreamed of a ministry for women students, DTS faculty wives had organized to train the wives.

Therefore, we have two women's ministries—one for wives and one for women students. (For information on developing a ministry to student wives, go to our Web site, www.newdoors.info, for the e-mail address of Carolyn Hannah, DTS student wives ministry adviser.) Some women are both and can partake of either fare. Occasionally we partner to bring in a speaker both groups enjoy or on a project for the school. But otherwise our ministries are designed to meet the unique needs of each group. In a secular school, ask the question, "Do wives and women students share the same needs?" If they do, structure a ministry to both. If they don't, keep them separate.

Where Do They Live?

Do most of the women live in the dorms or at home? Are you at a commuter school? Dorm life automatically brings women together socially. Usually activities are already planned and people are readily available for support and fun. It's hard to be lonely in the dorm.

But women on a commuter campus are more likely to come and go quickly. DTS is located downtown and housing is in short supply. Many women live in apartments throughout the city and local residents drive long distances to class. Even though many want to connect, it's a challenge.

At a commuter school you will need to offer activities and ministries when the majority of women are on campus, usually during the day. My office partners with the Placement Office to present a workshop to help women prepare to find employment when they graduate. We offer the same workshop at lunchtime on Thursday and Friday in order to accommodate class schedules. Evening or weekend events are more difficult for us, but they work at a school where most women live in the dorm.

Where Are They From?

Are women students mainly local, or have they come from around the nation or the world? If your campus is in a large city, women from small towns are often overwhelmed initially as they learn to navigate the traffic and find their way around. If they come from other countries, they may experience language and cultural barriers. Women who travel far to attend your school probably won't know anyone when they arrive.

What is the racial mix? Do your women tend to segregate by race or are they comfortable with one another? How will your women's ministry bring women with different perspectives together for the benefit of all?

We draw women from all over the nation and the world. Many

arrive alone and overwhelmed. They believe God has called them to a life of service but are uncertain where to find the needed resources. The first few weeks are critical to a healthy adjustment. This is true on most campuses. How will you help them connect and settle in? We'll show you.

We intentionally mix women of different races and nationalities together from the first day they are on campus. Often barriers never arise because the women feel loved and cared for as individuals and they have shared the experience of being new on campus.

We are also careful to recruit board leaders from different races and nationalities. As the board prays and plans together, women present different perspectives that might be overlooked if the leadership didn't reflect a mix.

If you draw women from a variety of places and backgrounds, consider it a blessing and communicate that attitude to your women. Instead of causing conflict or divisiveness, variety is a plus that can enrich the lives of women and model true Christlike love on the campus.

Are You at a Christian or a Secular Campus?

If you are at a secular campus, Christian women yearn to find one another and form a community where they can grow spiritually and encourage each other in their faith. Usually their values and standards are different from the college culture, and they appreciate a haven where they are accepted and strengthened to be salt and light on campus. A women's ministry can transform a Christian woman's experience at a secular college.

Sigma Phi Lambda provides a successful model of a Christian organization on a secular campus. That model will look different if you are planting a women's ministry at a Bible college, seminary, or school supported by a particular denomination. If Bible studies are common or students are required to take Bible classes, your structure may not need to include Bible study. At DTS our greatest need is for community and connection among women. Our ministry takes on an entirely different flavor from Sigma Phi Lambda.

Study the demographics of your women before you begin. Until you know who they are, you won't know how to structure a ministry to meet their needs. Is the need spiritual, social, or academic? Is there a primary need to focus on first? What's already in place? You don't want to duplicate what others are doing. After you assess the needs on campus, consider who will lead the ministry.

Who Should Lead a Campus Women's Ministry?

Is God showing *you* the needs on your campus? Do you have a passion to change the environment for women? Great! God put these desires within you for a reason. But are you a student, or a staff or faculty member? Your status determines how you should proceed.

Will your ministry be to students? If so and you are on staff or a professor, ask God to show you a student with the same vision and heart. Students will understand the campus from a unique perspective that staff and faculty cannot share. Other students will be more likely to join in if they are led by one of their own. A student organization is better student-bred and -led.

If you are a student, ask God to identify a woman staff member or professor to assist you. You may need a long-term advocate on campus or a woman with more experience to help you through conflict or crises. If you need financial assistance from your school, she may be instrumental in securing the budget you need to function. She may serve as the liaison between you and the administration, helping you to understand the system and to get things done quickly.

When the DTS women's board chairman had to make a choice between serving on the board or working to pay her tuition, I was able to get her a scholarship. When women want to use their board service hours for an internship, I can be their required supervisor. Certainly the staff or faculty member should not micromanage the organization. But partnering with her will benefit everyone.

Pioneer Profile: Pamela Reeve

"People often ask me, 'What is your passion?'" muses Pamela Reeve, former dean of women at Multnomah Bible College and Seminary. "I tell them I have a passion to know Christ; as for ministry, I see a need and move with passion to meet that need."

During her thirty-seven-year-plus tenure at Multnomah, Pamela observed the students' need for a program specifically designed to help women understand and meet the demands of ministry to and for women. Ultimately, she created the first bachelor's and first master's programs in women's ministry in the United States. She taught many of the classes, and even in partial retirement continues to teach and counsel the young women studying at Multnomah.

Originally an architect, Pamela became a Christian in her early twenties. She distinctly remembers the occasion when God asked her, "Would you be willing to go through life single for the sake of the kingdom of God?"

Despite concern for her financial future (with her father dead and only a few relatives in the country), as well as her emotional, physical, and social needs, she concluded that this was not a hypothetical question and answered "Yes." "I was so in love with the Lord that I accepted celibacy, not as a renunciation, but as an opportunity to devote my life to the Lord's interests." Her response to God's call commenced a journey marked by challenge, courage, and community.

Knowing that she had been called to ministry, Pamela gave up her promising career to become a teacher, and later principal, in a Christian high school. After eight years there, she found herself teaching at a local college and filling her off-duty hours in Inter-Varsity work and Bible studies for working women and high school girls. Frustrated that her ministry had been curtailed to "after hours," Pamela began praying earnestly for direction back into full-time ministry. In 1964, after eleven years "in the desert, with no signs, no markers, no footprints to follow," God opened up the position at Multnomah. Her time there would prove to be long, fruitful, and satisfying.

One of only three women on faculty at the time, Pamela taught Introduction to Counseling and Personal Development and Leadership in addition to fulfilling her duties as dean. Much of her time was spent counseling and mentoring the women students. This exposure to the students led to her discovery that the women needed specific training in women's ministry. In 1978, she designed the college-level program. In 1980, she initiated the first "Women in Ministry" conference at Multnomah, which opened in conjunction with a pastor's conference. Over six hundred women attended. "My goal for the conference was to give our women students a broad exposure to resources and material they could use for ministry," says Pamela. The conference was an immediate success, and it has been widely duplicated across the country in recent years.

We asked Pamela for her thoughts on what women need as they consider a life in full-time ministry. She replied, "True ministry flows out of a deep love for God. If you only are serving people, you're sunk! You are serving God! Women need somehow to be taught to get to know at a heart level the immensity and intensity of God's love for them. Tools and training for ministry, while vitally important, are secondary. I believe women should be good theologians, and I urge my students to apply their theology to every aspect of their lives and teaching."

In 1988, Multnomah approved the creation of a master's degree in women's ministry. It, too, was the first of its kind in the United States. By this time, Pamela had retired from her position as dean, although she continues to this day as a part-time professor, still mentoring and counseling students when she can. She is the author of several books, including *Faith Is . . .* and *Deserts of the Heart*.

Remembering her decision to follow Christ as a single person, Pamela exclaims, "I can't tell you of the wonder and magnificence of His love! I want to shout it from the housetops. He has met my every financial, social, and emotional need."

Claimed by at least three families as one of their own, with countless spiritual children worldwide, Pamela Reeve remains a model of godly womanhood for us all.

Determine Your Ministry Structure

How Will You Begin?

- Gather a team of interested women to pray, brainstorm, and plan.
- Write a purpose statement to help maintain perspective.

For example, our Women Students Fellowship Board exists "to foster community among DTS women for the purpose of honoring our God-given worth, maintaining high academic standards, building friendships and abiding fellowship, and developing ministry opportunities."

Sigma Phi Lambda exists "for the sole purpose of glorifying our Lord Jesus Christ and making His name great. This is done by providing a source of fellowship to Christian women who sincerely seek to know His person, His will and His ways. . . . Because of this purpose, the sorority is not presently nor will it ever be Panhellenic."

As you structure your board, programs, and ministries, you ask, "Does it line up with our purpose statement?" If not, you risk sidetracking the ministry.

- Write your constitution.

Becoming a student organization is often a lengthy process. You will probably need to apply for a charter. At some schools you are also required to apply for tax-exempt status and recruit a faculty adviser. To begin the process, you need to write your constitution. This is a document that describes the way your organization will function. It contains sections entitled Name, Purpose, Membership, Officers, Structure, Meetings, Methods to Amend the Constitution, Bylaws, and any other information particular to your organization. See appendix D for the DTS Women Students Fellowship Constitution. For Sigma Phi Lambda's constitution and information on how to begin a chapter, access our Web site www.newdoors.info.

How do you know what officers you'll need on your team? Again, look at your purpose statement. What are the greatest needs? Why do you exist? What will your calendar look like? What programs will you create to meet those needs? You'll need leaders to head up these ministries.

Decide on Your Programs

What will meet the needs of the women on your campus? Here are some ideas that worked for us and might help you get started.

Dallas Seminary

Orientation Ministry

The first few months on campus often determine whether a student thrives or fails. How can you help students acclimate quickly?

At DTS, before women arrive on campus, they receive an invitation to our welcome luncheon. They also have the option of joining a fellowship group led by a returning student. The first year we offered these groups, 90 percent of the women participated.

Our luncheon is held between two mandatory tests during orientation—so that we reach them the first day they are on campus before classes begin. We decorate the room, serve a delicious lunch, and play games that force them to get out of their chairs and interact. Living the same experience bonds them quickly.

During lunch the board chairman and I welcome the women and explain what to expect. We use drama and other creative methods to help them laugh and relax. After lunch they meet with their fellowship group and receive a map and an invitation to a brunch the next day. Informal brunches are held in homes and apartments on Saturday morning, but the women often stay into the afternoon. At these brunches, relationships are birthed.

The fellowship groups continue to meet monthly during the fall, but usually women take the initiative and form communities after the brunch. Whether or not a new student attends all these gatherings, she still has a friend and resource in her fellowship group leader. Getting off to a good start makes a tremendous difference!

Retreat

Nothing bonds women like a block of time away. What kind of retreat would work for your campus? Can you get away to a retreat center, a local hotel, or even a facility on the campus overnight?

We carpool to a country retreat center about an hour out of Dallas. It's quiet and green, and there are enough rocking chairs on a porch by the lake to accommodate almost everyone. We hold this retreat early in the semester before "crunch" time, and we only stay Friday night through Saturday afternoon to suit homework demands. Although the retreat devours a sizable chunk of our yearly budget, it's worth it.

To learn how to organize and implement a retreat, read chapter 10, *Offer Exciting Events*. Adjust to your budget and time frame.

Brown Bags and Seminars

Are there subjects of particular interest to women that are not addressed in their classes? Are there women speakers they would enjoy but will not have the opportunity to hear unless you organize the event? Are there women's issues that need to be highlighted on the campus?

At DTS since most professors are men, women seldom hear ministry taught from a woman's perspective. In addition, most receive minimal training in women's issues such as postabortion syndrome, eating disorders, and lesbianism—issues they will face in ministry. Our enrichment coordinators plan a smorgasbord of gatherings that focus on women's needs and issues.

Graduating Women's Luncheon

What kinds of celebrations warrant a party you can host? What will women remember about their college days that will last a lifetime and affect their future involvement with the school? A strong women's ministry often takes the initiative to make memories.

We treat our women graduates to a sumptuous luncheon complete with crystal vases and fresh flowers. I purchased the vases on sale and use them year after year. I give them a print of Jesus holding a lamb to remind them of who they are and what He is sending them out to do. You'll find this print framed in offices and homes all over the country and the world—a symbol that bonds us together. We recruit women alumna to speak and encourage the women as they set out to serve. We photograph the class and send out complimentary copies. What kinds of memories can you make on your campus?

How Often Should You Meet to Implement Your Programs?

We learned to focus on key needs and not to do too much. Women students are busy with assignments, work, or family responsibilities. We are careful not to overload our calendar with activities during midterms and finals—and not to burden our leaders with unnecessary meetings.

The DTS board meets monthly during the fall and spring semesters for about an hour and a half. We meet at a time during the day that is convenient for everyone. We travel to a bed and breakfast for a spring training camp to transition between the old and new board and to prepare for the year ahead. Also, we ask the board to support one another's activities. Most women students can't commit to much more.

This is a sampling of programs at DTS. What works on a secular campus? Let's look at the programs of Phi Lamb and how they originated.

Sigma Phi Lambda (Sisters for the Lord) at University of Texas

Junior Trisha Adams had a dream. She dreamed of a sorority that was not exclusive like the Panhellenic organizations. Its motto would be, "You choose us. We don't choose you." She dreamed of a Christian community on her campus composed of women from different denominations yet united in Christian love and purpose. An organization that propelled women deeper into an intimate relationship with Jesus through prayer, Bible study, and mentoring.

In 1988 Trisha gathered a team of like-minded women and founded Sigma Phi Lambda on the University of Texas campus. They began with five founders and eight charter members—thirteen in all. During the fall they tried out their ideas and formulated them into a constitution. They joined the UT rush for the first time in the spring and netted nine pledges—almost doubling their membership.

Today her dream has taken root at eleven other colleges where women students have established Phi Lamb sororities—and several other colleges are investigating the possibility. Phi Lamb has grown to impact thousands of women. The 2002 pledge class at Texas A&M bulged at two hundred. All but three of their chapters are on secular campuses.

Until four years ago, the UT officers were responsible for helping new chapters get started. But now a seven-member alumni board oversees this process. They meet with all the chapters' officers for a retreat in August to maintain continuity and encourage the students as they prepare to lead their sororities.

How did they structure their ministry? What programs are in place to serve their members? How similar are the original organization and its sister chapters?

Phi Lamb's Programs

Phi Lamb requires their members to attend a local church, be involved in a Bible study of their choice, meet with a Phi Lamb prayer group once a week, and attend 80 percent of their meetings and a retreat each semester.

They also join together in community service projects. The Texas Tech Chapter requires four hours of community service each semester, according to 2001 President Mandi Waldrip. "We minister to places like the Ronald McDonald House and Women's Protective Services. Through Phi Lamb, Jesus has become more real. It has influenced every aspect of my college life—especially my prayer life. It's where I found my friends," says Mandi.

Members meet once a week to sing, pray, share, conduct business, and hear an inspirational speaker. Phi Lamb dues range from $50 to $100 a semester, but women who cannot pay are exempt. It's a mother's dream!

"Phi Lamb is a great evangelistic tool. Our pledges are mature Christians, new believers, and even some seekers. The officers meet with every new woman to assess needs and have the opportunity to present the gospel," says Mandi.

Would you like to know more about planting a Phi Lamb chapter on your campus? Go to our Web site at www.newdoors.info to find their contact information. They will send you an "interest" packet to help you discern if God is leading you in this direction.

If you choose to partner with Phi Lamb, they will help you get started. "What is so amazing is to see the same spirit in each chapter. We ensure consistency and purpose by asking each chapter to follow the same constitution," says Bonnie Collins Turner, alumni board leader.

Trisha's dream has impacted thousands of college women in their quest to grow closer to Christ and each other. During pivotal years in their spiritual journey, Phi Lamb and other campus women's ministries have transformed lives.

What are they doing that inspires you? How will you structure your ministry and implement the programs for the women on your campus? Once you have determined your programs, you need women to lead them.

Choose Your Leadership Offices

Every organization needs a leader. The DTS board chairperson is a woman student chosen from the existing board by the current board chairperson and the adviser to women students. She serves for a year. Other offices include coordinators for retreat, orientation, special events, academic excellence, enrichment, and special events. Women also serve to support the board as publicity coordinator, secretary, historian, and affirmation coordinator.

Phi Lamb officers are elected and each corresponds with an assigned member of the alumni board for guidance and support. Their slate includes a president, vice president, chaplain, treasurer, and secretary. Every group will take on a different flavor. Choose your leadership positions to fit your needs.

Work with the Administration

Stay on Track

To be most effective, ministry needs consistency in purpose and vision. On a campus most students are cycling in and out every four years. Who is around for the long haul? Who passes on hard-learned lessons and ensures the team doesn't get sidetracked? Often the faculty adviser, women's ministry director, or dean of women works closely with the student-led ministry and can be the consistent thread needed. Include her graciously and seek her counsel.

If your school does not provide a woman leader for students, identify a woman working in the Student Services or Dean's Office and ask her to be the liaison between your group and the administration.

If you are a student, what is your attitude toward the faculty and staff? Do you resent their involvement? Are you willing to learn from their experience? Certainly, the adviser should not run the ministry, oversee meetings, or be involved in the details. But her expertise, experience, and understanding of how to work with the administration can be an asset to your organization.

Be Flexible and Cooperative!

Who keeps the calendar at your school? Be sure you check the school's calendar before you schedule activities or events. Be known as a flexible organization taking other group's plans into account and not insisting on your own way.

Every school operates differently. If it is a private or religious institution, it must consider the opinions of supporters and donors in its policies and decisions. You may not always understand the reasons behind restrictions placed on student organizations, but you will honor God and earn a good name for your group by cooperating with the administration and abiding by its guidelines.

Resolve Conflict Together

Conflict is inevitable in any ministry. Your adviser probably has experience resolving conflict and should be alerted if parties clash. One year a conflict arose at DTS between two student organizations. The board president tried to handle it on her own but only made it worse. By the time I learned of the conflict, several women were wounded and angry.

The board president asked me to intervene after the damage. When we sat down to talk I suggested that if she had come to me earlier, we could have averted hurt feelings and ill will between the two organizations. She agreed. Then we prayed together and brainstormed how to deal with the dispute. We gathered all the involved parties, apologized, and talked out our differences. Take advantage of your adviser's expertise!

Provide Role Models and Mentors

Many women earn undergraduate and graduate degrees while in their twenties. Of course, there are older women students on campus too. What is the attitude of the younger women students toward older women professors, staff, and students? Most younger students yearn to connect with an older woman for mentoring and discipleship. But like in a church, the older women won't volunteer their expertise and wisdom. They must be asked!

A campus women's ministry can be the matchmaker that links older and younger women in mentoring relationships that benefit both. How can you facilitate these relationships? Invite older women to your events. Interview them and find out who has the desire and time to spend with younger students. Then link them as appropriate.

DTS offers a four-year master of theology with a women's ministry track and a two-year master of arts in Christian education with a concentration in women's ministry. We attempt to include the women who teach and administer these degrees in what we do. Ask influential women on campus to speak at your seminars, brown bags, and retreats. Many are right under your nose—treasures who have a heart for younger women they see regularly. Don't overlook them.

How Will You Create Your Own Campus Women's Ministry?

In a nutshell . . .

- Evaluate your campus atmosphere
- Decide who should be the key leader of the ministry
- Determine your ministry structure and programs
- Choose the officers to lead those programs
- Work with the administration
- Provide role models and mentors

Women on campuses everywhere are hungry for the relationships, encouragement, and inspiration that a women's ministry provides. Is God calling you to be His initiator? If so, step out and go for it! Women's lives can be transformed through a women's ministry on the campus just like in the church or on the mission field.

Chapter 16

WHAT'S HAPPENING AROUND THE NATION?

*W*e've looked at two women's ministry models—DTS for the Christian campus and Phi Lamb for the secular campus. Now let's take a look at other schools. As you read about these women's ministries, compare and contrast their organizational structures. As you study their designs, you can mix and match ideas that will work for you.

You will notice that many campus leaders are mentioned by name. These women have graciously consented to have their contact information included on our Web site. If you desire more details about a particular ministry, take advantage of their expertise.

Gordon-Conwell Theological Seminary (Boston, Massachusetts)

Historically, Gordon-Conwell has welcomed women faculty and students to all their educational programs. A. J. Gordon was a well-known advocate, in his day, of women's ministry. Today Gordon-Conwell's flagship degree for women is a new doctor of ministry specializing in effective ministry to women under the direction of Alice Mathews, Ph.D., distinguished associate professor in women's ministries.

Participants attend three two-week intensive residencies, one each year for three years. During the first residency, students focus on understanding women as listeners and learners. They explore a variety of gender issues in the church and society that impact women and answer questions like, "How do women know what they know?" and "How do women make moral decisions?"

During the second year students study women in the Bible and throughout church history. They investigate what the Bible teaches and how history shapes women's lives—what they can and cannot do, how they are to live as God's women in a fallen world. The last year builds on the work of the first two residencies and focuses on how to establish effective women's ministries today. The final residency also equips students to minister to women in pain, dealing with a wide range of issues requiring counseling and mentoring. For doctoral candidates seeking to understand women through a biblical and historical grid and who want to plant stellar women's ministries, this program offers challenging opportunities.

Also unique to Gordon-Conwell is the student-created Women's Resource Network, an organization that ministers to women in a variety of ways on the campus. They secured a small classroom in the academic center and turned it into a WRN lounge—with comfortable chairs and a small library on relevant issues—where women gather for prayer, conversations, discussions, and small group meetings.

The WRN also organizes one or two low-key retreats each year and small group Bible studies in the dorms as well as special seminars with visiting speakers. Dean of Students Lita Schlueter oversees WRN, while the director of programs for women acts in an advisory capacity.

Pioneer Profile: Alice Mathews

"It's never too late; nothing with God is ever wasted," testifies Dr. Alice Mathews as she thinks back over a rich history. Here are some of the highlights of her journey.

- Alice and Randy Mathews married over fifty years ago. Randy, now retired, served the Lord as a pastor, missionary, and church planter in Europe. Their first church was in a small town in Wyoming, where Alice focused her energies on her four small children. "My ideal was June Cleaver, and I gave myself heart and soul to being the best house-keeper, wife, and mother I could be. However, although I was committed to the domestic role, my intellectual life was suffering." But God gave Alice a friend who shared her love for theology and challenged her to work through a chapter of the Greek New Testament each week. They met for their "Greek morning" each Thursday for five and a half years.

- After two decades in youth ministries, Alice was challenged to join two friends in a outreach ministry to women in Paris, France, where she and her husband worked as church plant-ers. At age forty, Alice says, "I discovered the joy of minis-tering to women for the first time!"

- Returning from the mission field in 1980, Alice and Randy made their home in Colorado. Alice was soon invited to join Denver Seminary's staff to set up a public relations office.

- In 1981, the seminary's academic dean asked her to teach a course in women's ministry. When she asked what he wanted included in the course, he responded, "Teach whatever you want." This sent Alice on a lifelong search through the Scriptures, history, and culture to learn more about ministry to and by women.

- In 1985, Denver Seminary sent Alice to an intensive summer program at Columbia University in theological education management. On the final day each participant was asked, "If you could do anything in the world five years from now, what would it be?" She answered, "I would be a full-time professor in an evangelical seminary." The next question was, "What will it take for you to get there?" The answer—a Ph.D.!

- After a two-and-a-half year search for a program that would study the culture and its effect on women, Alice discovered a new doctoral program in religion and social change at the University of Denver and Iliff School of Theology—right down the street! She graduated eight years later at the age of sixty-five.

- In 1994, The Seminary of the East brought Alice on as dean of their Philadelphia center. This difficult move came on the heels of the loss of their only son to a drunk driver, but this was clearly the next step in God's plan. Randy says, "My wife followed me all over the world all those years. Now that I am retired, it's my turn to follow her."

- In 1997, Dr. Haddon Robinson invited Alice to run the D.Min. program at Gordon-Conwell Seminary in Boston. She and Randy postponed their retirement plans, and she now serves as Lois W. Bennet Distinguished Professor of Educational Ministries and Women's Ministries. She teaches seven courses in women's ministries as well as mentors individual women who are blessed by her teaching and wisdom.

- Alice is the author of *A Woman God Can Lead,* and is working on several other books to inform and equip Christians to better minister to and understand women, the unique ways they learn, their stress and family patterns.

Has God given you an exceptional mind and a desire to devote your life to scholarship and academics? We hope Alice's journey encourages you. Naysayers insisted that Alice had no future in institutions of higher learning, but she refused to be swayed by their pessimism and cynicism. Today she is impacting women all over America and especially future women leaders. She's an inspiration to women who think academic ministry is unattainable.

The Master's College (Santa Clarita, California)

Women make up over 55 percent of Master's College student body. The sheer number of women on campus provides ample opportunity for ministry both horizontally—student to student, and vertically—administrator to student.

"One of the most significant ministries of women to women on our campus," says Director of Women's Ministries Betty Price, "is the leadership of our women resident directors. Each of them shepherds a dorm of eight-five to one hundred women students while they train and disciple four women resident assistants. As a team, these RDs and RAs minister to the women in their dorm. The RDs are very mature, spiritually strong young women, some single and some married, approximately aged twenty-five to thirty-five. Because of their crucial role of leading, shepherding, planning, dealing with serious emergencies, counseling, speaking up front, and other things, they have a major impact on the women of our campus."

The Master's administration has stepped up to the challenge of ministering to its women students as well. Price teaches three classes for women students, leads a monthly small group of twelve Student Life staff women, and counsels and mentors students one on one. Her department coordinates a weeklong student-and-staff-led orientation program, "WOW" (Week of Welcome), for three hundred-plus new students each fall, including a four-day retreat for the 130-plus members of the orientation staff. They also plan women's chapels and seminars throughout the school year, and facilitate summer overseas ministry opportunities for women students.

At Master's, women students minister to each other both formally and informally through discipleship and mentoring, which the administration greatly encourages. Women lead small groups in the dormitories, serve as assistant or coleaders on all coed summer missions teams, and colead all of the WOW coed groups during orientation week.

Multnomah Bible College and Seminary (Portland, Oregon)

The home of one of the foundational women's ministry programs in the country, Multnomah's campus is shared by both the 601 college students and the 257 seminary students. A mix of married and single, resident and commuter, undergraduate and master-level students makes for a diverse population. Almost half of the undergraduates are women, and the seminary records a 38 percent female presence. The needs of, and opportunities to serve, women at Multnomah are great.

As dean of students and chaplain to women at Multnomah Seminary for the past fourteen years, Carley Wecks wields strong influence over the seminary's ministry to women students. "As a woman in charge of student services, I am able to coordinate social activities, weekly prayer times in the dorm houses, and discipleship groups for the women. I provide individual and marital counseling for the women and couples. Each fall I coordinate, along with another faculty woman, a daylong spiritual formation retreat for the upper division masters women. In the spring, the graduating women coordinate an overnight retreat."

Women participate in both master of arts in pastoral ministry programs, including a specialty in women's ministry, and also in the master of divinity program. At least two of the women in the M.Div. foresee a ministry as hospital chaplains.

The seminary also sponsors a monthly group time for the seminary women designed to provide social and spiritual interaction through the dorm houses, although open to all the women. These times foster opportunities to pray together, encourage one another, and address topics unique to women. The discipleship groups are geared to allow the women to "debrief" regarding classes, chapels, and so on in the context of an all-women group, as well as voice prayer requests and personal struggles. These gatherings also allow them to interact regarding their internship programs. An additional woman faculty member supervises the internships for those in women's ministry, and meets every other week with them individually.

The college and the seminary have a combined Wives Fellowship program organized and run by the wives themselves. Included in the ministry are weekly care groups, a gleaner's program, e-mail prayer chains, retreats, and monthly group meetings. The seminary offers a Spouse Enrichment Program that allows the spouses (mainly wives) to apply a variety of educational experiences toward a certificate that allows them to "walk" with their husbands at graduation.

Wecks reflects on the effectiveness of the school's ministry to its women. "As I watch the women enter and then leave the school, the area of change I see most is their confidence level in the ability of the Lord to use them in ministry. Having other women as role models, having been stretched through student ministry and internship programs, and finding God sufficient in the inevitable struggles of seminary life matures them into women who know God's grace and in gratitude seek to serve Him and know Him better."

Southern Baptist Theological Seminary (Louisville, Kentucky)

Southern launched The Office of Women's Programs in the fall of 2000 when they hired Sharon Beougher as its director. Its purpose is to meet the growing needs of women students and provide women role models.

Shortly after Beougher began her ministry on campus, a group of students approached her asking to start an organization for female students. The group's name is FOCUS, an acrostic for their purposes, which are to:

F oster relationships among women at the seminary in a way that will provide fellowship and support

O rganize discipleship groups among women in order to sharpen each other "as iron sharpens iron"

C oordinate special programs and events to encourage and equip women

U ndergird the administration as they seek to provide a practical program for women in leadership

S eek scriptural guidance regarding women in ministry

Beougher serves as faculty adviser. One of her goals is to provide "professional mentoring" to graduating students. She envisions matching students with professionals in their areas of common interest—a woman with a desire to work in women's ministry with someone who is doing it; a woman who is called to missions to be linked with a missionary; a woman who aspires to teach with a teacher; and so on.

The Office of Women's Programs facilitates accountability groups and programs with special speakers. Southern hired a part-time associate director to assist Beougher as well as an associate director of women's programs for women at affiliated Boyce College. They also have begun a master of arts in Christian education with a focus in women's ministry.

Student wives are also cared for at Southern through the Seminary Wives Institute, a program designed to give ministers' wives biblically based and practically applied teaching. They are taught by seminary faculty as well as faculty wives and guest speakers.

As Southern commenced their formal campus ministry to women, seminary president Dr. Albert Mohler wrote a letter to the campus community, stating, "Women are here by invitation and they are fully welcome. They bring their gifts, wisdom, scholarship, and calling to the Southern Seminary family. We are richer for their presence, and our churches will be richer for their service." Beougher is grateful to minister on a campus that is "very supportive of the women's programs."

Trinity Evangelical Divinity School/Graduate School (Deerfield, Illinois)

The Student Government Association includes a women's student representative who provides a voice to the faculty and administration regarding the concerns facing women students and, with her women's committee, ministers to the women students on campus. Community Life Coordinator Rima Butler serves as a facilitator for these various ministries and works directly with the Residence Life staff and the residents in her living area. "This has taken both formal and informal dimensions," she says. "It seems that a lot of the ministry of encouragement and challenge that is occurring at TEDS takes place on a deeply relational level. I regularly spend time in informal counseling and prayer. However, beyond that there are many opportunities for women to gather and spend time in Bible study and prayer from their own initiative."

In the fall of 2001, the women hosted their first retreat co-sponsored by TEDS/TGS and the EFCA Women's Ministry. In spring 2002 they hosted a one-day women's conference spearheaded out of the Student Development office of Trinity College. "It is our desire," reflects Butler, "that out of these we will continue to grow and develop our women's ministry here on campus and provide training and direction for those women continuing on in women's ministry."

At TEDS, student wives are cared for too. There are significant ministries reaching out to both wives of students and international women sponsored through the Community Life Office but primarily student run. These provide times of study, fellowship, and connection in a transitory time of life.

Wheaton College (Wheaton, Illinois)

Dr. Edee Schulze, dean of student life, oversees women's ministry at Wheaton, an interdenominational Christian liberal arts college where women comprise approximately half the student body. The dean of student life, working through the Student Development Office, provides services that meet the unique needs of these young women, including mentoring and referrals or counseling for eating disorders, depression, difficult family situations, gender roles, and more.

To help them adjust to campus life and grow strong in their faith, Discipleship Small Groups provide opportunities for Bible study, support, prayer, and fellowship. The Residence Hall program facilitates the development of women through floor social activities, relationships, and programs on same-sex floors. Women can participate in worship dance or choral groups as well as various intramural sports.

Dr. Schulze cares deeply for the women students she serves. "It's very rewarding to stand at the crossroads with female students when they have pressing or challenging issues and help them sort out what needs to happen next. I've been privileged to see female students turn from destructive lifestyle patterns to making positive choices, to watch desperate and depressed young women return from an emotional wilderness and gain a stronger sense of themselves and of God, to witness God's work of healing relationships these young women have with family, friends, and men, and to celebrate the successes of life—from getting a date to getting a diploma."

Methods of ministering to women students are as different as the schools they attend. Evaluate the needs of women on your campus and appropriate any ideas we've shared here that will best fit your situation. Be creative. While administrative support and involvement is important, student participation is vital. Implement the Transformation Model and watch the lives of women students change.

PART 4

CONVERTING THE TRANSFORMATION MODEL CROSS-CULTURALLY

Chapter 17

Strategies That Work Worldwide

*M*any churches in my country are led by women who have no training. Will you take a team to train them in the spring?" Celestin's eyes danced as he spoke about his native land, Rwanda, in Central Africa. They darkened as he described the 1994 genocide massacre, when over eight hundred thousand of his people were murdered by warring tribes—among them five family members.

With the deaths of so many men, women step up as pastors rather than leave their churches leaderless. But most are discouraged. The needs are overwhelming. They have few resources—many don't even own a Bible. Celestin informed us that there had never been a women's ministry conference in Rwanda. He wanted to sponsor the first—and he wanted me to lead it!

"I'll pray about it," I responded, butterflies already fluttering inside. *Where is Rwanda? Why does he want me?* I had traveled extensively growing up, but I had no experience on the mission field.

Celestin Musakura's six-foot frame towered over the American women he invited to lunch. His ink-black skin and bright orange

African flowered shirt turned heads as we paraded into Bruno's Italian Restaurant. Although he was completing his doctorate at Dallas Seminary, he organized and often led training in Africa five or six times a year. His ministry, ALARM—African Leadership and Reconciliation Ministry—began training male pastors, but now his passion extends to equipping women leaders and pastors' wives.

Five months after lunch at Bruno's, our team of five, including Celestin's wife Bernadette, hopscotched across three continents en route to Kigali, Rwanda's capital, where we trained eighty-four women leaders from all over the tiny nation.

Can you counsel grieving women or teach the Bible? What have you learned from walking with the Lord that could encourage women in other countries? I never imagined God would call me to Africa, but He did. He might call you too!

Adapt the Transformation Model

Women on every continent want to minister to one another. Women's ministry happens naturally but, just like with the Rwandan women, they hear what's happening in America and they want it too. The Transformation Model is cross-cultural. Of course, it must be adapted in other countries to fit their needs and methods—but the heart of it is transferable. Women everywhere want an intimate relationship with Jesus, to know the Bible, and to connect and serve.

We interviewed experienced women missionaries who shared principles and projects that transform lives in other cultures. Take what you have learned in parts 1 and 2 and adapt it to your own missions setting.

Think Outside the Box!

Since biblical times women have obeyed the Great Commission by planting churches, preaching, healing, and teaching across the world—sometimes alone. Examples include New Testament women Priscilla and Lydia as well as more contemporary models like Amy Carmichael (1867), Mary Slessor (1848), and Lottie Moon (1846). Their noble work continues, but now new doors are opening for women in cross-cultural women's ministries—both short- and long-term.

Do you love women in your church or community but also hear God's call beyond your borders? Is your primary calling at home but you also hear a secondary call to missions? Is it possible to do both? Does a global heart beat within you but circumstances hinder you from living overseas?

Today a missionary doesn't necessarily need to uproot permanently. Missions in a postmodern world looks different! New methods and strategies give women unheard of opportunities to minister cross-culturally. Tools like e-mail, satellite, and the Internet help us connect anywhere in the world in an instant. With faster travel, we can target a group and return intermittently to build and equip them—for the purpose of growing them so that one day they won't need us. Missions has a new face!

I (Sue) dismissed missions—in fact, the idea scared me—but God opened short-term doors that broadened my perspective and enriched my ministry at home. His plan for you may include surprises—short-term projects, living in another land, or maybe even in another part of your city. Does your pulse race as you read these words? If so, God could be calling you to missions! How will you know? Ask God for direction and learn all you can.

Cross-cultural ministry is more than packing your bags and setting out with good intentions. Women who impact others across the globe are savvy. They proceed with a plan. And they network with others.

What would you need to know to oversee a missions ministry in a church? How do women today prepare themselves for high impact, short-term trips? How do you know when God is calling you to uproot for a long-term commitment? In this section, we'll explore key components to cross-cultural ministry.

Determine Your Scope

"For a long time missionaries could go anywhere in the world and do almost anything with the assurance that it would be useful and productive. But we can no longer go anywhere without risking overlap or interference with the legitimate work of others. We are part of *a global missions movement* and we must find our most valuable and productive roles," says missions strategist David Mays.[1]

Kathy Appleton, director of missions at Irving Bible Church, agrees. Every week requests come across her desk for money and support. Mission organizations and individuals clamor for her attention and resources. This deluge drove Kathy to focus her efforts and determine her scope.

"Otherwise our ministry would have been request-driven and at the mercy of where other people wanted us to go," she says. "Now we are strategically driven. We want to go places and do ministry that helps national leaders!"

How can you ensure that your ministry is strategically driven?

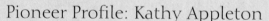

Pioneer Profile: Kathy Appleton

Kathy was fearful—but she confessed her fear and asked God to help her overcome it. He answered by sending her all over the world and putting her in charge of a megachurch's missions ministry with a budget of over $500,000.

"I was a school teacher for ten years, enjoying my home and family. But I knew God was working to overcome the fears I let control me. The Scriptures, Amy Carmichael, and Jim Elliott, even my pastor as he preached, 'Ask God to Throw You In over Your Head'—everywhere I turned, God was saying 'I see your fear as sin and an insult to Christ.'" God enabled her to loosen her grip on comfort and safety.

When IBC asked the congregation to pray about joining a short-term mission team to Veronish, Russia, Kathy was first to sign up. "It was a faith building experience," she says. "It wasn't practical to go. We had small children and money was tight, but God was faithful. I needed $2,500, and it came in to the penny. I was on the way to the mall to buy walking shoes, size 6½, when I stopped by a friend's house. Before I left, she offered me a new pair of shoes that didn't fit her—size 6½ walking shoes! They fit perfectly."

The Russians won her heart. During her first mission trip, God planted the same vision in both Kathy and a Russian deacon—IBC and the Russian church should join together as sister churches. The IBC elders loved the idea, encouraged her to "dream big," gave her the resources, and suggested she lead ongoing trips back.

In 1996, on a Saturday night, Kathy prayed, "Why, Lord, have you put missions on my heart?" Sunday morning, an elder stopped her. "Our mission's budget is now $100,000. We believe it is time to hire a missions coordinator, and the elders are unanimous—we want you!"

Kathy felt totally inadequate, but God has equipped her. In 2001, seventy-two people served on her mission team, sending 150 on short-term trips to India, Africa, Russia, Guatemala, and the Canary Islands. Her ministry supports thirty-six full-time missionaries and organizations.

In her first year as missions director, almost the entire church staff ministered together in their Russian sister church. The day before their departure a woman in the church pulled Kathy aside and whispered, "Do you realize that all our leaders are on that plane? Have you thought about what would happen if it went down?" Years before, she would have shared this woman's fears—

but no more! She is no longer paralyzed by fear, and her church, the world, and God's work benefit as a result. A favorite verse: "There is no fear in love. But perfect love drives out fear" (1 John 4:18).

Create Your Strategy

Whether you belong to a small church, a large church, or a parachurch organization, strategy is critical. Examine these three different examples and apply their experiences to your own setting. (Many of the leaders mentioned in this chapter can be contacted through our Web site, www.newdoors.info.)

A Small Church Strategy: Creekside Bible Fellowship (Weekly Attendance 150)

What about small churches that are doing well even to keep themselves financially afloat each year? Can they participate in world missions? You bet!

Creekside Bible Fellowship found itself asking, "How can we get our church members better involved in missions?" The leadership spent time in prayer, asking for guidance on how to approach missions with purpose, making the most of their resources. Then they mapped out a strategy.

How does a church of any size develop a strategy that fits its character and resources? Creekside's leadership considered issues like:

- What is our *passion?*
- How can we *practically* affect the world for Christ?
- What are *our* resources? What do we have to offer?

The missions budget at CBF now includes monthly support for five missionary families, including its former pastor, who departed in 2000 to plant a new church in Indiana. The other families originated within the church body, leaving to minister around the world: Papau New Guinea, China, and in short-term missions virtually everywhere.

The other primary focus has been to partner with a Mexican church in Nueva Laredo, just across the Texas/Mexico border at Laredo, Texas. Lance Ward, CBF's pastor, said, "We were looking for an established church that we could help—help them spread the gospel, with training, resources, supplies, building—and let *them* be the church in their culture. We did not want to plant a new church, but come alongside one that could use our help and encouragement."

Why Nueva Laredo? "It's close," explained Lance. "Visits to Iglesia Bautista Kerigma are pretty affordable for those who want to be involved." The first such visit took place in March 2001, when twelve Creeksiders drove 450 miles in two vans for a week's stay. Each paid under $400, covering the cost of transportation, lodging, and food. They thought they were going to share the gospel door to door, but when they arrived it was apparent that there were other priorities. They adapted to the need of the moment, remembering that they were there for the nationals, not to fulfill their own agenda.

The week's events included a kids' night program for the many children in the neighborhood, a marriage and infertility conference, a showing of the *Jesus* film, visits to a prison and an orphanage, and painting the church. Little outright evangelism was accomplished, but the nationals felt loved. That feeling was intensified when the pastor realized CBF's intention was to partner with them—not just visit once.

"We want to keep him encouraged, share our resources with him—books, sound equipment, immediate financial needs we may be able to help meet—anything to keep him from burning out," reflects Lance. "Chuy (the Mexican pastor) is doing his job virtually alone, for almost no pay. He needs our encouragement."

So, yes, a small church can have a great impact on world missions. Focus your energies, be realistic but not afraid to dream, pray for God's leading.

A Large Church Strategy: Irving Bible Church (Weekly Attendance 2,500)

In creating their strategy for missions, Kathy and her team asked questions like:

- How has God gifted *us?*
- Where is *our* heart?
- Where are *we* most experienced and qualified?
- Where are *we* already connected?

After prayer and lengthy discussion, her missions team created a strategy focus limiting their work to three areas.

First, they determined they would minister within the 10/40 window, an area of the world situated between the tenth and fortieth latitudinal parallels. This area includes the Middle East, India, and much of Southeast Asia, countries that historically have been hostile or resistant to Christianity. These parameters provided basic geographic borders. Within those parallels they narrowed the focus even more and adopted an unreached people group— the Kutchi. Approximately 1.5 million live in Gujurat, a state of India. They will work with this group in a long-term relationship, investing extensive resources in the Kutchi's physical and spiritual welfare.

Second, they decided to partner with nationals they knew and trusted. Leaders from Africa, Europe, Romania, and Cuba were already working with them and had connections in their homelands. Working alongside these leaders was smart for reasons we'll explore later.

Finally, the team chose to target children at risk—especially orphans and street children. This emphasis fit with work they were already doing in Russia and Romania.

The results of their strategies?

- The *Jesus* film has been produced in the Kutchi language.
- Trans World Radio is broadcasting the gospel message throughout the state of Gujurat.
- Relief and shelter was given to the victims of the January 26, 2001, earthquake.
- Nearly six hundred people from the church have participated in a short-term mission trip.
- One thousand orphans in the Penza region of Russia have heard the message of Christ and have received humanitarian aid.
- Partnerships have been developed to equip leaders in Russia, Romania, Africa, and Cuba.

Scope and strategy make the difference!

A Parachurch Strategy for Russia

At least 80 percent of Russian church members are female. Yet training for women's ministry was almost nonexistent. However, in 1992, three women spread a map of their native Russia across a table, stretched their arms over it, and prayed. Teardrops spotted the vast expanse. Their request? Lord, send us training so we can minister to women in our churches!

Was their request too big for God? No, but the answer was almost a decade in the making. A national women's ministry training project, "Christian Women in Partnership—Russia," was birthed in 1999. God networked key Russian and American leaders and a variety of parachurch mission organizations to fashion an in-depth, long-term training program for gifted Russian women leaders. The goal is to reach and transform thousands of Russian women all over Russia's eleven time zones. It's happening! How did God orchestrate this amazing story?

God crafted a beautiful mosaic etched at different times in different places all over the world to answer their prayer. "We felt like we were skiing behind a 747," says Gail Seidel, a key American player.

Puzzle Piece #1: God Prepared the Curriculum

At the same time the three Russian women prayed, American missionary Wendy Wilson was developing a seven-course curriculum for women in Eastern Europe. She works with Biblical Education by Extension International (BEE). The courses were translated into Romanian, Bulgarian, Czech, Hungarian, and Polish. They also decided to translate the courses into Russian even though there was no existing place to use the material.

Puzzle Piece #2: God Prepared Three Women in the East

Valentina

In 1992, Valentina Karchazhkina, a former Communist Party leader and proponent of Marxist philosophy, heard John Maisel speak at Moscow State University. John is the president of East-West Ministries International (EWMI). Valentina gave her life to Christ and grew quickly in her faith. A former linguistics professor and fluent in English, she was hired in EWMI's Moscow office to minister to women.

Vera

In 1998, Vera Kadaeva heard John speak at a Russian women's conference. The daughter of a Baptist pastor, Vera was persecuted for her faith even before she became a Christian and, after accepting the Lord during her college years, spent time in a mental hospital as the government tried to reindoctrinate her to atheistic communism.

Liz

American Liz Loeffler has served as a missionary for Greater Europe Missions (GEM) since 1993 and began ministering in Moscow a year later. She was on loan to BEE in their Women's Ministries Department and then in 1998 to EWMI, where she assisted Valentina. The two Russians, Valentina and Vera, and American Liz shared a vision to train Russian women and began meeting in Moscow to consider the possibilities.

Puzzle Piece #3: God Prepared Women in the West

In 1998 in Dallas, John Maisel initiated a meeting with Gail Seidel, a missionary on furlough with BEE, and Gwynne Johnson, a BEE board member. John expressed his desire to see a nationwide women's ministry training program birthed. Within an hour, all three agreed to invite their Russian colleagues to a strategy meeting in Dallas to explore what God might do as they pooled their resources. However, the meeting was delayed due to scheduling problems.

Puzzle Piece #4: God Prepared an Indispensable Russian Man

During this delay, God enlisted another key player. Peter Konovaltchik was the head of the Union of Evangelical Christians-Baptists of Russia (UECB). This umbrella organization includes the majority of evangelical churches in Russia, and Peter wielded tremendous influence over them. As he saw the vast need for women's ministry, he blessed the idea of a national women's ministry training program. He was instrumental in promoting the ministry within individual churches throughout Russia. Without his endorsement, the vision that God was working out in John and these key women in both the East and the West might never have materialized.

Puzzle Piece #5: God Prepared Additional Women

In January 1999 Russian and American women met for two days at a Dallas home to hammer out a comprehensive strategy. Valentina, Vera, Liz, Wendy, Gail, and Gwynne were there along with others who would later serve as faculty, on a Dallas board, or on a national board of reference.

Simultaneously on the other side of the world, God was preparing the hearts of twenty-one Russian women leaders throughout the eleven time zones to respond to an invitation to participate in that strategy. Their decision would not only transform their lives but those of thousands of their sisters.

Here is the strategy:

- Five regions were identified across Russia.
- Three Russian women leaders were selected from each region by the Russian Baptist superintendents. (Several others were later invited, making the number of students twenty-one.)
- Twenty-one students travel to Moscow three times a year for training in the seven-course curriculum. (The courses are: Discovery Bible Study and teacher training, a women's ministry "how to" class, Spiritual Life, Evangelism and Discipleship, Marriage, Family, and "Developing a Discerning Heart" counselor training.)
- The instruction lasts for six years. Students make a long-term commitment to intensive training.
- Classes are taught by a Western faculty. The students read books and complete weighty assignments between classes.
- In groups of three, the students establish regional women's ministry training centers. The first centers opened in the spring of 2001. Centers are up and running in seven locations stretching from Moscow in the west to the island of

Sakhalin off Russia's eastern shore. They are teaching women the same curriculum they learned in Moscow.

- The goal is to birth additional local training centers and ultimately smaller training centers in individual churches. This strategy will potentially equip over 2,300 Russian women leaders.

Imagine the impact on Russia if even a portion of the dream is realized.

Here's What the Training Means to Russian Students

I've waited twenty-one years for training like this.

You have taught us how to smile.

I had no idea that I'd ever teach the Bible. God made me adequate for that.

I hope my students will love me as much as we love you.

Here's What the Training Means to American Faculty

I never imagined that I would be traveling to Moscow on a regular basis to be part of a teaching team for a project of this size. What a privilege it has been to connect with women from a different country. We speak different languages, face different challenges, live in completely different worlds, and yet, we love the same Lord, have the same dreams for our families, share many struggles, and have grown to love one another.

—Mary Dean, IBC
Director of Women's Ministries

When we first met the Russian women, they lacked confidence. Our training and personal interaction with them has helped them to grow in their understanding and abilities to equip their Russian sisters. They are now enthusiastically spreading the love and hope of Jesus Christ across their vast country. And their faith in God and commitment to women's ministry training has been an inspiration to me personally.

—Joye Baker
Research and Teaching Assistant
DTS Christian Education Department

Pioneer Profile: Wendy Wilson

"I feel like I'm riding a wave—and it's been a wild ride!" says Wendy. For eighteen years Wendy has trained women leaders in Romania, Bulgaria, Hungary, the Czech Republic, and Russia. After many years of patience, perseverance, and careful interaction with church leadership, now she is seeing the women she has trained begin to train others. Listen to Romanian Lidia Schiopu, one of Wendy's first students:

Dear Wendy,

This month I traveled to the Romanian city Zulau where the pastor of Pent church invited me to encourage women there to start a group. So we had a meeting and more than 100 women came. And afterward, I met with 12 women who decided to start to study. I met there a woman who knows you; she attended your courses in Debrecen some years ago. We had a very good time! You know where the pastors are interested. It's great!

Also, Dalia is traveling to Zalau every month. Angela travels to Hateg, Livia to Moldova Noua. Maricica has groups in many places. Camelia goes to Dej to help there. Ani has a group in Cimpia Turzii. You know Ani was so timid (like me—ha!) but now she is going to other places. And these are just a few! We cannot control how quickly the work is developing now. Sometimes, I say "wait" but there is such enthusiasm!

My dear, I would tell you so many things. I would share my soul, my feelings, my joys and sorrows, my deceptions and victories. But I cannot communicate all this things in English very well. Anyway, I praise God for your impact in my life, for your wise advice and for your patience. So many times I remember all these things and I try to do the same with others. One day we will see and understand more and maybe we'll be so overwhelmed how God worked in us and through us.

Much love,
Lidia

Seventeen years ago, Wendy began her work with BEE by training Romanian women. Now there's an army of trained Romanian women building into the lives of their sisters all over the nation. How did it happen?

"In the early 1980s when the communists were in power, BEE sent me out to encourage pastors' wives, but soon it was clear that the real need was to develop women to shepherd their own," says Wendy. She began with nine groups of eight women meeting in homes in different cities.

Every three months for six years, Wendy spent two days in each city. The first day she taught the group courses on how to study the Bible, mentor other women, spiritual life, and evangelism and discipleship. The second day she visited one student in her home.

"For real impact, ministry must be done in the context of relationship building," insists Wendy.

As Wendy's training spread to other countries, she developed a curriculum that was transferable—effective in any culture and easily reproduced by her students. "When the nationals were trained in Eastern Europe, I thought I'd be out of a job—but women's ministries is blowing open all over the world—and God is taking the model to other places."

Today Wendy oversees teams of American and national trainers as the resource person, troubleshooter, and curriculum adviser. She worked almost ten years hammering out her women's leadership training curriculum, but she is willing to share it with others. To contact Wendy, see our Web site, www.newdoors.info. "It works anywhere," said Wendy. "The facilitator is the one who makes it relevant in each particular culture."

Wendy travels often, choosing to invest her life in God's women all over the world. "I've worked hard," she admits, "but obviously this work is on God's heart. I've been available and others have been faithful partners. What a privilege!"

Why Is This Strategy Working?

Notice that these ministries were not territorial. They combine vision and resources and don't care who gets the credit! Also, the Americans and Russians share leadership. Both have overcome language and cultural barriers to work together toward a common dream. Americans have been willing to be led by Russian women with less training and fewer resources because the Russian women better understand what works in their own country. Strong leaders humble themselves and submit to others' ideas for the greater good.

As a result God answered the tearful prayers of three Russian women who prayed over a map! How? He sculpted the lives of called men and women. He placed them in crucial places at particular times. He orchestrated their days so that they crossed paths and came together to carry out His plans. They are ordinary people just like you and me who were willing to listen to God and follow Him. God can use you to impact your world for Jesus too!

But can it happen without a strategy? Not a chance! Now Celestin's African ministry is considering a similar strategy tweaked for Africa. The land is purchased in Nairobi, Kenya, for the training center. What's God going to do in the lives of African women? With a strategy and a God who uses ordinary people, there are no limits!

What Are the Advantages of a Strategy?

By using a bullet rather than buckshot approach, you are a good steward of the money and people God entrusts to you. A hit-or-miss plan is difficult to evaluate, but with a narrow focus, evaluation is easier—and so is impact! When you determine your scope and even publicize your strategy, you can say yes or no to the plethora of requests. When you decline, you are able to explain, "It isn't that what you want to do is wrong and what we want to do is right. It is just that we all have limited resources and this is where we believe God wants us to invest our efforts." You deny requests without guilt, knowing that God will provide for their needs in other ways.

You research the target areas—you don't have to be an expert on every place in the world. But you become an expert on some.

You can connect multiple short-term trips into long-term projects. Creekside employs this strategy in partnering with Iglesia Bautista Kerigma. If the goal is training leaders, train them in stages. If evangelism, follow up when another team returns. If discipleship, a return trip provides accountability. Whatever the ministry, a return trip increases productivity. With a strategy you are assured of a visible, significant impact!

People on your teams invest in long-term relationships. On the first few trips you earn trust and credibility. Follow-up trips are more productive when solid relationships between the team and nationals already exist.

Put in the time up front to plan and prepare carefully. Depend on God every step. Don't be afraid of big plans because He is a big God! Remember: it won't happen without strategic planning, prayer, and a limited scope.

Involve Your Church Leaders

When Creekside planned its trip to Nuevo Laredo, the pastor didn't feel obligated to go—he was on fire to go! This personal journey by twelve members of CBF gave them firsthand experience and a renewed heart for spreading the gospel. The project galvanized our elders and staff. Their wholehearted support, seen through their participation and publicity from the pulpit, encouraged our members to move forward with the plan.

At IBC, pastoral staff are encouraged to join or lead a missions team once a year and a sizable amount is set aside in the church budget for that purpose. When they return, they will naturally build a global perspective into their ministries at home. If you want a church that loves the world, supports missions, and wants to participate, that's a surefire way. If your church can't afford staff-funded trips, encourage the staff to send letters to friends and family for support. If God wants them to go, He will provide.

Chapter 18

PARTNER WITH NATIONALS

Did you observe that in Russia and Rwanda we were invited by nationals? Our seminaries, colleges, and companies are full of men and women from other countries. Seek them out and learn from them. God may connect you with a Christian national who wants to minister back home and needs your resources. If you work together, you both will benefit and so will the kingdom of God!

Nurture the Relationship

What Are the Advantages of Working with Nationals?

Cultural

Your friend has connections that will take you years to develop. She knows the language and is already accepted and trusted by her peers. She is culturally adjusted and understands the political climate.

Financial

It's more cost-effective. What does it cost to support a national's ministry in a developing country? About $50 to $100 a month!

Most nationals will work in ministry an average of twenty-two years. You have invested between $132,000 and $264,000 for twenty-two years' work!

What does it cost to support an American overseas? On the average, $4,500 a month. That's $648,000—but that's just the total for twelve years, the average length of an American missionary's career. Two of those years are spent raising support and two years on furlough. That leaves eight years for ministry, including language training.[1]

You do the numbers! Even if we invest $30,000 to put a national through seminary, we're still light years ahead. Even better than bankrolling nationals at an American seminary, send them to seminary in their own country. The cost is less and they are more likely to go home—those who study here often don't.

The World Is Smaller

World conditions are conducive to partnering with nationals. We live in a communications/information-based world—we faxed our outlines to Rwanda for translation before we left! Ease of travel makes it practical. You can fly anywhere in the world in twenty-four hours.

Access

Nationals can go where we cannot go. There are sixty-six nations and states that significantly restrict missionaries. National leaders are accepted in ways we will never be accepted. In addition, they continue to serve God long after Americans go home.[2]

They Need Our Resources

They know their own people's needs and they know how to reach them. But in two-thirds of the world, they need Western money and technology. When we traveled to Rwanda, not only did we pay our own passage, but we raised $10,000 to bring the

Rwandan women leaders to the capital city. They didn't have enough to feed their children. Certainly they could not afford to travel to the capital. But women in our church sponsored women with small donations of $10 and $15 dollars, and soon we raised the money to bring them all.

In 2001 IBC underwrote a portion of the operating costs for an African ministry for $36,000. This covered the payroll for a portion of their staff and included a new hire to work with children and orphans. This ministry trains thousands of men and women every year. Can you think of a better investment?

"Of all children born today, 80 percent live in developing countries in Asia, Africa, Latin America and some parts of Europe, where extreme poverty is prevalent."[3] In these countries, two million pastors minister—but in Africa, for example, 86 percent have no formal training or resources; many are without Bibles.[4] I remember the faces of the Rwandan women as we handed out Bibles in their own language. Afterward they danced and sang with glee.

It's Just Plain Practical!

Partnering with nationals is productive. You jump start your vision and accomplish far more long-term. Does this mean there is no longer a need for American missionaries to live overseas? Of course not. But the number needed is far fewer today. And we need to send them into places to do the tasks that nationals don't have the resources to do. On the Russia project, Liz Loeffler lives in Moscow, returning to Dallas when necessary. She is vital to planning and communication between the team members here and there. Melody Wilson, a law school graduate turned missionary, bases herself in Moscow but travels to visit and undergird the women's ministry regional training centers throughout Russia. Her skills and support are indispensable.

Partner with National Churches

"What's amazing is watching the nationals do missions themselves," says Lyndsay Murray, a nineteen-year-old who spent a year as a foreign exchange student in Moscow. She also invested time in her church's sister church in Penza, Russia—and now the Penza Russians have birthed missions in Murmansk, a region of 1,117,000 people below the Arctic Circle. Lyndsay's church and the nationals send combined teams to Murmansk—a truly cross-cultural experience for all involved and a great witness to the people there that Christ can break down any walls that separate us!

Patrick Johnstone writes in *The Church Is Bigger Than You Think*, "What is advocated is a partnership in servanthood each to the other so that the Church becomes what God always intended—a perfect Bride for His Son to co-reign with Him through all eternity. We have fallen far short of that ideal, therefore every effort must be made to repair broken bridges of understanding and fellowship and establish practical working relationships at every level so that we, the Church, might be one in love, the power of the Holy Spirit and vision for a lost world."[5] What better way than to partner in missions with national churches!

CAM International has invested over 110 years in Central America. Now they support Latin American nationals as missionaries to the Middle East. In places where Americans cannot go due to political prejudice, these Latin Americans are accepted and more productive.

Missions today is in a time of transition. Americans partner with nationals to provide resources—people and money—and the people serve short- or long-term, depending on the needs. We must always ask "Where?" and "Why?" before moving ahead. Accountability and impact are evaluated constantly to make good use of the gifts God has given. As the planet grows smaller, we can reach more of it for Christ—if we use new methods and mind-sets.

Pioneer Profile: Marion Pattillo

"We had sixty requests for housing rehab in our adopted neighborhood, but I couldn't shake a sense of urgency about the house covered in black plastic that was home to three ladies," says Marion, executive director of Metro-Link, an inner-city ministry in South Dallas. The owner, Pleasant Rochelle, was ninety-two and bedridden with Alzheimer's. Her fifty-six-year-old daughter, Catherine, was caregiver to both her mom and her own thirty-one-year-old daughter Sharon, who smiled and clapped but couldn't talk. They had been on a rehab program list to replace their roof for five years. Part of the ceiling had already fallen on the dresser across from Pleasant's hospital bed, although the black plastic kept the rain from soaking her.

Marion's husband heard the concern in her voice and responded, "Even if we have to hock something to pay for the roofing materials, we will get the job done." But in forty-eight hours the money came in, as well as a crew to replace the roof that would keep the three ladies dry for Christmas.

First, they moved Pleasant out of her hospital bed into a wheelchair and rolled her into the living room. Five minutes later a tree limb crashed onto the old roof sending the roof, ceiling, insulation and attic contents plummeting into the bedroom where Pleasant had been lying only moments earlier. As they constructed the new roof, they found the walls so rotten there was nothing to attach the roof to. "The Lord held the room together with the wings of angels and the prayers of His saints," proclaims Marion. She often sees God's work in zip code 75215, the neighborhood Metro-Link has adopted.

She oversees the daily business of this multifaceted ministry—community development, housing, education, health, discipleship,

Bible studies, and family services—but God has been preparing Marion for this role all her life.

Marion grew up in a preacher's home in Corpus Christi. As a teen she helped Hispanics speak and read a new language. In her studies at Baylor University, she majored in literacy journalism, where she learned to teach and write materials for adults with limited education. After graduation she taught at Baylor and then headed the Literacy Journalism Department. Under her direction, four Waco community centers opened literacy workshops staffed by volunteers whom Marion trained.

After Baylor, she taught men and women job skills. Later, she worked as assistant administrator at John Peter Smith Hospital for indigents in Fort Worth, Texas.

In 1985 when she married Nick, they decided to leave big city life and moved to a lakeside community in Waxahachie. Soon they learned their sleepy little community was actually third in crime per capita in the state. Again God called her to minister to the poor and hopeless. The police chief and chamber of commerce appointed her to head up a crime prevention committee. Under her leadership, crime dropped 54 percent, ninety-eight new homes were constructed, a $2.5 million Salvation Army Boys and Girls Club was built for at-risk youth, sixty crack houses were bulldozed, and a hundred new jobs were brought to the area. In addition twelve churches worked together to repair twenty-five homes.

In the summer of 2000, Marion was enlisted to lead Metro-Link, a new ministry that links God's people and resources to serve inner-city neighborhoods in need.

"We find practical ways to demonstrate God's love to our neighbors through small acts of kindness," says Marion. Volunteers have adopted 220 homes in South Dallas, an area with high poverty, crime, and unemployment. Every week dozens of volunteers visit homes to pray and keep track of their needs. They paint and maintain homes. They mow yards and plant flowers. They deliver food and clothing to homes, read to children, and help with job placement, rent/utility assistance, health care, legal assistance, and GED training.

"It's being faithful in the little things," testifies Marion, and over and over neighbors have trusted Christ as a result. Is God leading you to minister to your neighbors across town? How can you prepare? Find an inner-city ministry and volunteer. Talk to experienced women like Marion Pattillo. There is probably a mission field in your backyard.

Minister Their Way!

When I (Sue) was a child, we lived in Rhodes, a Greek island in the Aegean Sea. My father was a Coast Guard officer. One weekend as we drove through the tiny villages, my mother pointed out mammoth masses of metal rusting in the fields. "American missionaries brought tractors to help farmers," she explained, "but left them behind when the peasant farmers refused to adopt American farming methods. Now they sit rusting in the fields, without parts, as a reminder of American arrogance."

Dancing with Elephants!

Our best intentions can do damage! Listen to a story Africans tell about Americans:

> Elephant and Mouse were best friends. One day Elephant said, "Mouse, let's have a party!" Animals gathered from far and near.
>
> They ate. They drank. And nobody celebrated more and danced harder than Elephant. After the party was over,

Elephant exclaimed, "Mouse, did you ever go to a better party? What a blast!" But Mouse did not answer.

"Mouse, where are you?" Elephant called. He looked around for his friend, and then shrank back in horror. There at Elephant's feet lay Mouse. His little body was ground into the dirt. He had been smashed by the big feet of his exuberant friend, Elephant.

"Sometimes that is what it is like to do missions with you Americans," the African storyteller commented. "It is like dancing with an elephant."[6]

In our enthusiasm, we Americans often arrive as "fixers" and "rescuers." We bring our technology and money, assuming nationals will submit to our methods and ideas as a result. When we encounter resistance, we are wounded and return home feeling like unappreciated parents. Often we never understand that we have disrespected a culture. In our hurry to achieve our goals, we forget to honor timetables, learn courtesy from another perspective, and develop relationships. We never mean to hurt anyone but, in our excitement, we can do more harm than good.

Do no harm—better yet, do great good! How do we dance with Mouse without harming him? How do we empower Mouse so that he directs the dance?

Examine Your Motives

Short-term missions is not a way to get other people to pay for your summer vacation. Long-term missions is not a way to escape problems at home. We don't go because we need to appreciate our blessings. We don't go to expose our youth to suffering. We don't go to expand our minds or to embrace a global perspective.

We don't send church members so they will give more to our missions projects or because they need a bonding experience. These are by-products of the experience, benefits for us, but they will never empower or sustain us in the midst of the work.

It's not about us—it's about them—and even more, about God! "Watch your motives," warns Kathy Appleton. "Even the motive of loving others is the wrong motive. The real fuel is a love for Christ and a passion to see Him glorified." When you are knee deep in mud, throwing up in a dirty bucket, or reworking your lesson for the third time, that's the motivation that keeps you going.

Select Your Team Carefully

Who should minister cross-culturally? Who should lead your team?

Missions is not for sissies. If your idea of roughing it is slow room service, you're not ready. Ministering in another culture requires maturity, humility, and flexibility. The latter quality is so important, we'll devote an entire section to it.

On the other hand, missions is a great place to learn to live Philippians 2:3, "Do nothing out of selfish ambition or vain conceit, but in humility consider others better than yourselves." Your team leaders need to be seasoned, your new recruits teachable.

Walking into another culture with a project is far different than attempting the same ministry in your own territory. People there don't think like you, talk like you, or work like you. They may not like you because they've been exposed to obnoxious Americans. Before they will hear you or trust you, they insist you respect their culture and have their best interests at heart.

Much up-front work must be done before you begin the actual project. A team member with an attitude that says, "You'd better accept me the way I am" will sabotage your efforts.

A Russian Experience

Mary Bodien serves on the IBC Women's Ministry staff as arts coordinator. On a mission trip to Penza, Russia, she learned how difficult it can be to adjust to another culture. Exhausted from the transcontinental flight, the team was driven from the plane to the Russian church, where the pastor explained the rules for ladies. They learned that only immodest women crossed their legs. "I couldn't concentrate on anything else in the service," confessed Mary, "I was so concerned I would cross my legs unconsciously." Select a team who can adjust to these kinds of demands with a positive attitude and a sense of humor.

An African Experience

Our flight to Rwanda took forty hours, and our bags were lost. They contained all our conference supplies as well as our personal effects. We had no clothes, toothpaste, deodorant, curling irons, medicine, or supplemental food—only those things in our carry-ons.

We disembarked the plane and were whisked to the conference center—an open building with a cement floor. I (Sue) collapsed on a cot in our quarters with a full-blown migraine. The women had been waiting for us for two days, so Jackie and Alice left to teach the first session. I slept hard—my first rest in three days. I awoke suddenly, my migraine waning, to two discouraged women.

Exhausted and with no time to prepare, Alice had done her best. But children cried, women fidgeted, and about halfway through, a quarter of them stood up and walked out. Alice and Jackie had no idea why. They returned, looking to me for direction.

We prayed for God to help us understand and be overcomers. Then we processed what was happening. As I listened, suddenly I understood. Hundreds of women back home were praying for us. With all this prayer, these hindrances had to be part of God's plan! We discussed ways God might be allowing these struggles to promote His purposes. We learned that many of our students had traveled as long as we had, walking or riding a bus. They were exhausted too. We realized that our stylish clothes sitting in an airport in Belgium might be a hindrance to the women we were teaching. They had one change of clothes and so did we.

The hygiene in Africa makes close contact harder for Americans, but without deodorant, we realized it wouldn't be a hindrance much longer. All that had happened over the past three days would help us bond and understand the Rwandan women! We prayed again.

The next morning we learned that our students were from varied denominations and two tribes that had massacred each other. They gathered in groups by tribes, refusing to interact with those who had murdered their loved ones. Our first message that morning was on forgiveness, and we mixed them in small groups for discussion. Walls began to fall that morning—and by the last day the women were dancing and singing together.

We also learned that many of the women rode three hours each way on the bus every day to attend. And the bus left at 4:00—about midway into Alice's message the afternoon before.

We had turned to the Lord in our crisis and He answered. Find team members who have enough experience with the Lord to know what to do in a crisis. Find team members who have learned to depend completely on the Lord. Find humble servants who know that *only* by abiding in Christ can they accomplish anything. Cross-cultural ministry means that you are out of control! Usually that is when the adventure begins.

Prepare Thoroughly

How do you get ready? Learn about the culture. Find out whom you are serving. Talk to nationals visiting America first. Meet and pray as a team as you strategize and plan together. Enlist others to pray for you.

IBC's missions director binds a "prayer passport" booklet to hand out to the whole church. It contains pictures, goals, and prayer requests of everyone going on a mission trip for that season.

When I (Sue) joined the Russian faculty, we prepared by reading *Introduction to the Russian Soul*. We gathered monthly and then weekly before we left. We shopped for long skirts and scarves to cover our heads to teach. I left my diamond wedding ring at home and purchased a tiny gold band at a discount store. Makeup was limited to soft colors and nail polish stayed at home. Small jewelry was permissible but nothing flashy. All these adornments were obstacles to the Russian women, and we wanted to connect quickly. It was simply a matter of respect.

Flex, Flex, Flex

Missions is messy. Toss the mental picture you have created because it won't go as planned. Unexpected situations will probably arise and you will need to adapt quickly and with a smile. Your preplanned schedule often won't work. In Rwanda, we worked late into the evening altering our lessons. Some students had college degrees, while others could not read and had never attended a class of any kind. We needed to adjust our material accordingly. In fact we only taught about half of what we prepared.

Expect the unexpected. Unusual living conditions. Strange food. A new language. Unreliable transportation. Different customs and dress. Worship styles and ceremony unlike anything you've experienced. The lights may go out. The toilets may not flush—if you have any. And you may be misunderstood. But if you bring a flexible attitude and a sense of humor, these inconveniences will simply be part of the experience—little things really when you consider the God you represent and the good He can do through you.

Ziplocs Come in Handy!

"Wake up! Wake up, Peggy! We must start for the airport now. It is 5 A.M. but a blizzard is raging and there is two feet of snow over the streets. We cannot get the car to the door of the apartment, so you will have to walk about four blocks to the wider street where the car can pick you up." Pavel's voice over the telephone was concerned but determined.

She knew he would get her to the Kiev airport for her flight home if anyone could. But with the blizzard it would take at least eight hours. Peggy Hanley had been in Ukraine for three weeks teaching women about "contentment." She would teach two days and then travel to the next class. Now she was tired and ready to go home, although her mind played back to last night's hugs and singing. Even though she was freezing as she walked the long four blocks, she felt an inner warmth that comes from a job well done.

Pavel and his friend were waiting in his 1962 black Ford that sat growling on the street.

The two jovial Ukrainians leaped out to embrace her with a kiss on each cheek and a hearty greeting.

"Sorry you had to walk. Car is cold and keep on dying. We must hurry now to make it to airplane."

They threw her luggage into the trunk as Peggy crawled into the backseat by herself.

Her skirt was soaking wet and she was thoroughly chilled. But soon the old heater kicked in and she could feel her feet. It was Sunday, and in Ukraine snowplows don't work on Sunday. So they followed the faint tracks of cars in front of them, sliding and praying.

Peggy battled motion sickness and in her travels took medicine for it every day. She had taken her usual dose, but with all the sliding she became violently nauseated. She popped another pill and then took something for the stomach upset caused by the first two pills for motion sickness. She settled in for the long trip.

Two hours later she felt that sensation when you know it won't be long until you need to stop. In Ukraine, there are no nice "Exxon" gas stations with a lovely sit down toilet. Occasionally along the highway there is an outhouse near a bus stop—but the nice green forest is usually more desirable.

Peggy verbalized her need to Pavel.

"I must stop. Can you find a place?"

Out into two feet of snow she waded again and returned with a very wet skirt.

As she trudged back up to the road, she realized that the car had died and Pavel was desperately trying to get it started again—with no success! Cars in Ukraine were often unreliable.

Peggy prayed, "Lord, make me content with whatever You have planned for today. Here in the forest for the day, in a strange farmhouse for the night, whatever."

Finally the car turned over and chugged.

"This car very bad when we stop. We cannot stop again," Pavel repeated over and over as they continued down the slippery road. Peggy knew they risked missing her plane or worse if they stopped again.

Four hours. That sensation returned again. Suddenly it dawned on her why. All three pills she had taken were diuretics! Oh, no!

Five hours and she was uncomfortable. Five and a half. She shifted her weight from side to side. She crossed her legs. She twiddled her fingers. *I'm going to have an accident. I've got to think of something!*

Seasoned travelers always pack ziploc bags. They come in handy to carry clothes, medicine, makeup, whatever—and she had several ziploc bags in her carry-on that sat by her feet. Quietly she unzipped the case and emptied the baggie. Fortunately she was wearing a skirt.

A moment later she rolled down the window—"for some fresh air"—and tossed the bag onto the shoulder of the road. Below-zero temperatures would soon freeze it. She chuckled as she pictured whoever found it in the spring.

Seven hours—and because of the diuretics, she used another baggie and tossed it out before they hit the city limits of Kiev. Two puzzled Ukrainians in the spring! No disrespect intended—there are times when a creative alternative is required, and this was one of them!

Peggy says, "The two guys who took me to the airport still tell this *war story* as the worst blizzard they have ever traveled in. I tell it differently. Amazingly, I did have the peace of contentment, the lesson I came to teach—not because I could do that—but because God gave it to me when I asked for it."

Bomb Scares and Bad Plumbing

When I (Sue) was in Moscow, teaching for the Russia project, we had a bomb scare. Police came to escort us out of the rooms. Actually there was no bomb. A government election was planned in our room the next day, and they wanted us out so their German shepherds could sniff for bombs. But we didn't know that.

During another training session, the women stayed in a different hotel to save money. However, the heat and hot water didn't work and the showers barely trickled. But who wanted a shower with cold water and no heat anyway? The American team "sucked it up" and finished their mission without complaining (much). They tasted what Russian women face every day and returned home with greater compassion for their sisters and an enhanced appreciation of heat, hot water, and showers.

What would you have done in Peggy's or Sue's situation? Can you face these kinds of challenges with an attitude of adventure and a sense of humor? Remember: flexibility is not optional in cross-cultural ministry. Flex, flex, flex.

Give Your Host Wings

Conflict erupted during our Moscow trip. Each training session we provided our twenty-one students with a textbook—usually an American best-seller translated into Russian. The students wanted to copy the books and give them out to women in their churches. As they taught others, these books would be helpful. But copyright laws came into question.

In addition, Liz, the American anchor living in Moscow, objected. She wanted the women to learn to write their own material. Several of us felt her response was unrealistic and harsh. Why should they write their own books when we had already written them? I see now that she was right.

Don't give a man a fish—teach a man to fish! It's an old saying, but a good one for cross-cultural ministry. How do you prepare your host to go on without you? How do you empower her so that she picks up the baton? That's the long-term goal.

Wear her ministry shoes. What resources are available after you leave? Use them. Will she be using faxes, e-mail, the Internet, or a word processor? If not, don't use them either. Use her tools. What's her budget? Work within those parameters.

God gifts His children all over the world. Identify and equip women who can create needed curriculum and materials. One day your church may not send teams there. Or one day the borders may close to Americans. Begin now to prepare your host to stand on her own.

As you can see, we don't sugarcoat missions. It is challenging, but it is also rewarding if you go for God's glory and prepare yourself well. Doors to women's ministry are opening across the globe beckoning to everyday women like you and me. The Transformation Model is adaptable in any culture. If God is moving you toward the mission field, take these principles and get going!

How Do I Prepare Myself for Full-Time Missions?

Do you believe God wants you to minister cross-culturally as your life work? If so, you can choose from a variety of options. What do you want to do? Do you want to serve overseas? Are you ready to launch? If so, here's a suggested method to discern God's call and prepare.

Begin at Home!

Why go thousands of miles when another culture lives in your city? Immigrants from all over the world live in pockets of most major cities, transforming that area into a piece of their country. There you will find people who speak another language, order their lives by different customs, and often live in poverty.

Why not taste cross-cultural ministry there first? You may find your calling in the inner city. Certainly you will learn more about yourself.

> A journey of ten thousand miles may begin on a local bus. This is not glamorous. We may prefer *Afganistanitis,* that is, serving exotic people in exotic places. How much more exciting (and how much more under our control) that overseas trip may be than befriending Mexicans across town. After all, who knows but what they might show up on our doorstep for an exchange visit!
>
> Yet when these local Mexicans or Afghans or Vietnamese commend us to their families in their distant homelands, we will be welcomed there for long-term mission rooted in relationships.
>
> In any case, what benefits us, or our grandchildren, is not the top priority. Mission is not therapy. Christ did not come primarily to enhance his own experience. He came to serve, and he started with what was near at hand.[7]

I (Sue) cut my teeth on inner-city ministry years before I ministered overseas. My husband and I traveled regularly to South Dallas to *Voice of Hope.* Kathy Dudley founded the ministry and developed a thriving program for youth, their families, and the elderly. In time she turned the ministry over to black leaders who emerged from within the ministry. My husband tutored in the after-school program. We attended conferences on racial reconciliation and participated in programs where we worked side by side with other races. We ministered in prisons and incarcerated youth camps.

Try your hand at home first. Many of the skills and qualities you'll need overseas can be learned right here. In addition, the needs are overwhelming and just as important to God. You may find that you are a missionary to your own back yard.

The Candidating Process

If you still believe God is calling you overseas, take a year or two and work through Kathy's three stages of candidate preparation.

If you have run with footmen and they have tired you out,
Then how can you compete with horses? (Jeremiah 12:5 NASB)

Stage One: Candidate

A candidate is an individual seriously considering the possibility of serving in career ministry. At this stage, ask God to show you how to best prepare yourself if God leads you into missions work. Connect with the missions pastor of your church and ask for guidance.

Take a missions class at a college or seminary. Read *Let the Nations Be Glad* by John Piper and other recommended books. Take an evangelism/discipleship course. Do a gifts and aptitude assessment. Write your personal testimony.

Strengthen your intimacy with God. Read *The Pursuit of God* by A. W. Tozer or *Knowing God* by J. I. Packer. Practice the disciplines of Bible study and prayer.

Become involved in an accountability group in your church. Ask your group to pray for your decision and involve them in the process. Participate in a short-term mission trip and initiate a friendship with an international student or worker.

Examine your family relationships. Meet at least once with a counselor or staff member to evaluate the health of your relationship with parents, spouse, and children. Consider what this move might mean to loved ones. How are they feeling about the ministry?

Research mission agencies. Begin to seek God's guidance for a team of sending partners. At the end of a year, if God has given you a firm heart commitment to pursue full-time ministry overseas, proceed to stage two.

Stage Two: Apprentice

An apprentice is an individual who is committed to entering career ministry and is actively taking steps toward investigating the type of ministry/agency organization that she hopes will send her. She has crossed the line from "I'm willing to go, but planning to stay" to "I'm planning to go, but willing to stay."

Pray to discern the will of God. Research options for full-time ministry. A useful tool is the MARC *Mission Handbook*.

Now it is time to learn all you can. Read Hudson Taylor's *Spiritual Secret, Shadow of the Almighty* by Elisabeth Elliot, and *Culture Shock* by Myron Loss.

Recruit twenty-five prayer partners and take on a leadership role in your church for at least six months. Become a small group leader, Sunday school teacher, or youth sponsor. Plan and lead a short-term mission trip. Meet with missionaries on furlough.

Determine the target area, target ministry, and sending agency. Meet with them and work through their requirements. Cultivate relationships with their leaders and ask God to show you the best fit. Then meet with the pastor or elders of your church and ask for their blessing. Is God giving you a green light? Has He sent up any red flags? If not, proceed to stage three.

Stage Three: Appointee

An appointee has completed the necessary requirements and has been accepted by a sending agency. What's left to do?

Now is the time to complete an in-depth study of your target area and type of ministry. See your doctor for physicals and discuss any health concerns. Set your house in order.

It's also time to raise support. Ask for help from someone with experience. Many missionaries dislike asking for help. Some even turn a deaf ear to God as a result. Don't! Remember: God commands that we all invest in His work. You are providing others an opportunity to use their resources for eternity. God always provides for those He sends.

As your departure approaches, arrange with the church to commission you. Then depart for the field with joy and get ready for adventure. Nothing satisfies like glorifying God according to your design and gifts. As you have submitted to this process, you can be fairly sure you are where God wants you. And you'll be leaving the Elephant at home.

APPENDIX A

IBC Women's Ministry Organization Chart

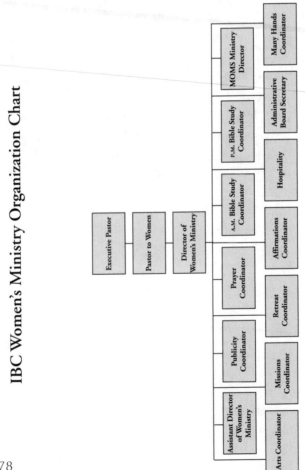

Executive Pastor

Pastor to Women

Director of Women's Ministry

Assistant Director of Women's Ministry

Arts Coordinator

Publicity Coordinator

Missions Coordinator

Prayer Coordinator

Retreat Coordinator

A.M. Bible Study Coordinator

Affirmations Coordinator

P.M. Bible Study Coordinator

Hospitality

MOMS Ministry Director

Administrative Board Secretary

Many Hands Coordinator

Sample Job Descriptions

Pastor to Women

Purpose of Position:
To train women to meet the needs of women, their families, and community through solid Bible teaching
To oversee the women's staff, board, and program

Reports to:
Executive Pastor

Relates Closely with:
Director of Men's Ministry, Community Life Pastor, Children's Pastor, Community Care Pastor

Responsible for:
Director of Women's Ministries, Women's Ministry Assistant Director, Fine Arts Women's Coordinator, Interns

Position Objectives:
Execute the purpose of the church
    —recruit, equip, and oversee women's board
    —oversee the development of new ministries
    —oversee the development of women's ministry staff
Cast vision for women's ministry
    —provide leadership in developing a long-term plan
    —develop a team of solid Bible teachers
    —dream big for the sake of the kingdom

Primary Gifts/Strengths:
Heart for God, solid Bible training, excels in art of teaching, encompassing leader, team player, teacher/visionary

Bible Study Coordinator

Reporting Relationship:
Women's Pastor

Primary Function:
To oversee the Bible study
Select and support a team of leaders to carry out details

Responsibilities:
1. To serve as administrator of the class
2. To call an assistant, with the Women's Pastor's approval, and train her to take over the class
3. To select, call, and encourage both an administrative team and a small group leaders team
4. To assist the Women's Pastor with leaders' meetings and to oversee the business agenda
5. To coordinate and partner with other board members helping with the class (Music/Drama, Children, Affirmation)
6. To oversee "kick off," "end of semester" events or any other special programs relating to the Bible study
7. To serve as the MC of the Bible study, responsible for opening prayer and announcements
8. To attend board meetings
9. To attend board training
10. To support Women's Ministry activities and other board members

Board Meeting Agenda

Date: _____ **Time:** _____ **Place:** _____

1. Devotional

2. Prayer

3. Women's Ministry Staff Reports

   - Pastor to Women
   - Director of Women's Ministries
   - Assistant Director
   - Arts Coordinator

4. Special Reports

5. Team Reports

   - Bible study
   - Prayer
   - Many Hands Mercy Ministry
   - MOMs Ministry
   - Fall Seminar
   - Hospitality
   - Evening Fellowship Dinners
   - Retreat
   - Publicity
   - Missions
   - Historian
   - Affirmation
   - Administrative Secretary
   - Teachers
   - Intern

6. Next meeting _____

7. Closing song or prayer

Sample Covenant Lesson

Lesson One

Women today need Bible study to keep balanced, focused, and Christ-centered in their busy worlds. And they also need to interact with women of different ages and stages (Titus 2:3–5). This Bible study is designed to meet both needs.

The study questions allow you to choose the study level that fits your lifestyle. And to provide even more flexibility, you may pick a different level each week depending on your schedule.

The A, B, C, D, *"core"* level questions require about an hour and a half weekly study time, yet provide a basic understanding of the text. For busy women, this level provides in-depth Bible study with a minimum time commitment. All students are asked to complete the core questions. Most core questions will be covered in your group.

The *"digging deeper"* level questions require outside resources such as an atlas, Bible dictionary, and concordance. This level will challenge you to learn more about the history, culture, and geography. You will also be looking up parallel passages for additional insight. These questions are marked with one diamond.

The *"summit"* level questions are for those who want to probe the text even more. These questions grapple with complex theological issues and differing views. You are encouraged to investigate deeper by using an interlinear Greek-English text and Vine's Expository Dictionary on your own. Also you may create outlines, charts and essays in seminary style open-ended assignments. Some with teaching gifts and an interest in advanced academics will enjoy exploring the "summit." These questions are marked with a double diamond.

The Garden Covenant

Have you ever sensed that you don't belong here?
Is there something deep within you that calls out
for another existence—a place of perfection, a place of peace?
What is it that speaks faintly,
"You are not who you were meant to be?"

The truth is that you don't belong here!
You were made for something grander
and far more beautiful.
Your forefathers tasted it
and a remnant of its memory remains within you.

Your oldest ancestors lived in a completely different realm of life.
Their Creator—and yours—designed a place of perfection,
in which His beloved would dwell, unlike any world
we can even imagine. We don't know how long
they lived there, but we do know their paradise ended.
They spoiled it!
And we still reap the consequences of their offense.

Does this seem unfair? Yes!
But God's nature required that He make it right.
And He has! World history is the unfolding of God's plan
to bring you back to the Garden.
And YOU have a part in this panoramic plan!

Pray and ask God to show you His plan of history
and your place in it.

Let's dig into the Garden!

The Garden Covenant

Lesson One

One

A. Why did God put man on the earth (Genesis 1:26–28; Psalm 8:3–9; Hebrews 2:5–8)?

B. As Adam and Eve carried out God's intentions, their primary purpose resulted. What is it (Isaiah 43:7)?

Two

A. Carefully observe Genesis 1:29–30 and 2:8–14. Describe the earth.

Describe the specific place God created especially for Adam and Eve.

What did they eat? What did the birds and animals eat?

Describe the sounds for them to enjoy.

From your observation, was the garden large or small?

What were the two trees planted in the middle of the garden?

What beautiful things could be seen in the land of Havilah?

B. How was the earth watered differently than it is today? Do you think it ever rained (2:6)?

♦ What was the Garden named? What does this Hebrew word mean?

Three

A. Describe God's relationship with Adam and Eve before the fall (3:8a–9).

B. Imagine you were able to relate to God that way. How would this kind of intimacy affect your knowledge and love for God?

Four

A. What was their job description (2:15)? What kinds of tasks do you think this job entailed?

B. What is the significance of the fact that "work" came before the fall? What is your attitude toward work?

Five

A. Imagine you are Eve. Describe a typical day in the garden from what you have observed in the text. What was life like before the fall?

Six

A. A covenant is an agreement between two parties that defines their relationship. God's part in the covenant was to provide for Adam's and Eve's every need. What was Adam's and Eve's part in the covenant (2:16–17)? Why?

B. Was this a conditional covenant or an unconditional covenant? Why?

Seven

A. A "serpent" shows up in 3:1. What does this verse tell us about him? Who is he (Revelation 12:9)?

B.   Why do you think he approached Eve instead of Adam? Was Eve present to hear the original command (2:16a)?

C.   What did he ask her (3:1b)? What do you think was his purpose in asking her this question?

D.   What did she answer (3:2)? How was her answer incorrect?

E.   What was the lie in 3:4?

♦♦   Until this time Adam and Eve had experienced only good and never evil. Why do you think God did not want Adam and Eve to know good from evil? In what sense was the choice to eat of the tree evil?

F.   What were the three reasons Eve decided to eat (3:6a)?

G.   Was Adam there during this conversation (3:6b)?

H.   What happened as soon as they swallowed? What was the first thing they did (3:7)? Contrast this with 2:25.

Eight

A.   Read 3:8–11. Adam and Eve did something they had never done before. What was it? What emotions were felt for the first time?

B.   What has already changed in the relationship between Adam and Eve (3:8–13)? How is their world beginning to change?

Nine

A.   Adam and Eve had broken the covenant. As a result they and all their descendants have reaped the consequences.

What two curses did women reap? What do you think this verse means (3:16)?

B. What curse did Adam and all men reap (3:17–19a)?

C. What curse did all men and women reap (3:19b)?

D. Who else reaped this consequence (3:21)?

◆◆ Adam is the representative head of our race. Read Romans 5:12–19. Why do we reap the consequences of Adam's sin? Although some claim this truth is "unfair," what has God done to rectify this situation?

Ten

A. Who first took life? For what purpose (3:21)?

◆◆ Blood was shed for the first time that day. What precedent and practice was established for the first time?

B. Why were Adam and Eve banished from the garden (3:21–24)? Will they ever be allowed to eat of the tree of life (Revelation 22:1–3a)?

◆◆ Eve had no name until after the fall when Adam named her. Why did he now name her? What does this imply about the relationship between men and women after the fall (2:19–20; 3:16b)?

◆◆ What does Eve's name mean and how does the meaning imply that Adam understood and believed the prophecy of 3:15?

Eleven

A. Even when man's rebellion was fresh in His heart, God began the process of reversing the curse and redeeming His creation. This primitive promise is woven into the serpent's curse. What was Satan's consequence (3:14–15)?

B. Do you like snakes? If not, how does your dislike reflect the truth of 3:15a?

C. Verse 15 also says there will be alienation between the woman's offspring and Satan. Biblical scholars agree that the woman's offspring ultimately refers to Jesus Christ. What is the prophecy hinted at in this curse? Who will crush Satan's head and what does that promise mean for mankind? for you personally?

♦ Read Hosea 6:1–3 and relate it to the promise of Genesis 3:15.

Twelve

A. The first three chapters of Genesis describe the way God wanted life to be and how man chose to rebel against Him. As a result, we live in a broken world. What are some of the daily struggles we all encounter as a result?

B. Are you realistic in your expectations of this world? When something "bad" happens in your life, do you try to explain why? What are some of the reasons that often come to mind?

C. Why do you think God gave us the freedom to choose whether or not to rebel against Him? What would we be like if we did not have a choice?

D. What have you learned about the character of God from the Garden Covenant?

APPENDIX B

Who You Are Becoming

Seven Qualities of a Godly Leader

1. **Maturing Christian**

   A maturing Christian not only has a personal relationship with Jesus Christ, but also is growing in Him. As a result, she is teachable, open to suggestions as to how to improve herself and her skills, and willing to step out and try new things. She is careful in setting her priorities and guards against becoming overextended.

2. **Diligent Bible Student**

   A godly leader knows that the Bible is the Handbook for Life and God's Love Letter to her. Therefore, serious Bible study and wholehearted application are part of her life.

3. **Persistent Pray-er**

   Reliance on God for power and ability is foundational to ministry, and prayer is the expression of that dependence. Therefore, we ask leaders to commit to pray for themselves, one another, the women in the groups, and the study at large.

4. **Responsible Worker**

   We depend on each leader to be diligent and punctual. If she arrives late or is complacent concerning the details of her tasks, the study will be chaotic and unorganized. This reflects poorly on our Lord.

5. **Servant Leader**

   Our goal as leaders is to be obedient to Paul's mandate:

   > *But we proved to be gentle among you, as a nursing mother tenderly cares for her own children. Having thus a fond affection for you, we were well-pleased to impart to you not only the gospel of God but also our own lives, because you had become very dear to us.*
   > —1 Thessalonians 2:7–8 (NASB)

6. **Team Player**

   Effective ministry is characterized by leaders who are willing to pitch in and help no matter how menial the task. Working together in harmony, listening respectfully to one another and supporting another's efforts are part of the team approach to ministry. Also a team player respects her leaders and works within the structure and guidelines for the overall good.

7. **Gracious Encourager**

   A godly leader realizes that God has extended His grace to her, and so she is able to extend grace to others. Women need to be affirmed. Take the initiative in encouraging class members with words, notes, etc. It is especially important that the leader be vulnerable and comfortable sharing her struggles as well as the lessons God is teaching her through them. This motivates others to do the same. The leader must be completely trustworthy, never repeating anything said in confidence.

What You Do

Our Goals as Leaders

The leader and coleader serve as a team to facilitate a discussion characterized by:

- a nonthreatening climate conducive to an honest exchange of ideas
- a flow of stimulating and meaningful interaction
- the presentation of God-honoring, biblically based insight

Although the leader is more visible, the coleader is equally important in accomplishing these goals.

Discussion Leader Responsibilities

1. **Put the Women at Ease**

   Caring for the women must be on the hearts and minds of the leaders from the moment the first woman walks in the door until the last woman leaves. Arrive early! Prepare your area and be ready to greet them as they arrive.

Do your best to see that everyone is physically comfortable. If the temperature of your room is distracting, see the class administrator.

Also, do your best to see that everyone is emotionally comfortable by initiating conversation before the class begins. Draw out the women by asking nonthreatening questions such as "How long have you lived here?" or "Tell me a little about yourself." Especially focus on the woman who seems shy or lonely. Remember, you set the atmosphere of unconditional love.

- **Be Other-Centered!** This is not the time to visit with your friends at other tables. You are your group's shepherdess!

  Proverbs 17:22 says, *"A cheerful heart is good medicine."* Many women are in dreary circumstances and have varied spiritual needs. Make walking into your group a highlight of their week!

- **Develop Good Listening Skills.** By intent, focused listening you convey value. Practice meaningful touch when appropriate.

Continue tender shepherding and nurturing throughout the class. *You may be the only reflection of Christ some women ever see!*

2. **Begin on Time!!**
The class administrator will begin the class on time from the platform. Usually, worship follows. Begin quickly after worship concludes even if only two or three of you are there. Late arrivals will soon learn they must be prompt. The reality

is that there will always be stragglers. Begin without them. Quickly and graciously greet them when they arrive. If you find you are seldom finishing your lesson, check to see if you are really starting on time.

3. Begin with Enthusiasm!

In a discussion, always call on someone who is enthusiastic for the first question. Get it off to an exciting start!

Keep your eyes off your paper as much as possible. Look at the women as they are speaking. In leading a written study, train yourself not to read sections like notes or the introductory paragraph on the lesson but instead to rephrase it and speak it out in your own words.

4. Assume Authority! (But Remain Gracious)

- Be firm but not bossy.
- Be gentle but stay in control.

Someone has to be in charge, and you are it!! The women expect it. Project your voice if you are soft spoken. Sit up and direct the group. You are there to keep the group on target and make sure that time is not wasted. This is a serious role, but don't forget to keep a sense of humor and have fun!

5. Encourage Discussion—DO NOT TEACH!

The leader does not "spotlight" herself but instead focuses on the women in the group. Her role is

- to direct the flow of the discussion
- to encourage interaction
- to set the climate or tone

- to guard against poor use of time
- to lead the group in an understanding of the material

We want to establish an atmosphere of unconditional acceptance where each member is free to share what she is really thinking and feeling. We may not always agree with a woman's view, but we can respect her person and therefore listen respectfully to her ideas. **The leader does not correct or "straighten out" the women in the group.**

The leader is to guard against being the one with all the answers. We want an atmosphere where each woman shares what the Holy Spirit is teaching her through God's word. Women need to feel they can ask their questions and not be made to feel foolish.

It is also imperative that a biblical perspective be presented. That is why the coleader's role is critically important. She graciously presents the biblical answer when no one else in the group has done so. Working through the lessons in advance prepares her for this role. In this way, women hear the biblical perspective, but no one in the group is singled out as the one with the wrong answer. As women continue studying the Bible, they soon discover God's perspectives for themselves.

In addition, the truth of God's Word is presented by the teacher in her lecture. As the leader, coleader, and teacher each faithfully carry out their respective part of the process, we see women coming to Christ as Savior and walking in His ways.

6. Call on the Women by Name

This is better than asking for a volunteer to answer the question because:

- usually the same few women volunteer
- waiting for volunteers consumes time and can cause the discussion to drag

This is also your greatest tool for maintaining control! Don't fail to use it!

You can bring out and encourage shy women while keeping the talkers from dominating. Call on the quiet women early in the discussion because often when they have participated and been affirmed, they find it easier to speak up. The best discussion is one in which everyone participates.

You can move quickly through questions which seem fairly obvious and bring out more discussion on other questions. For example, observation questions are those which can be answered easily right from the text. Often they require less time. You may want to call on one person for an answer and then move on. Sharing and opinion questions take more time and often bring out interesting discussion.

Try to call on everyone (except the talker who dominates) during the discussion. Vary the order around the circle when you call on people.

If a woman has not done her lesson, do not call on her. Be careful not to draw attention to her or belittle her. On occasion, someone will ask not to be called on at all. Honor her request but do your best to include her in ways she feels comfortable.

Your ultimate goal is to encourage natural interaction and conversation between group members. As the women become comfortable, hopefully you will see a more natural interchange occurring. This means you won't call on women as much because they are speaking up in response to one another. This makes the group less like a question and answer schoolroom session. However, this takes more skill on the part of the leader to control. If the group becomes chaotic and the quieter ones are not participating, step back in and take control. If not, let this more natural interaction continue but learn to sum up ideas expressed and move on to the next question when appropriate. You are responsible for the flow of discussion.

7. **Use Volunteers for Share Questions**
   Be sure to let the women know from the first that personal application questions are for volunteers only! To be called on might cause a woman to reveal something personal that she would rather not share.

   Be ready to share on personal application questions occasionally. One of the great benefits of discussion group is the therapy that takes place when participants open up about their struggles, fears, or feelings of inadequacy. The leader can set this in process by being open about what the Lord is doing in her life.

8. **Keep Up the Pace!**
   The pace of the discussion is determined by the personalities of the group members and the skill and preparation of the leader and coleader. Observe the pace of your group. Work with your coleader to discern the pace and together develop strategies to keep the group moving and interesting. Serve as a sounding board for one another.

   There are two extremes and each requires a different response.

   A. The quiet group which water-skis over issues (their pace is too fast!) This group tends to finish quickly. They share very little and seem content with pat answers. What can you do?

- Muster enthusiasm.
- Encourage, encourage, encourage.
- Be patient; intimacy takes time.
- Rely on the coleader to ask stimulating (not controversial) questions to spark interest.
- Draw out answers by calling on many women for each question.
- Don't settle for a pat answer.

B. The talkative group which never finishes (their pace is too slow). They are often busy talking but sidetrack and go down rabbit trails easily. This is often a group filled with women who love to talk and have interesting ideas to contribute. The problem comes when the more verbal women begin to dominate those who are less articulate and when the group can't get through the lesson. What can you do?

- Assume a greater air of authority.
- Illicit the more talkative women's help privately in drawing out quieter women.
- Cut off talkers (as graciously as possible).
- Coleaders can learn to interrupt a talker (graciously of course).

Whenever women become sidetracked, the leader must decide how much time she will spend there. Pursue a rabbit trail briefly if it is of common interest and time allows.

If a woman breaks down or shares a deeply personal struggle, the leader must be sensitive but also think of the group as a whole. The group often wants to spend the remaining time consoling, counseling, and fixing the problem. Allow a couple of minutes of tender feedback, but then step in and pray briefly for the woman. Assure her you will talk with her later, and do so. Then move on. **Do not discontinue working through the lesson!**

Do your utmost to finish regularly. It is good to finish as often as possible because a woman who has worked hard on her lesson may have questions that she especially wants answered. Ask God for wisdom on when to move ahead and when it would be better to spend additional time on a particular question.

9. **Be Sure Every Comment Is Affirmed!**

    The leader must be sure every comment is acknowledged in a positive way. Nothing feels more awkward than to express an idea and have it ignored. This conveys rejection. If no one else in the group interacts or responds to the comment, then the leader must affirm the group member with warm words like, "Thank you for your insight," or at least, "That's interesting." Try to respond as you would in everyday conversation, as naturally as possible. Never say by word, gesture, or facial expression, "You're wrong!" The way to handle a poor answer is to acknowledge it graciously, then call on someone you think will have a better answer or call on your coleader who is prepared with the biblical perspective. Affirming the women is a necessity!

10. **Control Your Own Talking!**

    The leader and coleader are in ministry to those in their group. We want to be sensitive to the group and allow this to be their time. If the group is a talkative group, the coleader should limit her talking and present a biblical perspective when needed. If the group tends to be a quiet group, she needs to talk to prime the pump and then back off when it is going. One way to evaluate if you are talking too much is to mark each question you answer.

Please do not talk while someone on the platform is talking. Direct the women's focus there.

11. **Maintain Unity of Spirit**

Never speak in a critical manner about any church, or denomination and do your best to discourage this kind of talking in the group. Politics is a subject to avoid as well. Redirect the conversation. This kind of talk is divisive, and can destroy the unity that we are striving to build. A woman may be offended if another group member slanders a group she grew up in or respects.

12. **Stay in Touch with Your Group**

It is very important to make periodic phone calls to your group. This is a way you have of checking their pulse to be sure everything is all right and to let them know that you are praying for them. This builds relationships. It lets them know you care. You may want to split the list with your coleader and switch names. Be sure to call a new member the first week to answer any questions and go over the guidelines. Seek out women in your group at church or invite a woman to lunch. You are a shepherdess—so tenderly nurture your flock.

Coleader Responsibilities

1. **Serve Together with the Leader to Put the Women at Ease**

2. **Help the Leader with Time Schedules**

Arrive early! Be aware of the clock and help the leader begin on time and end on time. Model punctuality for others. Don't go to the coffee bar after the study begins.

3. **Be an Enthusiastic Participant**

   Studying the Bible and gathering with others to discuss what we have learned is exciting and fun! Learn to express your excitement. Enthusiasm is contagious! You can set the tone for your group.

4. **Take Care of Administrative Responsibilities**

   Nothing frees a group leader more than knowing she can count on her coleader to take care of the paperwork. One of your responsibilities is to check the roll. Be sure a new member has a stick-on name tag the first week and a permanent name tag the next week. Encourage the women to wear name tags all year. This helps a new member or a visitor feel more comfortable.

   Prepare your table so that it is functional and attractive before the women arrive. Be sure each member has a message outline and all handouts at the appropriate time. Pass out sign-up sheets during announcements.

   Clean up your table at the end and stack materials on the designated table. Put name tags and attendance sheet back into the envelope.

5. **Present the Biblical Perspective When No One Else Has Done So!**

   The coleader participates naturally as one of the group except when the biblical perspective has not been presented or when the biblical perspective is challenged. Your leader depends on you to fill the gap when no one else can answer a question clearly.

   Please do not present this idea in a confrontational, antagonistic manner; but rather as a group member presenting another perspective on the issue. You may want to wait until after a little dialogue distances you from the poor answer before you make your point. Then pray that the Holy Spirit will convict the women listening as to the wisdom and truth of the biblical answer. Make it your goal to become as articulate and winsome as you can, but remember to leave the results to God.

6. **Help the Leader in Her Role as the Authority by Serving as a Supportive Model**
Be quick to quiet down when you see the leader is ready to begin. Focus on women in your group, not on friends at other tables.

7. **Be a Team Player with Your Leader!**
Let the leader know you are available and work together. This is your group too! If possible, pray for your group together. Sit across from the leader if possible. You need to be able to maintain eye contact with the leader.

8. **Help the Leader Keep Up the Pace!**
Learn how to help your leader move the group along. For example, a skilled coleader can learn to quickly pop in, graciously interrupt a talker, and then verbally hand the conversation back to the leader who quickly moves on before the talker gets a word in. The coleader can throw out a comment such as, "We had better be moving on or we'll never finish." Be creative to keep the flow of conversation moving and interesting.

9. **Affirm the Women in Your Group!**
Do this naturally during group interaction and whenever appropriate. Encouraging words are scarce and precious!

10. **Control Your Own Talking!**
Please don't talk while someone on the platform is talking.

Coleader's Checklist

Did I . . .

❏   pray with other leaders for the study at _____.

❏   arrive early to set up the table and greet women as they came in.

❏   hand out name tags from the envelope as each woman arrived. Make a temporary name tag in large print for new women.

❏   make a new permanent name tag for new women for next week.

❏   collect the prayer sheets and give them to the leader when she asked.

❏   take roll.

❏   as the administrator began announcements, pass out the announcement sheet. During announcements, hand out sign-up sheets and brochures. Pass them around the table when the event or ministry is announced. Keep the paper pile down!

❏   write unanswered questions on the "Unanswered Questions" sheet.

❏   act as timekeeper. Work out times and ways with the leader.

❏   collect name tags and "Unanswered Questions" sheet and

put in folder. Return and stack sign-up sheets, brochures, etc, on the main table. Please put your table sign there as well.

Thank you, coleaders. You are the *best!*

Appendix C

Covenants, Covenants
Ellen B. Theilen

Characters:

LESLIE SLOAN: Thirty- to forty-five-year-old woman who is planning to attend next season's Women's Bible Study.

SARAH: Leslie's friend who is urging her to enlist for Bible Study in the fall.

There are other characters that are in Leslie's imagination. These include a Broadway singer, two young girls, church members, and Bible Study attendees. Women can play multiple parts.

Setting:

Scene takes place at Leslie's desk in her home. Scene opens with phone ringing and Leslie enters and approaches desk strewn with papers, books, phone, and other office paraphernalia.

LESLIE: *[answering phone]* Leslie Sloan.

SARAH: Hey, Leslie—Sarah.

LESLIE: Oh hi, Sarah, what's up????

SARAH: Listen, I won't keep you. I just wanted to remind you to fill in your form for next fall's Bible study.

LESLIE: Oh, yes. I have it around here somewhere. *[She starts fishing through a pile of papers.]* What are we going to study?

SARAH: It's going to be great. It's on covenants.

LESLIE: *[Silently mouths the word "covenants?"]* How . . . interesting.

SARAH: I can't wait.

LESLIE: Uh . . . why do you think we're studying . . . covenants?

SARAH: I think to focus on God's faithfulness.

LESLIE: Of course. OK, well thanks for calling and I'll get to that form right away.

SARAH: Do you promise?

LESLIE: Sure.

SARAH: Say it.

LESLIE: I promise. I'll get it in this week. Thanks, Sarah. See
               you Wednesday.

SARAH: Bye, Leslie.

[Leslie hangs up phone and reaches for a dictionary at the bottom of the pile of books.]

LESLIE: OK, Mr. Webster. Let's see what you have to say
               about covenants. Although, honestly, I don't know
               why we have to study the whole fall on where nuns
               live. I mean, I guess Sue has her reasons, but . . .
               hmmmm here we go. . . . Oh! This is interesting. A
               covenant is: a promise . . . *[pondering]* a promise. . . .

[Leslie puts her hand on the side of her face, resting her elbow on the desk and looks off as if daydreaming and says, "Hmmm. . . ."]

[Use chimes or other sound effect to indicate a daydream. Spotlight up on Broadway singer/dancer very energetically dancing and singing, "Covenants, covenants, I'm all through with covenants, covenants, yeah . . . I don't know how. . . ." to the tune of "Promises, Promises" by Dionne Warwick and scene immediately blacks out.]

LESLIE: This could be a very lively study. I wonder what else
               it means? ". . . a binding and solid agreement to do
               or keep from doing a specified thing; compact. . . ."

[Leslie daydreams again.]

[Chimes and lights come up as several girls are on their knees with their hands clasped together up in the air as a person is standing over them with her hands on her hips. The girls on their knees say, "Linda

(use name of study leader), we covenant we will never, ever, ever bring our cell phones to Bible study again." Then the lights immediately black out on that scene.]

LESLIE: Possibly. . . . I wonder what else it means. ". . . an agreement among members of a church to defend and maintain its doctrines. Yes, maybe this is it. . . .

[Chimes and lights up again as Leslie daydreams.]

WOMAN 1:   All right. Who was supposed to set up coffee service this morning? *[Or substitute another task done in preparation for Bible study.]*

WOMAN 2:   *[sheepishly]* I overslept.

WOMAN 1:   But you covenanted!

WOMAN 2:   *[Puts hands on side of face]* AAAAAAAhhhhhhh!!!!

[Lights black out.]

LESLIE: Somehow I don't think that is it. OK, Mr. Webster, help me out here: ". . . a formal sealed contract." OK, I could see that.

[Chimes and lights come up on stage as two young girls are playing with dolls.]

GIRL 1:   I am going to tell your mother that you said a bad word.

GIRL 2:   Go ahead because I am going to tell your mother that you hit me with your Barbie.

GIRL 1:   No, you're not.

GIRL 2:   Am too.

GIRL 1:   I have an idea. Why don't we make a connavent . . . a . . . a connfen . . . a kuv-uh-nint to never in a million years tell on each other.

GIRL 2:   OK.

GIRL 1:   OK, now we have to seal it.

GIRL 2:   Seal it?

GIRL 1:   Yeah, it doesn't work unless you seal it.

GIRL 2:   Well, what can we seal it with?

[Both girls look around them and then an idea hits them simultaneously.]

[They slowly meet each other's gaze and start grinning. A second later each brings a hand up to her mouth, spits on it really noisily and then extends it to the other. Scene blacks out immediately.]

LESLIE: *[shaking her head]* I can't see _____ *[insert name of study leader or someone involved in the study]* sealing a covenant in that way. . . . But on the other hand, I can definitely see _____ *[use another woman's name].* I guess I had better just show up and find out exactly how God uses these things.

[Leslie picks up the pen and begins filling out the paper as lights fade.]

LESLIE: This could be very interesting.

ART DIRECTOR'S NOTE: We anticipated that our study on "The Covenants" might seem heavy and even somewhat daunting to some of our women, so we wrote a script that was intentionally comedic and a bit "cheesy." The scene was used, not as a part of a Bible study lecture, but as a promo for the upcoming "Covenant" series.

Conflict Resolution Covenant

As a member of the Women's Ministry Board, I agree to follow the biblical pattern for resolving conflict in Matthew 18:15–17.

> If your sister sins against you, go and show her the fault, just between the two of you. If she listens to you, you have won your sister over. But if she will not listen, take one or two others along, so that every matter may be established by the testimony of two or three witnesses. If she still refuses to listen to them, tell it to the church; and if she refuses to listen even to the church, treat her as you would a pagan or a tax collector. (in feminine terms)

This means:

1. If I am offended and cannot overlook the offense (Proverbs 17:9, 19:11), I will contain the conflict by "going and showing her the fault, just between the two of us." If I need counsel, I will consult the Women's Pastor or Director of Women's Ministries. I agree not to involve other parties as this can lead to factions (2 Corinthians 12:20; Proverbs 16:28; James 4:11a).

2. If the conflict is not resolved after I "go and show," I will work to resolve the conflict with the Women's Pastor and Director of Women's Ministries, the other party, and any "witnesses" who might help resolve the differences in a gracious and godly manner. I agree not to discuss this matter with those who are not directly involved.

3. If the conflict is still not resolved, I can "tell it to the church." However, I will not go to "the church" without informing the Women's Pastor and Director of Women's Ministries as well as the other party. If I meet with "the church," I agree

to invite the other party and women's ministry leadership to go with me so that we can all be heard at the same time.

Name: _____ **Date:** _____

Appendix D

Women Students Fellowship Constitution

Article 1: Name

The name of this organization shall be the "Women Students Fellowship of Dallas Theological Seminary."

Article 2: Purpose

The purpose of this organization shall be to assist in developing, organizing, and supporting activities for women students on campus. It also will serve to help acclimate women to campus and prepare them for ministry in whatever area God has called them to serve. This will be done through:

• Retreats
• Mentoring programs
• Informal lunches
• Guest speakers
• Social events
• Other programs/events as approved by the board

Article 3: Membership

Section 1. Membership is open to all women students at Dallas Theological Seminary.

Article 4: Structure

Section 1. The Women Students Fellowship Board is the governing body. It is made up of women students who are appointed by the board to reflect the diversity of women on campus. An honorary, nonvoting position is given to the Advisor to Women Students.

Section 2. The board chair is nominated in the spring by the current board chairwoman and the Advisor to Women Students. This nomination must by approved by a two-thirds majority of the board.

Section 3. The suggested time for a woman to serve as board chair is one year. The chair can not serve longer than two years.

Section 4. A board member must make a one-year (fall and spring semester) commitment, but can not sit on the board for more than three years.

Section 5. The board will approve a faculty advisor at the final board meeting each year for the next school year.

Article 5: Meetings

Section 1. The board will meet a minimum of seven times a year.

Section 2. The Women Students Fellowship will hold an annual student women's retreat or similar activity.

Section 3. Other meetings shall be held to help facilitate the stated purpose of the organization as stated in Article 2 above.

Article 6: Amendments and Bylaws

Any amendment of this constitution or addition of Bylaws must receive a two-thirds majority of all WSF board members. Such an amendment must have been distributed in printed form to all board members at least seven days in advance of the meeting at which the proposed amendment is to be considered.

ENDNOTES

Introduction

1. See www.census.gov.

Chapter 1

1. Personal correspondence with author Sue Edwards.
2. Dennis Sheridan, "Modern and Postmodern Challenges to Liberal Education," in *The Liberal Arts in Higher Education: Challenging Assumptions, Exploring Possibilities,* ed. Diana Glyer and David Weeks (Landham, Md.: University Press of America, 1998), 41.
3. Len Sweet, *SoulTsunami: Sink or Swim in the New Millennium Culture* (Grand Rapids: Zondervan, 1999), 17.
4. Ibid., 27.
5. Ibid.
6. Ibid., 400.
7. Ibid., 78.
8. Ibid., 83–85.
9. See www.barna.org.
10. Ronald Mayers, "Apologetic to Postmodernism: General Revelation and the Fifth Gospel" (Evangelical Theological Society papers, 1998), 21.

11. Sweet, *SoulTsunami,* 385.
12. Ibid., 410.
13. See www.barna.org.

Chapter 2

1. Don Simmons, "Know Your Stuff, Know Who You're Stuffing, and Then Stuff It," *Explorer Lite* #37, www.leadnet.org (21 may 2001).

Chapter 3

1. *Washington Post,* 13 March 2001 (or see http:// washingtonpost.com/wp-dyn/articles/A944-2001Mar13.html).
2. Vickie Kraft, *Women Mentoring Women* (Chicago: Moody, 1992), 47.
3. Ibid., 47–48.

Chapter 4

1. *Washington Post,* 13 March 2001 (or see http:// washingtonpost.com/wp-dyn/articles/A944-2001Mar13.html).

Chapter 5

1. George Cladis, *Leading the Team-Based Church* (San Francisco, CA: Jossey-Bass, 1999), 1.
2. Ibid., 25.
3. Ibid., 139.
4. Ibid., 121.

Chapter 6

1. Bruce Wilkinson, *Walk Thru the New Testament* (Atlanta, GA: WTB, Inc., 1995), 4.
2. Ibid.
3. *Purpose* (Irving, Tex.: Wisdom Works Ministries) Issue 5 (September 1998).
4. George Cladis, *Leading the Team-Based Church* (San Francisco, CA: Jossey-Bass, 1999), 21.

Chapter 9

1. *Dallas Morning News,* 15 May 2001.

Chapter 12

1. You may contact *Peacemaker Ministries* at mail@HisPeace.org or visit their Web site at www.HisPeace.org.

Chapter 13

1. John Gray, *Men Are from Mars, Women Are from Venus* (New York: HarperCollins, 1992), 5.
2. The primary scriptural passages pertinent to this debate include the following verses: Genesis 1:27–28; 2:18–24; 1 Corinthians 11:3–16; 14:34–37; Galatians 3:28; 1 Timothy 2:8–15. Our commentary on this debate is not meant to be exhaustive or thorough, merely an introduction.
3. See *Women in Ministry: Four Views,* ed. Bonnidell and Robert Clouse (Downer's Grove, Ill.: InterVarsity Press, 1989).
4. See the CBMW Web site, www.cbmw.org, "Fifty Crucial Questions."
5. See the CBE Web site, www.cbeinternational.org, "Who We Are."
6. Elizabeth Inrig, *Release Your Potential* (Chicago: Moody, 2001), 176.

Chapter 17

1. David Mays, personal correspondence with author Sue Edwards.

Chapter 18

1. Hank Paulson, "The Third Paradigm in Missions," *International Partnerships, Networking and Nationals,* 4 October 2000, 1.
2. Patrick Johnstone and Jason Mandryk, *Operation World* (Waynesboro, GA: Paternoster, 2001), 2.
3. Patrick McDonald with Emma Garrow, *Children at Risk* (Monrovia, CA: Marc, 2000), 15.
4. Celestin Musakura, "ALARM" brochure, Dallas, Texas, www.africalarm.org.
5. Patrick Johnstone, *The Church Is Bigger Than You Think* (Pasadena, CA: William Carey Library, 1998), 210.
6. Miriam Adeney, "Short Term Missions Today," in *When the Elephant Dances, the Mouse May Die* (Pasadena, CA: Bill Berry, 2000), 8.
7. Ibid., 11.